LOVE'S LABOR

LOVE'S LABOR

Essays on Women, Equality, and Dependency

Eva Feder Kittay

Routledge • New York and London

Published in 1999 by
Routledge
29 West 35th Street
New York, NY 10001

Published in Great Britain by
Routledge
11 New Fetter Lane
London EC4P 4EE

Library of Congress Cataloging-in-Publication Data

Kittay, Eva Feder.
    Love's labor : essays on women, equality, and dependency / Eva Feder Kittay.
        p.   cm.
    Includes bibliographical references and index.
    ISBN 0-415-90412-9 (hc. : alk. paper). — ISBN 0-415-90413-7 (pbk. : alk. paper)
    1. Equality. 2. Dependency. 3. Caregivers. 4. Women's rights. 5. Equal rights
    amendments. I. Title
    HM146.K59 1998
    305—dc21   98-18629
                                                                           CIP
                                                                           Rev

Dedicated to
my children, Leo and Sesha

Contents

Preface

> Eldora Mitchell is nearly as old as the century, and for her it has
> been a life of love and service. Starting at the age of 12, when she
> went to work scrubbing white people's floors to help her family.
> Later, she cleaned hospital rooms to feed her own children and
> cared for her grandchildren while their parents were working. In her
> 60s, she nursed her dying husband and her elderly mother.
>
> Now, at 95, frail and slowly going blind, it is Mrs. Mitchell's
> turn.... Mrs. Mitchell has about $8,000 in savings and no long-
> term health insurance. What she does have is her family and her
> expectation—that they will do for her as she has done for the previ-
> ous generations . . .

So begins an article that appeared on the front page of the *New York
Times* (Rimer 1998, 1) just as I was completing the book you have before
you. The same article ends with the story of Martha Perry, forty-nine,
who gave up her job and daily life with her husband to care for her
mother-in-law. After the death of her mother-in-law, she served as a
round-the-clock caregiver for six months for her ailing eighty-five-year-
old mother before finally returning to her husband and her job. What is
Martha Perry's job when she is not taking care of family? She is the manager of a group home for disabled adults.

Both the older Eldora Mitchell and the younger Martha Perry have
spent their lives doing what I call *dependency work*, the work of caring
for those who are inevitably dependent. The dependency work on which
the reporter focuses is familial and largely unpaid[1]—the paid work these
women did was either domestic labor (itself not dependency work in the
sense discussed here, but closely aligned with it) or dependency work
proper, such as managing the group home for disabled adults.

The strength and strains of a life of dependency work are captured in these stories, as are the involved histories of race and sex in dependency care. The *Times* article is at once a paean to the strength of African-American family life—to the network of help the extended family in African-American communities provides—and a shameful testament to poor health conditions, economic strains, and a warranted history of mistrust of institutional arrangements that are the legacy and products of racism. Although the African-American community is featured in this story, the article cites a remarkable figure: One in four American families is caring for an elderly relative or friend "doing everything from changing diapers to shopping for groceries." This one-in-four figure does not include the work of caring for other dependents such as young children, the ill, and the disabled. In these families, no less than in the families featured in the story, the dependency worker is likely to be a woman. The fact that women largely bear the burden of dependency work is a legacy of tradition, of sexism, and of a sexual taboo against men being involved in the intimate care of women's bodies.[2]

In the stories of Eldora Mitchell, Martha Perry, and the other women (and some men) featured in the *Times* article lie the point and purpose of my book. I began this project in response to an invitation to speak on the topic of "Elusive Equality" as the keynote speaker of the Helen Lynd Colloquium Series at Sarah Lawrence College. Since philosophers and feminists alike had written volumes on the topic of equality, it was not clear to me what I could add to the topic. As I began to explore the burgeoning literature by feminist scholars, especially legal theorists, questioning the ideal of equality, I began to see that there was a consideration missing from many of the accounts. I began to see that while equality often entailed women crossing the sexual divide between women's work and men's work, equality rarely meant that men crossed over the divide to the women's side: our side—women's—the side where work was largely, though not exclusively, unpaid or poorly paid care of dependents. Simone de Beauvoir has written that "woman has always been man's dependent, if not his slave," that "the two sexes had never shared the world in equality" (Beauvoir 1952, xx). But it seemed now that this dependency was a derivative dependency, derivative of the care of dependents. This view was one that I had already encountered, if not in a fully articulated form, in the work of Susan Okin. Okin (Okin 1979) detailed how the great political philosophers of the Western tradition envisioned a role for women in political life only when they reconceived the role of women in the family—suggesting thereby the intimate relation between women's situation as caregivers and their exclusion from the public domain. It seemed to me that one could delineate a critique of the ideal of equality that I call the *dependency critique*.

The dependency critique is a feminist critique of equality that asserts: A conception of society viewed as an association of equals masks inequitable dependencies, those of infancy and childhood, old age, illness and disability. While we are dependent, we are not well positioned to enter a competition for the goods of social cooperation on equal terms. And those who care for dependents, who must put their own interests aside to care for one who is entirely vulnerable to their actions, enter the competition for social goods with a handicap. Viewed from the perspective of the dependency critique, we can say: Of course, women have not achieved equality on men's side of the sexual divide—for how could women abandon those they leave behind on their side of that divide? Their children, their elderly parents, their ill spouse or friend?

Yes, equality has been elusive for women and will continue to be so unless and until better institutional supports are put in place to enable women who wish to leave the exclusive domain of home—the haven for dependencies that no political theory could abolish by proclaiming all men [sic] to be equal—without jeopardizing the well-being of those they love.

Focusing on dependency, however, also allows one to see that as some women leave behind many traditional roles, other women fill those roles. The process creates greater differentiation among women. This indicates that while dependency and dependency work offer an important connection between women, they also give rise to a rift between those who do dependency work and those who have found other means to fulfill traditional responsibilities. The source of division is still more disturbing as women raising children on their own increasingly swell the ranks of the poor and suffer from the stigma attached to solo motherhood (even as its incidence increases), just as the condition of other more privileged women improves. To what extent, I wondered, are the "welfare wars" over the fate of poor solo mothers—a war now lost to welfare "reform"—a reflection of an ideal of equality for women that does not seriously consider the role of dependency and dependency care in women's lives?

These reflections on dependency were, I realized, prompted in part by a personal situation that made questions of dependency especially salient for me. My daughter is a lovely young woman who is profoundly dependent and will always be. Her conditions of severe mental retardation and cerebral palsy have meant she can never carry on a life without constant assistance. I have lived with my daughter's dependency for twenty-eight years and have had a long time to absorb the meaning and extent of dependency.

Out of these considerations grew the idea for this book.

My original hope was to formulate a new theory of equality that embraces dependency, for I failed to see how any progressive movement, at this historical juncture, could do without an egalitarian ideal. If there was something amiss with the ideal, it was in its formulation—not in the concept of equality itself. To provide such a theory was not possible in this book. There was too much work to be done in simply clearing the ground for an idea as radical as an equality that embraced dependency rather than defining itself against dependency. So this book is but a propaedeutic to some future theory of equality.

This book is as eclectic and yet as knit together as the concerns that gave it birth. Some of the material is very theoretical, some is more empirical, and some is deeply personal. Many of the chapters were originally written as separate articles, and have been revised for this book in order to have them read as a single work. My hope is that the reader will be willing to make the voyage with me, through my different voices and through my different but related concerns. I recognize, nonetheless, that some readers will pick and choose, and so I have been careful to include cross-references that will direct these readers to ideas that are key points for the chapters they want to explore.

In these prefatory remarks I would like to offer a few cautionary notes that will, I hope, forestall criticisms that may keep a reader from fully grasping my intent. First, a question I frequently encounter: Why focus only on the more extreme dependencies? Dependency is found not only in the case of a young child who is dependent on a mothering person. A boss is dependent on his or her secretary. Urban populations are dependent on agricultural communities. Persons on farms are dependent on electrical workers. Professors are dependent on janitors, and janitors are dependent on engineers. And so on. We are all *interdependent*.

My point is that this interdependence begins with dependence. It begins with the dependency of an infant, and often ends with the dependency of a very ill or frail person close to dying. The infant may develop into a person who can reciprocate, an individual upon whom another can be dependent and whose continuing needs make her interdependent with others. The frail elderly person, like Eldora Mitchell, may herself have been involved in a series of interdependent relations. But at some point there is a dependency that is not yet or no longer an interdependency. By excluding *this* dependency from social and political concerns, we have been able to fashion the pretense that we are *independent*—that the cooperation between persons that some insist is *inter*dependence is simply the mutual (often voluntary) cooperation between essentially independent persons. The argument of this book is that our mutual dependence cannot be bracketed without excluding both significant parts of our lives and large portions of the population from the domain of equality. To this end, I explore the implications for political and social life of the most fundamental dependency—not only for the dependent, but also for those who care for the dependent. As we draw out the implications of dependency for social and political life, we come to a new appreciation of our interdependence—because no one escapes dependency in a lifetime, and many must care for dependents in the course of a life. Rather than denying our interdependence, my aim is to find a knife sharp enough to cut through the fiction of our independence.

A related point derives from the seemingly one-sidedness of the dependency I portray and the lack of reciprocation I presume on the part of the dependent in the relation. I begin with the case of a dependent who is unable to reciprocate not because I assume it to be the most typical case, but because it is the case most in need of consideration if one is asking about the social responsibility to the caregiver. That social responsibility diminishes as the dependent is more and more capable of reciprocating and as the dependent is less than totally helpless. The less helpless and more capable the dependent, the closer the relationship begins to approximate relations between equals.

But for us to consider demands of dependency, we have to look at the whole range of possibilities—especially the portion that most diverges from relations among equals. This strategy then begins with the assumption of our dependence, asks what is required for the more demanding cases, and then presumes that we modify those demands as we think about relationships in which the persons are able to respond with reciprocity. The alternative strategy, the one which I believe has failed us, begins with the assumption of equality and then tries to make adjustments for the *non-normal* condition of dependency. If we try to accommodate the most needy, we have a better chance of capturing the requirements of justice for all. This is an insight captured in John Rawls's "difference principle," but one which, I will argue, is too narrowly applied within his own theory of justice.

Another cautionary note concerns the gendered nature of the discussion concerning dependency work, mothering and caring. Care of dependents is not inevitably nor exclusively the province of women. But it is *mostly* women who are dependency workers. Care of children, and the raising of children is not exclusively the work of mothers. I have witnessed, firsthand, how competent a father can be in the daily, hands-on care of a dependent child, and I am convinced there is nothing inherently gendered about the work of care. Nonetheless, to ignore the *fact* that most of the care of children is done by mothers, and to call this work of caring for children parenting rather than mothering is a distortion that serves women poorly. I therefore follow other feminists who have called the care of a child mothering, acknowledging that fathers, too, can be excellent "mothers."

This said with respect to the clearly gendered terms "mother" and "mothering," and since women primarily care for all dependents, I must comment on my reliance on a non-gendered term, "dependency worker," to speak of those who care for dependents. Resorting to a non-gendered term is meant to reflect a vision inherent in my notion of dependency work. Namely, that while this labor is now largely gendered, it need not be. This book is, in part, about a more equitable distribution of dependency work. The work of caring for dependents must be, as all work should be, distributed not by gender (or race or class) but by skill and inclination. The non-gendered nature of my terminology is meant to be consistent with that vision.

The reader will also notice that I have chosen to use the female pronouns for dependency workers. As there are no English gender-neutral pronouns, I also employ the female pronouns for dependents. This use, then, should be seen as a convention—one intended to counter the conventional use of the masculine as the generic pronoun.

A book on dependency must above all acknowledge the author's own dependence on all the persons involved in making such a book possible. There are so many to thank and there are so many different sorts of things for which to thank those who have helped.

First, I must thank Margaret Grennan and the many dedicated caring dependency workers who have helped attend to my daughter over these many years. Their devotion, their attention and responsiveness have taught me much of what I have tried to communicate in this volume.

Maureen MacGroggen and Linda Nicholson gave me the confidence that this was a valuable project when they contracted the book for the wonderful Thinking Gender Series—which they had initiated. The American Association of University Women (AAUW) enabled the initial work on the book by granting me a Founder's Fellowship. Traveling around the country and meeting the women who raise such funds that support so much scholarship by women was an inspiration.

I want to express my gratitude to Elfie Raymond for the initial invitation to speak on equality (the impetus for this book), for reading drafts of several chapters, for helping me come up with useful terminology to express some of my ideas, and for the many ways in which she has taught and inspired me since I first was her student as a college sophomore.

A number of persons have read most of these chapters, albeit in an earlier form. Diana Meyers has offered her sage advice on most of the chapters, as they have appeared in various versions and stages of development. I have benefited from our many talks on these and related topics, and am grateful for our long friendship in which a commitment to women's moral voices has been paramount. Ellen Feder—whom I am proud to count both as a former student and as a current friend and colleague—helped me determine that the collection of essays, in fact, constituted a book.

Other colleagues have read portions of the book. Robert E. Goodin has not only inspired my thoughts on an ethic of care based on vulnerability, he has been kind enough to read and comment on several versions of Chapters One to Four. Many thanks to John Baker for his interest in my approach to equality and for reading and commenting on earlier drafts of many chapters of the book. Chapters Three and Four published in a slightly different form as "Human Dependency and Rawlsian Equality" (Chapter Ten of *Feminists Rethink the Self*, edited by Diana T. Meyers [Colorado: Westview Press 1996, 219–266]), have also been read and commented on by several colleagues, including Susan Okin, Annette Baier, Susan Brison, William Kymlicka, George Sher, Anthony Weston, Jonathan Adler, Michael Simon, Kenneth Baynes, Alistair MacLoed, Leigh Cauman, and Neil Tennant—as well as a number of anonymous reviewers. I have benefited from their comments even if the current version does not reflect all their astute advice.

Chapter Five is a revised version of two separate papers: "Taking Dependency Seriously: The Family and Medical Leave Act Considered in Light of the Social Organization of Social Organization of Dependency Work" (*Hypatia* vol. 10, no. 1 [Winter 1995] and reprinted as Chapter One of *Feminist Ethics and Social Policy*, edited by Patrice Di Quinzio and Iris Marion Young, [Bloomington: Indiana University Press, 1-22] 1998). This chapter benefited from the helpful comments of Iris Marion Young and Patrice de Quinzio, Lisa Conradi, and Amy Baehr. Iris Young deserves a special thanks for guiding me in the direction of considering welfare as an application of my theoretical work. The material on welfare reform grew out of a paper originally given for the Philosophical Exchange at SUNY-Brockport and printed in their proceedings: "Women, Welfare, and a Public Ethic of Care," in the *Annual Proceedings for Philosophical Exchange* 27:1996-1997. I thank Joseph Gilbert for the invitation and comments. An amplification and further development of this paper was published as "Welfare, Dependency and a Public Ethic of Care" in a special issue of *Social Justice*, (vol. 25, no. 1, April 1998), edited by Gwendolyn Mink. The paper has primarily benefited from the knowledgeable and thoughtful suggestions and editorial guidance of Gwendolyn Mink. I also want to thank Nancy Hirshmann, Martha Fineman and Joan Tronto for their comments. The material in Chapter

Five is importantly inspired by the women on welfare whom I have known and worked with, especially Kelly Telgalo and Terry Scofield, and by the marvelous women on the Women's Committee of One Hundred: Guida West, Gwendolyn Mink, Ruth Brandwein, Sonya Michel, Eileen Boris, Kim Christensen, Deirdre English, Heidi Hartmann, Pat Reuss, Frances Fox Piven, Diana Pearce, Cynthia Harrison, Mimi Abramovitz, Linda Gordon, Felicia Nestor, and many others. I learned an enormous amount from their knowledge and dedication to women and welfare.

Chapters Six and Seven are revisions and amplifications of "Not *My* Way, Sesha. *Your* Way. Slowly" which appears as "Not *My* Way, Sesha, *Your* Way, Slowly: 'Maternal Thinking' in the Raising of a Child with Profound Intellectual Disabilities" (*On Behalf of Mothers: Legal Theorists, Philosophers, and Theologians Reflect on Dilemmas of Parenting,* edited by Julia Hanisberg and Sara Ruddick [New York: Beacon Press]). Sara Ruddick's brilliant editing was essential as I turned these deeply personal thoughts into an academic paper. I also want to thank her for reading other chapters in various stages of development and for her support throughout this project.

Westview Press, Indiana Press, and Beacon Press, as well as *Hypatia* and *Social Justice* have been very accommodating in permitting the use of part or all of previously published material.

A number of outstanding current and former graduate students have helped with various stages of this process. Emily Lee helped sort out various drafts of early material in preparation for assembling and revising them for the book. Sarah Miller's efforts, with those of Jenny Hansen, were invaluable as they collected references, checked quotations, and gathered vital empirical data. Earlier in the process I had the research assistance of Barbara Andrew, Barbara LeClerc, and Eric Steinhart. I thank them each for their assiduous efforts. Important, as well, has been the input of some of the students and others in my graduate seminars on feminist theory—especially the seminar of 1991, affectionately called Femsem.

The Department of Philosophy was kind enough to allow me leave time and to put the resources of the department at my disposal. I am indebted to my Chair, Edward Casey, for his willingness to offer the support of the department throughout the many years I have been engaged in this project. A special thank you to Virginia Massaro, Letitia Dunn, and Martha Smith for their services and support. Anne Gallette provided secretarial help that kept my office at home functioning well enough for me to write.

Portions of this book were written in a beautiful and peaceful house in Maine, made available by the generosity of my dear friend, Donald Sussman.

I wish to recognize those persons in my life who have been at the center of my thoughts on the labors of love. First, my mother—my earliest and best teacher of love's labors. Next my two children, Leo and Sesha, who never cease to reward me for my own labors of love. And finally, my life partner, Jeffrey, who has shared with me the care of our children, the writing of this book, and a life of mutual love, respect, and concern. Thank you Jeffrey for reading and thinking about this book and for providing the inspiration and hope that men and women can one day share the world in equality.

Introduction

Dependents require care. Neither the utterly helpless newborn who must be cared for in all aspects of her life nor a frail, but functioning, elderly person who needs only assistance to carry on with her life, will survive or thrive without another who meets her basic needs. Dependency can be extensive or brief, with the extended dependency of early childhood or a temporarily incapacitating illness. Dependencies may be alleviated or aggravated by cultural practices and prejudices, but given the immutable facts of human development, disease, and decline, no culture that endures beyond one generation can be secure against the claims of human dependency. Questions of who takes on the responsibility of care, who does the hands-on care, who sees to it that the caring is done and done well, and who provides the support for the relationship of care and for both parties to the caring relationship—these are social and political questions. They are questions of social responsibility and political will. How these questions are answered will determine whether the facts of human dependency can be made compatible with the full equality of all citizens—that is, whether full citizenship can be extended to all.

How a social order organizes care of these needs is a matter of social justice. Traditionally women have been those attending to dependencies. The labor has been seen as part of familial obligations, obligations that trump all other responsibilities. Women who have been sufficiently wealthy or of sufficiently high status have sometimes been presented with an option to confer the daily labor of dependency care to others— generally other, mostly poor and ill-situated, women. Poor women who have had dependency responsibilities along with paid employment have often relied on female familial help. The gendered and privatized nature of dependency work has meant, first, that men have rarely shared these responsibilities—at least with the women of their own class; and, second, that the equitable distribution of dependency work, both among genders and among classes, has rarely been considered in the discussions of political and social justice that take as their starting point the public lives of men. This starting point has determined not only moral, social, and political theory; it also has determined the shape of public policy.

Elusive Equality

> When I do not see plurality stressed in the very structure of a theory, I know that I will have to do lots of acrobatics . . . to have this theory speak to me without allowing the theory to distort me *in my complexity* (Lugones 1991, 43).

Within the course of Western political and legal theory, claims made on behalf of a universal conception of humanity have had a progressive thrust. From her own position of difference, Lugones challenges us to construct theory that addresses those who see not the face of a liberator but the visage of an oppressor in the image of a universal humanity. The questioning of inborn privileges and hierarchies is our inheritance from the egalitarian traditions that frame the legal and political doctrines prevalent in modern democratic institutions. But increasingly, social movements reveal the exclusionary aspects of the universal doctrines, so much so that the challenge posed to feminists by Lugones cannot go unheeded. Group identities are an unwelcome intrusion of difference into the ideal of equality. Partiality and perspective threaten to tear the benevolent blindfold off the figure of justice.

No one who pursues these concerns desires to undermine hard-won assumptions of moral and political parity. Still, some insist that the liberal ideals of impartiality, neutrality, and equality itself, cannot bring about the egalitarian vision they are meant to foster. These ideals seem especially resistant to efforts to put plurality into the very structure of our theories. Many contemporary voices have insisted that equality will be formal, or even empty, until perspective and difference are acknowledged and incorporated within the fabric of political theory and practice.

Equality has served some daughters of the Enlightenment very well. It steered a movement that has culminated in the affirmation of women's right to enfranchisement in all Western nations. In the United States, after thirty years of equal rights legislation for women, its mandate covers everything from sports to education to the participation of women in the armed forces. Women in the United States have made progress under its banner.[3] Women occupy positions from astronaut to CEO and are now nearly half of the workforce.[4] Sexual harassment is recognized and prosecuted in courts of law. Women and men attend college in equal numbers. The achievements are impressive indeed.

Yet the idea of equality has not served all women equally well. In the United States[5], women continue to be excluded from the more prestigious and well-paid occupations[6], to be ill-served medically, and to still be, by and large, the sexual prey of men.[7] Although early abortions are now legal throughout the nation, only geographically or financially well-situated women have full access.[8] Women's wages remain well below men's, with only small increases achieved in the years when equal pay and antidiscrimination legislation have been in force.[9] Thus it is hardly surprising that women are economically in a far more precarious position.[10] Two-thirds of poor and homeless persons in the United States are in households headed by women. This looms as a specter for the middle-class as well as the working-class mother who contemplates divorce or who fears her husband will leave her and her children. The fate of children follows that of the mothers—the impoverishment of women has meant the impoverishment of children.

Equality-based policies have failed women in the public arena as well as in the private sphere, neither achieving their goal in representation in political office[11] nor in sharing of domestic chores and childrearing responsibilities.[12] Despite liberal commitments to the ideal, equality continues to elude us. In a nation such as the United States, where the women's movement (especially in its most organized forms) has so unrelentingly marched to the tune of its ideal, can we attribute "the marked contrast between the expectations and achievements of the women's movement" (Norris 1987, 144) to an unwise reliance on its dominance?

No doubt many impediments to a sexually egalitarian society derive from the imperfect implementation of laws already in place, and from the grip—one might better say, the stranglehold—social convention has had on the formation of gender identity. In recent years socially, as well as fiscally conservative politics and reactionary social and religious movements, have gained force, perhaps in part as a response to liberal gains. These forces, generally hostile to gender equality, work to impede and undo women's gains. But not infrequently, conservative gender politics appropriates liberal rhetoric, as we will see when we look at the fate of welfare "reform" in the United States.

Vigilance in the enforcement of laws already in place, together with efforts to reshape the socialization of girls and boys, will do much to equalize power and resources between men and women. But the pace at which we move toward substantial equality even as the formal barriers to equality have fallen, the direction of some change, and the uneven distribution of the benefits of advances among different groups of women, have underscored the qualms of feminists who question the goal itself.

In this book, I wish to explore one direction of such questioning, one which I believe holds promise in redirecting social and political theory as well as feminist strategies. The inquiry begins with a self-understanding of democratic liberal nations as an association of free and independent equals. I want to challenge this self-understanding for we are all at some time dependent. Many of us, mostly women, also have to attend to the needs of dependents. The notion that we all function, at least ideally, as free and equal citizens is not only belied by empirical reality, it is conceptually not commodious enough to encompass all. I call this challenge the dependency critique of equality.[13]

In making the case that equality will continue to elude us until we take seriously the fact of human dependency and the role of women in tending to dependent persons, I make use of a variety of voices. In Part One, "Love's Labor," I engage in a constructive philosophical project to establish the moral significance of dependency and its care, that is, the labor associated with it that I call *dependency work*. In Part Two, "Political Liberalism and Human Dependency," I interrogate the most thorough vision of liberal egalitarianism of our time, the work of John Rawls, and conclude that the norms and values underlying both the theory and the practice exclude the concerns of dependency. Here I use a critical philosophical voice. In Part Three, "Some Mother's Child," I move away from recognizable philosophical idioms as I engage with concrete realities: The first of these are policy questions that pertain to dependency and those who do the work of dependency care—dependency workers. I examine two policy initiatives undertaken in the United States in recent years, the Family and Medical Leave Act of 1993 and welfare "reform," concluding that these practical policies—like theoretical liberalism—do not acknowledge the nature and contribution of dependency work. I explore policy proposals more consistent with the concerns I highlight. While I suspend the abstract tone of philosophical discourse in favor of a more sociological and political style, the tone is recognizably academic. Chapter Six, in Part Three, begins with a deeply personal account of my own encounters with dependency, in particular with that of my own daughter—a young woman now—who is severely disabled. The final chapter of Part Three combines the personal, the sociological, and the philosophical as I rethink Sara Ruddick's categories of maternal thought in terms of the experiences of mothers of severely disabled children.

The many inflections—from the abstract to the concrete, from the constructive to the critical, from the impersonal to the personal—have been necessary for carving a path through a conceptual and psychological thicket. The encounter with dependency is, I believe, rarely welcome to those fed an ideological diet of freedom, self-sufficiency, *and* equality. It was, after all, as a rejection of dependency on the feudal lord that Rousseau (echoing the sentiment of his day) declared the equality of men [*sic*]. But the deeper dependencies of infancy and early childhood, frail old age, disease and disability, do not vanish in a revolution. We have no lords to fight for this independence. So we have built fictions. But these fictions damage us and with the demand of women to be included in the ideal of equality, we find the limit of an ideal based on our putative independence. Therefore we have to use our multiple voices to expose the fiction and rebuild a world spacious enough to accommodate us all with our aspirations of a just and caring existence. That is the thesis and the method I am pursuing here.

My approach to the question of feminism's relation to the ideal of equality differs in significant ways[14] from other approaches feminists have taken in criticizing equality. The critiques take place in the context of lively debates, especially in feminist legal theory, concerning the value and nature of the ideal of equality. Though these debates deploy critiques that are different than my own, they are relevant to the dependency critique. Therefore, I want to begin this journey with the question: What does it mean to question the goal of sexual equality?

Equalities

A bumper sticker declares that women who seek equality with men lack ambition. Marilyn Frye has mischievously called sexual equality still another "fine and enduring patriarchal institution" (1983, 108). These quips succinctly put forward a thesis that equality presupposes the measure of man as the measure of humanity, and so obstructs our vision of what the world could be like if women were truly free of male domination. The charge is not without merit. But one wants to know, is this a charge against all and any conceptions of equality, against the *concept* of equality itself, or against some particular conception?[15]

The *question of equality* fragments into *questions of equalities*.[16] Equality *for whom*?[17] Equality *by what measure*? Equality *of what*?[18]. Equal *to what*? Equal *to whom*? Entitling her essay "Equalities," feminist legal theorist Martha Minow (1991) asks us to consider the different perspectives and norms which deem one situation equal to some and unequal to others, equal by one measure, but unequal by another, equal with respect to some stipulated factor, but unequal with respect to the desired one.

Minow is a theorist who, utilizing her own critical writings on equality, as well as those of other feminists, has tried to shed light on the quest for justice sought by various groups. Minow suggests that feminist challenges to equality highlight: first, the need to contest norms implicit in decisions that likes have been treated as likes; second, the importance of respecting the perspectives of the excluded; and third, the importance of questioning the fairness and uncoerced character of the status quo. These considerations, she points out, are relevant not only to women, but to the many groups seeking equality.

To understand the import of these challenges, consider that the demand for equality is, at its simplest: a demand by X, a group or individual we can call "the constituency," to be equal to Y, a group or individual we can call "the reference class," with respect to Z, some social good or capability. If we take Z to be equal protection under the law, then the reference class (whose members presumably have such protection) determines the standard of treatment that constitutes the equality sought. But when the constituency differs from the reference class in a manner that is pertinent with respect to the attainment of Z, then the failure to achieve equality may be as much a problem of having taken the reference class as the standard for measure, as it may be a failure of the constituency to be sufficiently like the reference class to be comparable with respect to Z.

For instance, Minow analyzes the decision in *Hernandez v. New York*. The Supreme Court rejected the claim that a Latino criminal defendant (here a member of the constituency group of Latinos) was denied equal protection under the law when the prosecution used the power of peremptory challenge to eliminate potential jurors who were Latino. The plurality concluded that the defendant had failed to establish intent on the part of the prosecutor to discriminate against Latinos. Minow argues that in this case the monolingual English speaker—or the non-Spanish speaking English speaker—serves as the norm for jurors and thereby renders the presence of the bilingual juror problematic. Instead, this case might have made the presence of jurors who were not proficient in the language of the defendant a deficiency in the administration of justice. To uncritically accept certain persons as the norm is to accept the status quo as fundamentally nonproblematic. But the inclusionary[19] nature of the ideal of equality reveals the difficulty of its realization where the perspective of those who are dominant hold sway, where the norms which stand behind principles of universality and impartiality go unquestioned, and where the status quo is complacently accepted.

Equality as Sexual Equality

Perhaps it is easier to say what assumptions underlie particular legal decisions than what assumptions underlie such vast and malleable concepts as equality. Equality is not only difficult to attain; it is, first off, difficult to define. What makes defining this concept so formidable is the apparent simplicity of the idea, on the one hand, and on the other, the numerous and sometimes conflicting suppositions buried in each evocation of the concept. To say persons are equal is simply to say that they are identical in relevant ways. Justice then seems to demand that if persons are identical in relevant ways, irrelevant considerations must not enter into their treatment. And, as the brief consideration of *Hernandez v. New York* suggests, what is considered relevant and irrelevant is subject to contestation, for the criteria for relevancy can be set so that hierarchies (wittingly or unwittingly) are perpetuated. In its simplest formulation, equality is compatible with hierarchy and privilege, as was clear to Aristotle who could consistently insist on the equality of citizens and the ideas of "natural slavery" and the subordination of women. For Aristotle, all the "relevant" differences necessitated exclusion of slaves and women. That is, neither slaves nor (free) women possessed all the components of rationality requisite for citizenship in a polity.

Conceptions that are more modern sever the determinants of birth from the determinants of one's life chances. John Stuart Mill put it this way:

> For what is the peculiar character of the modern world . . . ? It is, that human beings are no longer born to their place in life, and chained down by an inexorable bond to the place they are born to, but are free to employ their faculties, and such favorable chances as offer, to achieve the lot which may appear to them most desirable. . . . In consonance with this doctrine, it is felt to be an overstepping of the proper bounds of authority to fix beforehand, on some general presumption, that certain persons are not fit to do certain things (Mill 1986, 22).

One of the few great male champions of women's equality, Mill promulgated a view of equality he thought consistent with women's aspirations. His view is familiar to us in the concept of equality of opportunity. On some understandings, those for example that embrace affirmative action, fair equality of opportunity can necessitate different treatment. But it is not out of place to note that even Mill supposed that women, not men (categories defined by what one is born to be on Mill's view), would take on childcare and domestic responsibilities. Mill, seeing the injustice of women assuming *both* domestic responsibilities (especially mothers too poor to hire servants) *and* other employment, restricted the liberty of occupation to unmarried and childless women or to the very wealthy. Gender equality so conceived could, as Mill understood, serve only the few and privileged.

"The root meaning of equality is negative," Michael Walzer writes. "It aims not at eliminating all differences but a particular set of differences, and a different set in different times and different places" (Walzer 1983, xii). Mill was mostly concerned to see certain impediments to women's equality end. His vision did not encompass the possibility that men and women would share domestic duties such as childcare.

But what about the more recent demands of "equality feminists"—feminists who have couched women's demands in terms of equality? We can, I believe, point to three identifiable formulations of the demand for gender equality.

The first deems gender difference to be a morally illegitimate basis for the distribution of fundamental rights and duties, and for the division of advantages from social cooperation—including economic benefits, liberties, political participation, and so forth. It asks only for an end to hindrances based on gender that impede equal opportunity and access to what is socially valued.

The second also looks to the elimination of gender bias in legal, social, and political institutions, but as a strategy for ending sexual domination. It demands gender-neutral policies in all major institutions, especially the law.

The third seeks, more positively, the inclusion of women into all the spheres from which they have been excluded. Here the demand is for positive strategies that result in the equal enjoyment by both sexes of the resources and privileges now concentrated in the hands of men.

When equality is claimed, the presumption is that members of the *reference class*, those from whom the demands are made, all share certain privileges. The expectation is that when the demand for equality is satisfied, the *constituency*, those seeking equality, will be included, as a group, and thus benefit collectively and individually by their inclusion. This presumption underlies each of the other formulations of sexual equality.

Feminist Critiques of Equality

> We might . . . think of feminists as having chosen or drifted toward the second of two possible responses (1) creating a world in which

> women cease to be the objects, and start becoming the subjects (or agents), of competition; or (2) creating a world in which women cease being merely the subjects, and start becoming the objects, of compassion. . . . The feminist ethos that emerges thus is not one in which women are to imitate how men act toward each other in the world of competition, but rather one in which women imitate, in their relationships with one another, certain aspects of how women are supposed to act toward men (Lugones and Spelman 1987, 244).

Throughout women's struggles many have assumed that expanding the possibilities for women clearly necessitated demanding that which men had hoarded for themselves.[20] But this seemingly obvious proposition overlooks the ways the standards of equality are established by the hopes, aspirations, and values of those already within the parity class of equals. They become the reference class for what is understood as human, and for what benefits and burdens are to be shared. In this way, the presumption of humanity as male—and of a certain class and complexion—underlies much of what is striven for in the name of equality.

The review of feminist critiques of equality that follows lays the groundwork for the development of the relation between women's inclusion into the ideal, the fact of human dependency, and women's historic role in tending to dependents. I first survey two critical approaches that have dominated feminist theory—both of which come largely from the feminist legal theory. Women's differences from men, both physiological and cultural, are the basis of the *difference critique*. The difference—not in properties possessed, but in hierarchy and power—constitutes the basis for the *dominance critique*. A third critical approach sees both gender equality and its feminist critics ignoring the importance of race, class, and other differences in shaping the leading ideals of justice for women. I have called it the *diversity critique*. The final critique that I discuss, the *dependency critique*, forms the basis of this book. Exploring the moral and political significance of the dependency critique and the possibility of recuperating a conception of equality that incorporates dependency will be the task of the remaining chapters.

The Difference Critique

The difference critique addresses the suppression of difference inherent in the first formulation of equality, namely, that gender difference is a morally illegitimate basis for the distribution of fundamental rights and duties. The difference theorist, pointing to the predominance of male-set standards in all areas of public life, argues that demands to be equal *to men* forces women to accommodate themselves to conditions that comport poorly with their physiques and lives. The negative intent of the first formulation is inadequate because even when gendered barriers are removed, women are not competing for goals with the same "equipment" (the same bodies, values, socialization, etc.) nor on the same terms (e.g., responsibilities and expectations) as men. The contested assumption is the normative character of the reference class of men, especially white, middle-class men, who implicitly set the standard for participation in the equal opportunity to compete for social goods. This critique has given rise to intense debate over such issues as pregnancy and maternity leaves, joint custody, and comparable worth.

Feminists, in a number of areas of both theoretical and practical import, have asserted the importance of women's difference from men. They have claimed that women make moral decisions differently from men, that there is an identifiable epistemological stance that is attributable to women, and that we require laws and policies recognizing woman's particular role in procreation and parenting. Difference feminists reject the "notion that all gender differences are likely to disappear or even that they should."[21] They urge special treatment so that women will not be disadvantaged in the workplace and other public institutions. Alternatively, they argue that the workplace must be altered to accommodate women's special interests and needs. Equality feminists have responded that it is better to eliminate all differences that are not innate and to analogize women's situation to men's situation in the remaining cases. But it is just the strategy of analogizing women's situation on the model of men's that so irks the difference exponents, for it appears to accept the male as the norm for humanity.

Defenders of the "equal treatment" approach, particularly in law, retort: First, this approach is aimed at getting the law "out of the business of reinforcing traditional, sex-based family roles" and at appropriately altering the workplace to make possible the "accommodation to parental needs and obligations," and making these concerns central, not peripheral issues of the workplace (see Williams 1985, 352-353). Second, continues William, the equal treatment approach does not accept the male as standard, but attempts to fashion a model of the androgynous worker.[22] Third, the equal treatment approach rejects the notion that distinctively female functions are something additional to males. They argue that to accept that women have something *additional* is once again to accept the standard of humanity as male. Better to insist on equal treatment and redefine the standard of humanity to include concerns previously limited to women and to exclude sex-based concerns not directly relevant to the issue at hand.[23]

Minow (1990), noting the difficulties of either ignoring difference or acknowledging it, has spoken of the "dilemma of difference." If we ignore, let us say, the difference between men and women workers with respect to childbearing, we have no adequate way to make demands relevant to pregnancy and employment. If we insist on women's special needs, we run the risk that employers will resist hiring women because of the extra cost of pregnancy leaves. Minow suggests that the way out of the dilemma is to see that differences are not properties attached to individuals per se, but are always relational, as is equality itself. We are different *from* another and we are equal *to* another. At the same time, when that we assert that another is *different*, we imply that we, too, are different—*different from them*. For instance, to insist that difference is the property of a deaf child in a class of hearing children—and so the deaf child must accommodate herself to her hearing peers—is to ignore the fact that the hearing child is also different from the deaf child. Neither hearing nor deafness is inherently a difference. Instead the difference is in the relation these children bear to one another.

The Dominance Critique

It may be argued that to affirm women's difference—when difference has historically been conjoined with women's subordination—is a gambit at best, foolhardy at worst. The dominance critique addresses the second formulation of the demand for gender equality, which construes equality as a strategy to eliminate subordination and hierarchy. This critique questions not equality legislation's suppression of difference, but its efficacy in ending male domination. The dominance critique urges that not only is equality in a patriarchy nothing but equality to men, but adds that the ideology of gender neutrality masks or ignores ways in which men and women are differently situated in society with regard to *the possession of power*. Not equality and difference, but subordination and domination are the relevant parameters for feminist change (MacKinnon 1987). The dominance critique opposes both gender neutrality and the affirmation of difference, asserting that domination precedes difference.[24] By this, its exponents mean that the only salient differences between men and women are those that become the basis for (or better still, are the product of) domination. Neither policies based on women's differences nor policies based on their sameness are useful to the elimination of domination: Gender neutral policies can only benefit those women who need it least, who are least different than men because they are least subject to men's domination, and policies which acknowledge difference reinstate attributes that have significance only by virtue of dominance.[25] Thus, for example, policies of equal pay for equal work only helps those women who are already sufficiently privileged to occupy jobs that men occupy.[26] But acknowledging that pay inequity is causally related to the different employment of women's and men's work is also to acknowledge that equalizing salary scales of *similar* or *comparable* occupations may not bring about the end to subordination. In Sweden, pay scales are near parity (in part because of a conscientious effort to make pay comparable across positions that men and women are likely to hold), but a different form of subordination is in effect. Sex segregation in employment is very extensive—far more so than in the United States. Positions of power and prestige still accrue to men.[27]

Those who dominate have the ability to create difference and then use that difference to justify domination and inequality because they have the ability to make their own perspective the one that defines both the problem and the solution. Where the playing field is not level and where the dominant group has the power to define the issues, gender neutrality in the law does little to alter the patterns of hierarchy and power. Modeling the women's movement on the Civil Rights movement in the United States, the dominance approach advocates enlisting the power of the State to equalize the power discrepancy between women and men. The dominance approach has been pursued especially with respect to situations in which men prey on women sexually, namely, sexual harassment and pornography.[28]

By pointing to the ways in which women and men are differently situated vis-à-vis power, exponents of the dominance critique intend to circumvent "difference." Thus one would suppose that this approach would not come up against "the dilemma of difference." But the dominance approach can be seen as another variety of the difference approach, where the difference is a difference in power. This difference becomes the defining mark of women, indeed it becomes another essentialism,[29] one in which woman is defined as victim. Such an ascription, it is argued, undercuts the autonomy of women and makes it hard to see how they can assume the role and responsibility of full agents in the moral and political domain. Here the dilemma of difference reemerges. If we ignore the difference in power between men and women, we ignore the difference in starting position of the different groups. Gender neutrality will only perpetuate those differences that are already in play. If we highlight the difference, we run the risk of reducing women to mere victims.

The Diversity Critique

Those who criticize the failure of equality theory and legislation to acknowledge differences between men and women often speak as if the differences they identify pertain to *all* women and to *all* men. Theorists who put forward the dominance critique often speak as if all men were in possession of powers that all women lacked. In this way they share the presumptions that *all* men are in possession of some things women lack in more or less equal measure and that women will benefit in more or less equal measure as they overcome the *gender-based* inequality. Although some difference feminists have turned the lens of difference to the situation of women themselves, women of color have been critical of difference exponents who suppose that there are sufficient similarities among women (and among men) to give rise to policies that equally favor women in all their variety. Policies that simply address *women* fail to take into account problems arising from the intersectionality of race, gender, class, disability, age, and so forth.[30]

Although dominance feminists have at times stressed the disparate impact of equality on different groups of women, maintaining that the women most likely to benefit from policies of equality are those least like women (i.e., with respect to power), women of color have pointed out that men are themselves not equally situated. Bell hooks best expresses this critique of equality for women when she writes: "Since men are not equals in white supremacist, capitalist, patriarchal class structure, which men do women want to be equal to?" (hooks 1987, 62). Women from the most oppressed groups, hooks proposes, "are more likely to see exaggerated expressions of male chauvinism among their peers as an expression of the male's sense of himself as powerless and ineffectual in relation to ruling male groups, rather than an expression of an overall privileged social status." She suggests that these women's early suspicions of feminism stem from the formulation of feminist goals in terms of equality to men.

We can identify this critique as the diversity critique. It speaks to the diversity amongst women, which fails to be recognized in the demands of sexual equality, especially when those demands arise from the perspective of women whose primary affiliations are with dominant white middle-class men. Because the diversity critique aims at all formulations of sex equality that mask intra-gender, as well as cross-gender, inequalities, the diversity critique is neither opposed to nor does it necessarily support other feminist critiques of sexual equality. We can say that it is orthogonal to them. That is to say, however one looks at the question of gender equality, the diversity among both men and women needs to be taken into account.

The Dependency Critique

The dependency critique responds critically to the third formulation of sexual equality, the inclusion of women into an association of equals, an inclusion that gives women access to the rights and privileges previously held by men. Even this more positive formulation is inadequate. The third demand asks for an equal share of the pie. Yet, the dependency critique maintains that a pie composed of the dreams and aspirations of men is not sufficiently nourishing. What is left out is just what is omitted when society is supposed to be an association of equals. The dependency critique avers that such a conception of society, while an immensely important progressive ideal, is a limiting and limited ideal in the context of woman's subordination for a number of reasons.

First, the conception of society as an association of equals masks the inevitable dependencies and asymmetries that form part of the human condition—those of children, the aging and the ailing—dependencies that often mark the closest human ties. Therefore the presumption effectively obscures the needs of the dependents within society and women's traditional roles in tending to those needs. This presumption is brought to light in the question raised by Bernard Williams (1973a): If inequalities brought about by different childrearing practices and opportunities made available by parents to their children are to be rectified, can the privacy of the family be sufficiently respected? Some writers have concluded that this is a genuine problem in reconciling the autonomy of the family with the demands of equal opportunity.[31] From the vantage point of the dependency critique, we see these conflicts instead as an incoherence in the ideal itself.

Equality was first understood as a relation between heads of households, whose families constituted their inviolable domain—but equality is also understood as an equality among individuals and thus appears to reach into the family. When it attempts to extend its reach, we see the deficiency of its conception in dealing with persons who are dependents due to age, disability, or disease. For when laws address a dependent within a family as an individual to whom equality is due, the state appears to overstep its role vis-à-vis that individual responsible for the dependent, and to limit the freedom of one citizen while promoting the equality goals of another. Yet, why should it be thought that the freedom of a family head is constrained when laws are made to pertain to a dependent within the family? It is only because there remains a residue of the notion that the family head is the one to whom the law is oriented—that those who are his dependents are within his domain, not within the legal domain (unless, of course, he fails to properly attend to his charges). But if the family head is the one to whom the law is directed, then the ideal of equality pertains to the heads of the household and not to the dependents within it. So we see that what looks like a conflict between the ideals of freedom and equality is instead a conflict between two different understandings of the subject of equality.[32] As the understanding shifts between an equality that pertains to each individual and to only independent persons, we miss the fact of dependency. As we try to understand the relation between equality and dependency, we discover the urgency of effecting substantial changes in our understanding of dependency and its consequences for social organization.

Second, the presumption of equality obscures the extent to which many of our societal interactions are not between persons symmetrically situated, even when they are between individuals who might otherwise be autonomous. Moral, political, and social theories have left us with a moral, and often, legal vacuum in domains where women are likely to be at one end of the asymmetry. The dependency critique shows that what is required is an appreciation of the inevitable variety of human interactions and a more adequate understanding of what is morally acceptable in asymmetric relations.

And finally, the equality possible when society is only conceived of as an association of equals has trained our gaze on one side of the sexual division of labor: the inclusion of women into the male half. As we look toward a change in gender roles, we must seek strategies that aim to redistribute the labor on the female half. But as we do, it is of special importance to explore the possible relation between policies of equality that advance a few privileged, usually white upper and upper middle-class women, and the growing impoverishment and deteriorating conditions of lower middle-class and working-class women and women of color. As middle-class women abandon dependency work, is that labor merely redistributed among other less well-situated women? Nearly a decade before national welfare "reform," Marilyn Friedman (1988) pointed out that cutbacks on welfare force women into the service sector of the economy—often into domestic service, thereby doing the domestic work that maintains many middle- and especially upper-income families. Her observation that "many low-income women now occupy a *class* position in relation to middle- and upper-income families which parallels the position which the traditional wife occupied in relation to her husband" (1988, 147) should alert feminists to the dangers of ignoring the importance of dependency work in maintaining structures of domination and subordination that are tied to, if not entirely determined by, gender.[33]

I have saved discussion of the dependency critique for last not only because it serves as the basis of what ensues, but also because I hope to highlight its contribution in light of the other critiques. Other feminist critiques of equality offer the possibility that we can extend their analyses to other excluded groups. The ideal of equality, as we currently find it formulated, underplays the specificity of various sorts of exclusions. The gain in generalizing the feminist critiques is the identification of the nature of those legal structures and strategies that resist and those that accommodate these varied differences. But then perhaps gender is put into a bag of differences, and that itself once again marginalizes the issues that confront women. The dependency critique hones in on one particular feature of women's difference, her historically assigned role as caregiver of dependents. The difference is contingent. Women need not be the caregivers of dependents. The fact of their having historically been so has pervaded their lives such that it has thrown doubt on the aspiration that they will ever share the world with men in equality.

Exponents of the dominance critique will be quick to point out that this is a difference that is tied to women's subordination. Care of dependents—dependency work—is most commonly assigned to those in a society with the least status and power.[34] Furthermore, attention to diversity cautions us not to assume that this is still another universal attribute of women, for not all women care for dependents. Caring labor is assigned to women differently depending on race, class, ability and age, and men of marginalized groups are often also assigned to care for dependents. In developing the dependency critique, we need to draw on the insights of the difference, dominance, and diversity critiques.

First we should see, however, that the dependency concerns which motivate the dependency critique are not reducible to either issues of difference or dominance. Dependency work may confer difference on women. But it is not a difference whose desirability or disadvantage we should be debating. Whether the work of caring for dependents is viewed as desirable or not—as conferring advantage or disadvantage—it is work that must be done by someone. Rather than ask if women's care of dependents results in them being marked as different, we need to ask whether doing dependency work excludes those who do it from the class of equals, and if so, what we must understand and do to end this exclusion.

Similarly, with respect to dominance and dependency, we can recognize that if the world were to magically become a place where no domination could be found, there would still be dependents in need of care. The dependency critique considers, then, the inescapable fact of human dependency and the ways in which such labor makes one vulnerable to domination.

Finally, while the diversity critique cautions against falsely generalizing from the dependency concerns of some women to all women, we cannot even begin to address issues of equality between women without examining the place of dependency work in the lives of women and in the social order. Dependency issues form the nexus of women's lives with men and with other women. Where women subordinate other women and where women dominate other women and other men, we are likely to find dependency matters at issue. To heed the insights of the diversity critique, attention must be given to the dependency critique.

I have argued that the dependency critique is not reducible to other feminist critiques of equality, nor to concerns of other groups who are also excluded from the ideal. Nonetheless an extension of its insights are suggested by the experiences of those women engaged in dependency work. Those experiences highlight the ways in which members of human communities are engaged in interdependencies. They emphasize the fact that the independent individual is always a fictive creation of those men sufficiently privileged to shift the concern for dependence onto others. Understandings of equality that remain based in the independence of individuals, whether they call for equality simpliciter or sex equality, will also exclude as they include.

Should Women Still Want Equality?

Ought women to continue to assert claims to equality or ought women's goals to be cast in different terms and be less marked by a philosophy steeped in patriarchal values? On the one hand, an overemphasis on equality, however formulated, misses the importance of the asymmetries and differences that are unavoidable and even desirable in human intercourse. On the other hand, the ideal is so intimately bound to progressive ideals of justice, freedom, and the elimination of oppression, that it is barely conceivable that a progressive agenda can do without some suitable conception of equality. Feminist theorists have questioned—often with much justification—*conceptions* of equality. These formulations are dominant but not exhaustive understandings.

The many responses to the dominance and difference critiques, which have been offered in recent years, engage the criticisms and search for better ways to retain the aspiration that men and women can share the world in equality. Martha Minow's strategy is to question the norms that define difference, rather than suppressing difference in favor of equality or underscoring difference and foregoing equality. Like the dominance critic, Minow takes difference not as marking the inherent characteristic of the one so labeled but as arising from a relationship where one party has the power to label another as different. A conception of equality, she argues, requires an appreciation of the relational character of difference and of the rights that are precipitated from the claims of equality.[35]

A number of other legal theorists have attempted to respond to the debate in ways that preserve the strengths of both the critiques of equality and of its defense. Christine Littleton argues for "equality across difference" (1987b) and Drucilla Cornell (1991) proposes a model that eschews equality in favor of equivalence. Nonetheless equivalence can be thought of not as a rejection of the concept of equality, but a refinement. Deborah Rhodes (1989) espouses a *disadvantage model*. She argues with Littleton that the problem with difference is the disadvantage that it brings and that a theoretical position should not try to get rid of difference, but only the disadvantage of a particular difference. Rhodes's *disadvantage approach* may be seen as a way to acknowledge the power differences between women and men—in exploring ways that law and policy can remediate disadvantages in women's situations—without defining women by their subordination. Nevertheless, the elimination of disadvantage is nonetheless an equalizing strategy. All of these approaches affirm the aspiration of equality even as the liberal articulations are questioned.

The critics of equality are right in thinking that equality will continue to elude us as long as we work within traditional articulations of equality. We need a conception that addresses the truths about human lives and human relations that feminists have uncovered in their labor to take women's experiences seriously. Borrowing from Walzer again, we note that our dreams of equality are shaped by the norms and values of the society in which we live—values and norms fashioned, in large measure, by those in power. When women are the ones who tend to care for dependents, their just demands will fall outside the compass of an equality fashioned by these norms and values.

If this is right, then what? Should we abandon the political ideals that provide the foundations of democratic society? Should women abandon their supportive, caring, and nurturant ideals, decline to have children, or decline to care for their children once born? And if they do, then what? Who would care for these children? How would the relational and nurturant needs of society, the binding of society, take place?

Neither option is conceivable. The present work is intended to clear the way for an understanding of equality that is compatible with dependency concerns, that understands not only the demands of fairness, but the demands of connection. The distinctive contributions of women's work in tending to dependents bring distinctive values. In the moral domain, this contribution has been identified as the voice of care. It is a voice that is too frequently preempted in the public domain by the voice of justice. Equality is an ideal of justice—its domain is rarely understood to include the values and virtues of care.

Feminist thinkers have begun to formulate a moral theory and a politics grounded in the maternal relation, the paradigm of a relation of care.[36] Their efforts to delineate an ethical and political model based on the nonegalitarianism involved in caring relations, together with the critical evaluation of egalitarian policies discussed in this chapter—and the possibility that policies of equality have a different impact on differently situated women—help stake the project I undertake here. Of special concern is that the achievement of equality, which uses white middle-class men as the measure, improves the lives of some women at the cost of a greater degree of inequality for other women.[37] An understanding of equality which asks only to share the goods of the dominant group without inquiring into the values and labor of those who are subordinated, risks merely shifting the burden of some members of the subordinate group to others who have less power—rather than distributing those burdens more fairly across the population.

Acknowledging human dependency and its consequences for those who do the work of caring for dependents, I will argue, is indispensable for finding a route around these obstacles to a truly inclusive feminism. The domains of caring and equality, an ideal of justice, need to be brought into a dialectical relation if we are to genuinely meet both the concerns of dependency and the demands of equality.

As the relation of the moral stances of care and justice has become elaborated, it has become increasingly clear that a simple opposition between care and justice is inadequate to the needs of our moral and political lives.[38] Although Gilligan is perhaps most responsible for presenting the two moral voices as opposing ones, in another context she describes an interaction between a young girl and a young boy that points the way to a different understanding. The girl wants to play neighbor; the boy wants to play pirates. A fair solution would be to play pirates for a certain amount of time and then switch to playing neighbors for an equal amount of time. But the young girl has another solution. She suggests that they play a game in which the neighbor is a pirate. Gilligan calls the girl's solution "inclusive" rather than "fair." In the fair solution, both games remain in their original conception. In the inclusive solution a new game emerges. There is a transformative potential here. To incorporate the needs and values which women have attended to, requires a transformation making equality truly inclusive. In the following chapter, I suggest that such a concept is adumbrated in the adage that "we are all some mother's child."

Part 1

Love's Labor:
The Requirements of Dependency

1

Relationships of Dependency and Equality

Reflections on Being a Mother's Child

My mother has been serving us dinner. My father and I are nearly fin-
ished eating. She alone remains unfed. A sigh announces the completion
of her task and the beginning of a well-deserved respite. She sits down to
eat. With a shrug and smile, and with a touch of ironic humor, she says,
"After all, *I'm* also a mother's child."

As a child I found this habitual remark confusing. As a woman, now
trained in philosophy, I can hope to articulate both the child's puzzle-
ment and the import of my mother's message. "*My mother is also a
mother's child.*" For a child who sees a parent as Hobbes (1966, 109) saw
his parties to the social contract, "as if but even now sprung out of the
earth, and suddenly, like mushrooms,"[39] the message never fails to come
as a realization. Yes, everyone is some mother's child. As good-natured
as the pronouncement was, it was a sort of self-assertion, an entitlement
claim. I could not understand the need for claiming the entitlement; first,
because I did not think that her desire to sit quietly and eat her own
meal needed justification; second, because I could not understand whom
she might think denied her rightful claim, against whom she was making
it; and finally (most puzzling of all), I could not understand how asserting that she too was a mother's child would be a basis for any entitlement. What was she thereby asserting? What was the claim in need of
assertion? And why was the fact—one might better say the truism—that
she, too, was a mother's child a basis upon which to make any claims?

Although a child (but old enough to be perplexed by my mother's
remark), I would feel uncomfortable that she did not join us at the table
and that she would wait on us even after a full day of work at her
salaried job. Mother would serve herself only when we had no more

23

unmet needs for her to attend to. In all fairness, however, both to my father and to the child I was, we did protest. Even my father, who took it for granted that kitchen work was women's work, was uneasy with my mother's refusal to sit with us and enjoy the food into which she poured so much effort. Still our protest was a paltry one. We never expected to, nor probably did we want to, curb her excess of altruism, and it was easier and surely more convenient to have her do it her way.

The discomfort we felt suggested that my mother's enigmatic pronouncement was implicitly understood, although I had to become an adult woman to understand the quiet vehemence that underlay the good humor. As a woman, I had to experience for myself the ambivalence with which so many women view our socially assigned role. It is an ambivalence that attaches to the joy we garner when we watch another thrive under our loving ministrations. The ambivalence is born of the desire to fulfil a vision of ourselves as good only when we attend to the needs of others, while failing to understand why others do not regard it as equally imperative to respond to us in a similar manner.

At the time I was trying to understand the relation of current feminist writings to conceptions of equality, I was struck by another version of the same expression that I remembered from those childhood dinners. A friend and I were listening to then Supreme Court nominee, Clarence Thomas, counter Anita Hill's accusations of sexual harassment. My friend had been a governess, a position that made her especially vulnerable to an employer's unwanted sexual attentions. While we were listening to Thomas with a skeptical ear, she remarked that as much as she wanted the truth exposed it was not her desire, nor did she think it was Hill's desire, to see Thomas publicly pilloried. "After all," she said, "he, too, was some mother's child."

My friend's cultural background was very different from my mother's and I was struck by the use of such a similar trope. Its meaning was clear in this context. Whatever he himself had done, there was someone who had cared for him, but was not to be blamed for his misdeeds; someone for whom his well-being and happiness were of central importance, who would be suffering if she were to witness his public disgrace. The empathy to Hill was also extended to Thomas, not directly (for he was thought blameworthy), but through his mother. The iconic representation of this fundamental connection between a mothering person and the fate of the individual she has mothered is located in the figure of the *Mater Dolorosa* where the suffering of Christ is imaged through the suffering of Mary. Although invoking universals is out of favor with progressive politics today, there seems to be something telling in the widespread appeal of this image and of the cross-cultural use of the figure of "some mother's child." The notion speaks to the relationship, forged through the care of a vulnerable dependent, and to the value that this relationship imparts both to the one cared for and to the caregiver. This relationship is ubiquitous in human society and is as fundamental to our humanity as any property philosophers have invoked as distinctly human.

In considering equality from the perspective of feminism's critique of the individualism and male-centeredness of the ideal as articulated in liberal philosophy, I came to recognize that the locutions "I am also a mother's child" or "He, too, is some mother's child" can be heard as "We are all—*equally*—some mother's child." And herein lies a claim to equality, one that is an alternative to conceptions which dominate discourse in liberal political theory. It is a claim with both moral and political consequences. Unlike most all conceptions of equality, it begins not with an individual (recall Shylock) asserting characteristics that pertain to him as an individual ("Hath not a Jew hands, organs, dimensions, senses, affections, passions?") and entitle him to equal status ("fed with the same food, hurt with the same weapons, subject to the same diseases, healed by the same means, warmed and cooled by the same winter and summer as a Christian is"). Philosophical theories of equality are more likely to begin with our property as rational beings rather than as possessors of organs and passions, but the effect is identical. By virtue of some common property that we possess as individuals, we make claims to equal treatment, welfare, opportunity, resources, social goods, or capabilities.[40] To have hands, organs, a vulnerability to hunger and pain, or to be rational, are properties that an individual possesses by virtue of who that individual is. Instead my mother asserted her equality by invoking a property that *she* has only in virtue of a property *another* person has. She is the child of a mother only because another person is (or was) someone who mothered her.

By plumbing the depths of this bit of maternal wisdom, I had hoped to come up with a feminist understanding of equality and thereby resolve the quandary of a feminism—itself the spawn of the Enlightenment ideal of equality—compelled to criticize its self-originating conception. After several years, I feel less certain that I have a new concept of equality to articulate. Nevertheless, I do think that by considering how being a mother's child gives one a claim to equality we see the contours of a new notion. Yes, the statement identifies a similarity between all persons, but not every similarity between humans will serve as a basis for the moral and political claim to equality. An answer to the question of whether this shared relation can serve as a basis of a moral and political claim to equality will be deferred until we look more closely at the relationship which the mother-child relation so often exemplifies, but does not exhaust: the relationship between a dependent and her caregiver.

We Can't Go Out the Same Door We Came In

Writing from her situation as a white middle-class woman having experienced divorce, Mary Ann Mason (1988) concludes:

> A family with children is not an egalitarian arrangement but a mutual-support society where all the members, children and father as well as mother, depend upon one another for emotional support and physical protection from the outside world. The degree of each member's contribution varies with age and over time, but nobody keeps score (Mason 1988, 15).

This nonegalitarian and gendered social arrangement sits nested within a political and economic arrangement which distributes rights and freedoms to those who participate in the public political and economic order.

Mason's vision presumes much. It presumes that the one who ventures into the outside world is treated as an equal with those outside the home, that the home is in fact protective for all within it, and that the structure of the family within the home is heterosexual. All these presumptions are in need of critical scrutiny. But let us, for the moment, limit ourselves to the rhetoric of equality—for the rhetoric of the public order is equality even if its realization with respect to non-gendered, as well as gendered, issues is imperfect.

While the ideal of equality itself is vested in the ideal of the moral and political integrity of each individual, Mason's lesson is that, although we may today enter a marriage as *individuals*, we can not go out the same door we came in—especially if we are women, and most especially, if we are women with children.

The gender asymmetry in this situation is crucial. It derives from the gender asymmetry in the division of labor. It is true that men, especially when they become fathers, get assigned the role of breadwinner—whether or not they choose it and whether or not they belong to a social class that gives them a range of possibilities for carrying out this responsibility. Given a breadwinner's responsibilities, it seems that neither can men go out the same door they came in. Most men assume their responsibilities, but so many abandon them. We want to understand why the sense of commitment that attaches to motherhood seems not to be as deep and pervasive a psychic change for the men who abandon their families and their obligations as provider. How much force can the obligation to provide for their children have in the moral consciousness of the men who abandon these responsibilities, even as they assume them for a second family? Perhaps the difference between men and women is found in the perception—that while the caregiver is not fungible, the breadwinner is. Perhaps psychosexual differences,[41] or differences in the depth of socialization for parenting account for the disparity. The same apparent motivations for abandoning a child—the love of another, the call of a profession, the despondency at difficult conditions, the despair at not being able to properly provide for one's child—are construed in dramatically different ways in the case of a woman versus the case of a man.[42] This gender asymmetry pertains across different classes and social situations—although under conditions of extreme need, even women are excused from their caretaking responsibilities, but only if they can hand over the child to one better able to provide sustenance.[43]

Except perhaps in dire conditions where expectations and assignments of responsibility alter, once a woman has a child—whether the child is conceived within or outside a marriage—she is no longer the individual she was before. (Dorothy Parker is said to have commented, "The trouble with having children is that once you have them, you have them.") Even the individual that she was before was shaped by the expectation that women take on the role of caregiver within the family. This expectation, modified through class, ethnicity, and race, shapes much of the economic reality women encounter outside the family and most of the roles they assume within it. That reality is marked by the responsibility—assumed or imposed—to care for dependents.

The aspiration of equality reaches to each individual's sense of integrity and self-respect. To this extent, it is an aspiration that cannot or ought not be abandoned. But to the degree that equality is tied to a particular conception of society, one in which persons are bound together by voluntarily chosen obligations assumed for mutual benefit and self-interest, society cannot begin to comprehend the difficulties and dilemmas created by the facts of human dependency. To paraphrase Wittgenstein, it is a picture that holds us captive. The bonds of a human society tie not only those who can voluntarily obligate themselves and who are equally situated to benefit from mutual cooperation. Dependents are not in such a position, nor are those who must care for dependents. And as long as the responsibilities for human dependency fall disproportionately on women, an equality so construed will disproportionately fail women in their aspirations.

If we begin our thinking not with persons as they are individuated nor with the properties that pertain to them as individuals, their rationality and their interests, but with persons as they are in connections of care and concern, we consider commonalities that characterize this relatedness. These would form the basis of a *connection-based* equality rather than the *individual-based* equality more familiar to us. The question for a connection-based equality is not: What rights are due me by virtue of my status as an equal, such that these rights are consistent with those of all other individuals who have the status of an equal? Instead, the question is: What are my responsibilities to others with whom I stand in specific relations and what are the responsibilities of others to me, so that I can be well cared for and have my needs addressed even as I care for and respond to the needs of those who depend on me?

The basis for such a reconceptualization rests on the centrality of dependency in human relations, the impact of the vulnerabilities of dependency on moral obligation, and the repercussions of these moral obligations on social and political organization. Dependency, as a feature of the human condition, has a crucial bearing on the ordering of social institutions and on the moral intuitions that serve to guarantee adherence to just institutions. Theories of justice, as Hume understood and Rawls underscored, are shaped by the circumstances of human existence that make justice both needed and attainable. A moderate scarcity of resources is such a circumstance because any social order is partially a response to some degree of scarcity. Yet it is equally clear that no society will continue beyond one generation if there are not persons who care for the young. No society—save those enduring the harshest economic, geographic, or climatic conditions[44]—can remain decent if some do not attend to the needs of the ill or disabled and the frail elderly as well as the young. Many moral theories can be and have been used to justify such moral obligations of both society as a whole and of particular individuals, but the obligations owed to those whose who give care, who attend to dependency, has not figured in moral, political or judicial discussions. At once sentimentalized and despised, dependency work has been unevenly distributed among genders, and even among women. The occlusion of dependency work combines with the inattention to dependency workers to make our obligations to those in need of care part of a system of exploitation,[45] one which diminishes the moral worth of the caregiver as well as the person cared for. A society in which such a system of exploitation is the norm cannot be said to be a society in which equality, as both a moral and social value, thrives.

To understand the demands of dependency work and why it calls upon a different social and political commitment if a true equality is to be achieved, we need to start with an exploration of the relationship of dependents to dependency workers. In the next section, I will attempt to characterize the relevant features of dependency and the relations of the individuals for whom the dependency has bearing. In later sections, I will consider the moral claims within and around relationships of dependency and propose an equality compatible with dependency relations.

Dependency in the Human Condition

Dependency is inescapable in the life history of each individual. Fineman has called these moments of early childhood, illness, disability and frail old age "inevitable dependencies" and grounds dependency in biology.[46] Yet it is also clear—from even a cursory examination of different societies and historical periods—that cultural dimensions as well as physiological constraints determine what counts as young, as ill, as disabled,[47] and as frail enough to be thought dependent. In this study, I provide parameters for consideration—parameters that are variously realized under different cultural conditions. Similarly, the understanding of obligations owed to the members of the class of dependents—construed through this hybrid of cultural and physiological determinants—is itself shaped by cultural and material conditions.

Nonetheless, there are identifiable states of our life history in which dependency is unavoidable, either for survival or for flourishing. The immaturity of infancy and early childhood, illness and disability that renders one nonfunctional even in the most accommodating surroundings, and the fragility of advanced old age, each serve as examples of such inescapable dependency. The incapacity here is determined neither by will nor desire, but by determinants of biology in combination with social circumstances. Less obvious conditions also render us dependent. Children who are well beyond the utter dependency of infancy must still count upon others for their flourishing. Even non-life-threatening illness can render one dependent for a period. In addition, under some conditions, a relatively minor disabling condition can render one seriously dependent either permanently or temporarily.

These are unassailable facts about human existence. While conditioned in fundamentally significant ways by cultural considerations, dependency for humans is as unavoidable as birth and death are for all living organisms. We may even say that the long maturation process of humans, combined with the decidedly human capacities for moral feeling and attachment, make caring for dependents a mark of our humanity.

Our dependency, then, is not only an *exceptional* circumstance. To view it as such reflects an outlook that dismisses the importance of human interconnectedness, not only for purposes of survival, but for the development of culture itself. I emphasize the most undisputed forms of dependency. Yet attention to just these embraces such a vast proportion of human interactions. My hope is that once we understand the implications of the clearest cases of dependency, we will appreciate the full range of human interconnection, and see how all moral and political concepts need to reflect these connections. To begin, we must see that regardless of how dependency may vary according to prevailing social understandings and technological constraints, the vulnerability of dependents creates a set of conditions whereby some persons inevitably must attend to the needs of others.

Dependency Work, the Dependency Worker, and the Charge

I have called the task of attending to dependents, *dependency work*. Although we sometimes speak of dependency care, I have chosen the word *work* to emphasize that care of dependents *is work*.[48] It shares features of other activity, traditionally engaged in by women, that feminists have underscored as labor. Affectional labor, for example, with its component of care and sexual attention overlaps with dependency work, but is not identical to it. Dependency work, when poorly done can be done without an affective dimension, and sexuality is, to a great extent, inappropriate in dependency work.[49] Furthermore, one can do affectional labor for one who is not dependent in the sense that I mean here. The affections a wife provides to a well and fully functioning husband, for example, is a labor that is not lavished on a dependent. Similarly, domestic labor, such as housework, while often done in conjunction with dependency work is not identical to dependency work.[50] Dependency work is done not only in the home, but in nurseries and hospitals as well. Still, where affectional[51] and domestic labor is assigned to women, dependency work is also assigned by gender.

I do not want to deny important differences between paid and unpaid dependency work. But we should note that whatever dependency work we pay for today has, at some time, been done by women as part of their familial duty. Therefore whether the work is currently paid or not, we can identify certain distinctive features that are common to both paid and unpaid varieties of dependency work and that have important moral, social, and political implications.

Those who perform this work, I have called *dependency workers*.[52] The dependency worker directs her energies and attention to an intended beneficiary, a *charge*.[53] The relationships forged between the dependency worker and her charge, I speak of as *relationships of dependency, dependency relationships*, or *dependency relations*, using these terms interchangeably.

A *charge*, in the sense I use the term here, is a person "committed or entrusted to the care, custody, management or support of another" (Webster's New International Dictionary, Third Edition, 1967). The use of the passive in the dictionary definition is instructive. It suggests a third party who does the committing or entrusting of the charge's care or management, and this, in turn, implies that such a commission is outside of the ability or entitlement of the charge. That incapacitation requires that another must be assigned to her care. Without these tasks being (often) assigned by another and performed by another, the charge would be bereft of life-sustaining resources. Because the charge cannot survive or function within a given environment—or possibly within any environment—without assistance, she needs to be *in the charge* of another for her care and protection. The dependency worker who is in charge of the dependent must have the power and authority necessary to meet the responsibilities of the work. In choosing to speak of the person who is dependent as the charge, I mean to emphasize both the responsibility that the role of dependency worker entails and the ways in which the well-being of the dependent person requires another to act in her best interests.

A Paradigm of Dependency Work

In order to understand its pragmatic requirements and its moral demands, we need to consider dependency work in the paradigm case of a dependency relationship. Such a paradigm will capture its salient features when the work is well-done and the relationship is a satisfying one.

The labor, when well done, is aptly characterized by Jane Martin's three "Cs": care, concern, and connection.[54] It is the work of tending to others in their state of vulnerability—*care*. The labor either sustains ties among intimates or itself creates intimacy and trust—*connection*. And affectional ties—*concern*—generally sustain the connection, even when the work involves an economic exchange. For the dependency worker, the well-being and thriving of the charge is the primary focus of the work.[55] In short, the well-being of the charge is the responsibility of the dependency worker. Such is the paradigm case of dependency work.

With respect to this paradigm, a few clarifications are in order.[56] First, to define dependency work as I have done appears to preclude reciprocal care. In the paradigm case, those who are cared for are unable to care for themselves, and so, one assumes, are incapable of caring for another while in this state. But interdependencies of caring relations are not only possible, they are common. Care may be reciprocated simultaneously. This can occur if neither party is too incapacitated, or if one is incapacitated in a way that the other party is not, or in cases where reciprocity can take place over time. A reciprocal arrangement, wherein there is an alternation of roles between the one who does the caring and the one who is cared for, is just a modification of the paradigm case.

Second, I have spoken as if the responsibility for the dependency work always falls upon a single individual. This reflects the prevalence of such forms of caregiving within our own society. Or rather, tasks that are best described as dependency work still take the form in which one person is expected to execute all its different aspects. Where the work has become rationalized and professionalized it tends to be less recognizable as dependency work. Nursing, traditionally done at home as unpaid familial women's work, has not only moved out of the home but has splintered into a variety of forms and functions. Some nursing work, but not all, continues to be dependency work in my primary sense. While there is no inherent reason why dependency work cannot be shared, at any given time it may be necessary that responsibility is assigned, if not to one individual, then to a few. Otherwise, there is the danger that at any particular moment, each caregiver supposes that another is looking out for the dependent when, in fact, no one is paying attention. Nonetheless, considerations bearing on the just distribution of dependency work, which are central to the project at hand, must assume that it is possible to divide some of the responsibilities. At times, bearing the full brunt of caring for another can be too burdensome and only by sharing responsibility can the work be made non-exploitative.

Finally, to speak of a dependency worker may suggest that dependency work is to be so distributed that it becomes the lifework of certain people, classes, or genders, thereby presuming a distinctive class of workers. This is, in fact, the current shape of things. But to define such a species of work and such a species of worker should not foreclose distributional questions. As I hope to make clear in subsequent arguments, it is precisely the current distribution of dependency work that requires revision.[57] While dependency work can be variously distributed and shared, as long as an individual is responsible for the care of another who is dependent on her, I call that person a dependency worker.

Situating Dependency Work Within a Practice

Although the dependencies with which I am concerned are inherent in the human condition, dependency work is normally situated in a practice.[58] Its requirements, its successes and failures, its practitioners and the specific implementation of care, connection, and concern are dependent on the practice. Need and vulnerability, no less than the appropriateness of response, are all evaluated, if not constituted, by the practice in question. But the practices are themselves ones that arise to meet the inherent dependencies of which I speak.

Maternal practice, as described by Sara Ruddick, provides a paradigmatic instance of dependency work. Ruddick identifies three features of maternal practice: preservative love, fostering growth, and training for social acceptance. Engagement in each aspect of maternal practice is dependency work. Nevertheless, not all dependency work is characterized by these same practices. Consider caring for the frail elderly. A preservative concern and respect may be more to the point than a preservative love; and in certain cultural circumstances, deference may be the preferred affect accompanying preservative behaviors. Care for the elderly requires fostering self-sufficiency and self-esteem rather than fostering growth. Rather than socializing for acceptance, care for the elderly requires stemming a disintegration of that social acceptability and sense of self-esteem which the individual attained while a vigorous adult.

The practice of caring for the severely developmentally disabled provides yet another paradigm of dependency work, distinguishable from the model of maternal care necessary for an "intact" flourishing child.[59] In Chapter Seven, I discuss in detail such differences in maternal practice. For now, consider that in the case of the significantly disabled child, preservative love and concern may have to be accompanied by a lifelong commitment to day-to-day physical care for the charge. Fostering development also becomes a lifelong project, but the notion of development attains a new sense. Socialization for acceptance may involve less effort directed toward the training of the charge and more to changing the expectations and grounds of acceptance of society itself. Different practices, then, differentially shape demands on the dependency worker.

Inequality, Domination, and Vulnerability in the Dependency Relation

While the dependency worker has responsibility for the charge, the dependency relationship does not authorize the exercise of power except for the benefit of the charge. Still the charge, by virtue of her dependency, is vulnerable to the actions of the dependency worker in ways that a more independent person is not.[60] Should the dependency worker neglect her duties, the fate of the charge hangs in the balance, and some intervention is critical. But the delicacy of the dependency relationship requires sensitivity in the manner of intervention.

It is useful to distinguish between the *inequality of power* in a relation of dependency and the exertion of *domination* in a relation of inequality.

The inequality of power is endemic to dependency relations. But not every such inequality amounts to domination. Domination involves the exercise of power over another against her best interests and for purposes that have no moral legitimacy. Characterizing domination in terms of the abusive power the dominator wields, Sara Ruddick writes, "Metaphorically, a dominator treats the dominated as if she were an "object of property." She continues:

> Dominators may care deeply for those they dominate; they may believe that domination is necessary for the eventual happiness and perhaps even the survival of the dominated. When caring dominators are benevolent and even-tempered, it is possible that neither they nor those they dominate recognize the character of their relationship. Dominating aims become evident, however, if the dominated develops projects and ambitions, attachments and sexual desires, that are disturbing to dominators . . . When confronted with incongruous willfulness, even a benign dominator is apt to reassert ownership, to confirm the relation of owner to object (Ruddick 1995, 213–14).

Domination is an illegitimate exercise of power. It is inherently unjust. The moral character of a dependency relation and its nature as a caring or uncaring relation is determined, at least in part, by how the parties in the dependency relation respond to one another, both with respect to the vulnerabilities of the dependent *and* to the vulnerabilities created for the dependency worker.[61] Inequality of power is compatible with both justice and caring, if the relation does not become a relation of domination. That the relation be a caring one is largely, although not exclusively, the obligation of the dependency worker.[62] That the relation not be one of domination is an obligation that equally befalls the dependency worker and the charge.

Both the dependency worker and the charge can transform a dependency relationship into one of domination. The dependency worker is well situated to abuse the vulnerable charge. The moral opprobrium accorded this behavior is strong, though not sometimes strong enough. At the same time, the usual ways in which we express annoyance and disapproval at the behavior of another, or vent frustrations in interacting with another when we deal with equals or even subordinates, are off-limits when we encounter certain very vulnerable persons. The charge may be abusive in ways she doesn't intend, and the dependency worker is bereft of the usual ways to cope with the injury.[63] In addition, the charge can exert a certain tyranny by the manufacture of false needs or by exploiting the worker's caring, concern, and need for the connection forged through the relationship. Marilyn Frye (1983) speaks of one who "grafts the substance of another to one's own."[64] To graft the substance of another to one's own is to fail even to recognize the integrity of the other who exerts her labor on your behalf. This is a special vulnerability of the dependency worker. Because of the charge's dependence upon her, and because of the ties formed through that relation, the dependency worker herself becomes vulnerable to the abuse of having her substance grafted onto another.

The danger of grafting the substance of another to one's own is surely more acute when the status of a charge (considered apart from her situation as a dependent) is higher than that of her dependency worker (for example, the immigrant nursemaid of a privileged young child). It is worth noting—and it is hardly beside the point—that in a situation where male dominance prevails, an inequality in status is found in each case where a woman mothers her own son.[65] At the same time, not all sons are equally valued by the society into which they are born. The relation between mothers and sons who are members of a devalued group has its own complexity.[66]

In the idealized construction of the paradigm case, the charge does not exert any authority or power over the dependency worker other than the charge's moral claim that the dependency worker meet her responsibilities. Likewise, the dependency worker restrains her power and exercises it only in the interests of the charge. The dependency relationship is, then, itself ideally not one of domination, even though it is between two individuals of unequal power. The inequality between worker and charge is one of capacity, although it may also be one of social status and even of power over life and death. Though the two may not even be moral equals—the charge may well be temporarily or permanently incapable of a moral response—the relation, at its very crux, is a moral one arising out of a claim of vulnerability on the part of the dependent, on the one hand, and of the special positioning of the dependency worker to meet the need, on the other.[67]

The relationship between the dependency worker and her charge is importantly a relation of trust. The charge must trust that the dependency worker will be responsible to and respectful of her vulnerability and will not abuse whatever authority and power has been vested in her to carry out these responsibilities. The dependency worker must, in turn, trust the charge neither to make demands that go beyond her true needs, to exploit the attachments that are formed through the work of care, nor to exploit the vulnerabilities that either result from the dependency work or that have resulted in the caregiver engaging in dependency work.[68] No doubt, such trust is often violated—more often than dependency workers and charges alike can permit themselves to acknowledge.[69] But unless this trust is respected often enough, it is difficult to imagine how the work of caring for dependents could be accomplished. The delicate emotional balance and restraint demanded of both parties, and the immense investment of emotional energies required to accomplish the work of dependency care, signal a highly affective relation between charge and dependency worker that demands trust.[70]

Precisely because of the significance of both affect and trust in these relations, the ties formed by relations of dependency are among the most important ones we experience. It often seems that to infuse caring labor into such a relationship (or a contact with another that is not yet a relationship) relaxes our own boundaries of self, which makes way for an emotional bond that is especially potent. These bonds can even transcend those of the human community and extend to all sentient creatures, especially those that "complete" the caring relation by responding to care appropriately.[71] When these relationships fail, not only is the immediate welfare of the charge at risk, but her long-range emotional well-being is in jeopardy. The dependency worker can also be harmed by the failure of these affective bonds.

An example is provided by the betrayal of a mother who invests her hope of happiness in her son in *The Women of Brewster Place*, a novel by Gloria Naylor. Matte is the mother of a young man who is charged with murder in a bar fight. Her son is released on bail obtained by using her house as collateral. Matte watches him move "through the parking lot almost singing" and Naylor says, "She took in his happiness and made it her own just as she'd done with every emotion that had ever claimed him."[72] (1983, 51). In a poignant scene that follows, we witness Matte's realization that her son has jumped bail, although he knew full well the implications for his mother:

> The vegetables were done, the chicken almost burnt, and the biscuits had to come out of the oven. She turned off the gas jets, opened the oven door, and banged the pan of biscuits onto the countertop. She looked frantically at the creeping shadows over her kitchen door and rushed to the cabinet and took out plates and silverware. She slammed the cabinet shut and slowly and noisily set the table for two. She looked pleadingly around the kitchen, but there was nothing left to be done. So she pulled out the kitchen chair, letting the metal legs drag across the tiles. Trembling, she sat down, put her head in her hands, and waited for the patient and crouching stillness just beyond the kitchen door (Naylor 1983, 54).

The awareness that her son has left comes at a moment when she assumes her caretaking role: the preparation of dinner.

Because Matte makes her son's joys and sufferings her own and invests her emotional life in him through her enabling actions, his betrayal, when he is grown, is all the more devastating. As an adult son, he is dependent enough to take her money, but not dependent enough to return home—nor loyal enough to evince concern for her well-being. The dependency relation with its requirement that the dependency worker invest some portion of herself in the happiness and well-being of another carries the potential both for deep emotional bonding *and* for vulnerability on the part of the one cared for and the caregiver alike.

The relation between dependency worker and dependent seems to hover between servitude on the one hand, and paternalism on the other. On the one hand, the dependency worker's self-respect is partially a function of how well she meets the needs of another, on the other, she has the awesome power to respond to and interpret the needs of a helpless other. She has too little power with respect to those who stand outside the dependency relation, and potentially too much power with respect to her charge. As we argue for ways to combat the powerlessness of the dependency worker vis-à-vis the world outside the dependency relation, we also need to be sensitive to the dependent's vulnerability to her caregiver's power within the relation. Paternalism in dependency relations is always a risk, but the proposals made in this book on behalf of dependency workers should diminish, not increase that danger. One who has her interests taken care of in an appropriate and just manner will be less, not more, likely to live her life through her charge, and less, not more, likely to find other ways to discharge ambition and power than through paternalistic behavior. A system that pays adequate attention to the dependency relation will be one seeking both to empower the dependency worker with respect to her own interests and, whenever possible, to decrease the dependency of the dependent as well. By relegating dependency to the status of an afterthought, neither caregiver nor charge are well-served.

Extending the Concept of Dependency Work

We can extend the notion of dependency work to cases where the other is not inherently dependent, that is, where the other is not a charge. Caring for grown children who are capable of caring for themselves—feeding them and attending to their needs as we see Matte doing in Naylor's novel—is an extension of dependency work that often goes with the maternal (and often paternal) territory. Beyond this, we can use the notion to cover the hidden dependencies of men on women. We can also include the ancillary or supportive but nonetheless crucial jobs women so often perform in the public workplace, many of which began as part of the familial duties expected of women. We can employ the term to cover what poet Adrienne Rich has called "world repair" (Rich 1979, 205), work done by those whom Marilyn Frye (Frye 1983, 168) calls "stagehands." In this extended sense secretaries, waitresses, and traditional wives are all dependency workers.[73]

In this book, I will confine the term "dependency worker" to its narrowest sense. I want to first show that as a society we cannot do without dependency work in the narrowest sense and that standard theories ignore this most fundamental work and form of relationship. If we get a theory that can bring in dependency relationships, in the narrow sense, and grant its participants full citizenship, then relationships of dependency in the extended sense will be included in a much more natural way. Therefore I exclude "wifely duties," for instance, that are not directed to those who are charges. A husband is not a charge of his wife, just as the boss is not a charge of the secretary, and so this is not dependency work in the primary sense. The wife, the secretary, the waitress, to mention but a few "service providers," are not providing their services to persons who are genuinely incapable of performing the duties performed for them by the dependency worker. Dependency work is labor that enhances the power and activity of another. It is work that caters to the needs of another. However, when this labor is exerted on behalf of those who could, at least in principle, perform these actions themselves, I want to speak of this as dependency work only in an extended sense.[74]

Professions such as medicine, law, teaching, and social work carry with them some implicit or explicit dictate to enhance the power and activity of the other—through improving the health or welfare or education of the professional's clients. The patient's well-being, even her life, is often dependent on her physician. The lawyer's client can be very vulnerable and dependent on the lawyer's expertise. The student is dependent to some degree on her teacher; as is the individual who receives the services of a social worker. Still these professional services are not dependency work, even in the extended sense. Dependency work is a type of a labor that requires its own definition—even if selecting its distinguishing features is difficult.

To distinguish these professional activities from dependency work, let us consider what some writers have claimed as distinguishing marks of the professions. Michael Bayles identifies the three necessary features generally singled out by authors writing on the subject: first, a rather extensive training; second, a training that involves a significant intellectual component; and third, a trained ability that provides an important service in the community (Bayles 1988, 28–9). Other common features he notes include: a process of certification, an organization of members, and autonomy, i.e., "the professionals are expected to exercise a considerable degree of discretionary judgment" (Bayles 1988, 28-29). Another writer speaks of the detachment as well as an intellectual interest and bent toward generalization required of the professional even as she deals with particular cases (Hughes 1988, 33). Still another speaks of these four essential attributes: "generalized and systematic knowledge;" "orientation toward the community interest rather than self-interest;" the internalization of codes of ethics promoted by "voluntary associations organized and operated by work specialists themselves;" and rewards (monetary and honorary) that serve as "a set of symbols of work, achievement and thus ends in themselves, not means to some end of individual self-interest" (Barber 1988, 36).

The other-directed and non-self-interested character of the work is surely similar to dependency work. But what varies significantly are features associated with status. The high status of the professions is indicated by the emphasis on their intellectual character, by a training that draws on "generalized and systematic knowledge," by the autonomy claimed for the professional, by the existence of self-regulatory codes of ethics, and by voluntary and autonomous organizations. The potential self-effacement of the other-directed character of professional work is offset by the autonomy, detachment, and achievement accorded to the professional. Perhaps most interesting of all is the method of compensation indicated by the last author. The monetary and honorary rewards are symbols of work achievement. The professional is thus set outside the self-interested competition for goods. But unlike the dependency worker (whose labor is also seen as not self-interested), the professional's work is interpreted as benefiting the community as a whole. When her obligations to do dependency work keep her out of the competition for goods, the dependency worker is marginalized. When the professional stands outside the fray, he stands above it. Rather than being seriously disadvantaged, he is exempt from its vicissitudes and is amply rewarded for his efforts. Of the two categories of labor in which devotion to the well-being of another is at stake, the status and remuneration goes to the professional.

The difference in status is connected to specialization. Sociologists speak of the *functionally specific* work of the professional compared to the *functionally diffuse* work of a mother, for instance.[75] The functionally specific work of the professional is, we can say, *interventionist,* not *sustaining.* The functionally diffuse work of the dependency worker, in my primary sense, sustains her charge by means of her (often daily) care. A range of needs get met. The skills needed to answer the demands may be trained for or not, may involve intellectual or manual abilities.[76] Whatever the need, as long as the dependency worker is capable of filling it, the responsibility to fill it falls to the dependency worker. The professional intervenes, and then steps away. The point of intervention is a carefully targeted set of concerns, for which the professional is specially trained. Once the intervention is complete, the professional's responsibility is over. The physician intervenes with diagnosis and prescriptions for care that others carry out. The lawyer intervenes between the client and the legal system, but her responsibility ends where the legal expertise ends. It is not the job of the lawyer to attend to the ills that created the need for the intervention, such as to pay debts or to take care of the injuries being sued for. The work of sustaining a dependent is not so well-circumscribed.

Significantly, careers that are precariously or newly professionalized, for example social work, are also ones in which the worker's role can lie on the border of sustaining and intervening. The responsibility of a social worker will include insuring that the work of sustaining the dependent gets accomplished—although the more professionalized the social worker, the more it will be her responsibility to assign appropriate tasks to others. Teachers—especially in the earlier grades—not only intervene with their expertise, but are often poised to care for the variety of needs of their young pupils. Nurses too, sit on the cusp of the distinction between the interventionist and the sustainer.[77]

The professions may be indispensable to the form of industrialized societies we have come to know. Dependency work, particularly in the primary sense, is indispensable to the maintenance and productivity of any society. In contrast to the visibility of the professional in our post-industrial age, the atomistic character of contemporary society makes dependency work especially invisible. Professional careers, demanding as they are, reward their associates with high pay, while dependency work is, when not unpaid, poorly paid labor. While professional work is held accountable to publicly acknowledged ethical standards, affectional ties importantly sustain dependency work. The professions are predominantly occupied by men; dependency work is mostly carried out by women. Women are so closely identified with dependency work that even the professions they enter into in the largest numbers—at least in contemporary Western industrialized countries—are ones thought to be closer to dependency work (compare, for instance, social work and early child education rather than law or medicine).[78]

Dependency Work and Women's Subordination

Although one can speak in gender-neutral terms about dependency workers, we know that it is women—in their roles as mother, sister, wife, nurse, and daughter—who have largely undertaken dependency work. Equally important, it is in their role as dependency workers that women have been made vulnerable to poverty, abuse, and secondary status.[79] Well-documented evidence has been adduced for the claim that it is within the patriarchical marriage—that is, a marriage in which the roles of breadwinner and caregiver are defined by gender—that women often suffer psychological, sexual, and other physical abuse as well as economic exploitation.[80] The partially hidden, partially known fact of spousal abuse aids and abets the economic exploitation. This situation depends on what is too often merely a serviceable fiction: Within patriarchal marriage, women accept a limit on their freedom to define and pursue whatever needs and aspirations are incommensurate with their dependency work—and the men, in return, will protect them from other men and provide "their" women with economic resources.[81] This "contract" effectively bars women's entrance into the public arena of political and economic participation. As the patriarchal marriage loses some of its grip, the promise, and responsibility, of equal opportunity opens before women. The Enlightenment vision, projected onto women, is that the paternalistic protectionism that infantilizes women will lose its sway and women will enter the world as equals.

But the Enlightenment vision leaves unchallenged women's role as dependency workers. The public space, within liberal political and economic theory, has largely remained the domain of free, equal, rationally self-interested beings. Entering that space does not free the dependency worker from responsibilities to her charges. The exercise of an unfettered, rational self-interest presumed possible for the putatively nondependent and independent worker is not possible for the dependency worker whose responsibilities to her charge remain primary.[82] Consequently, the inequality she experiences in a cooperative arrangement with a provider dogs her even as she enters the public sphere to play the role of provider herself. Not surprisingly, many women enter that public space by taking on the paid labor of dependency work. In what we might call a "dialectic of dependency," this labor again serves as a basis for the exclusion of the woman from the fraternity of equals in political life, even as it permits her a measure of economic independence. For the work of caring for dependents, whether paid or unpaid, requires—morally, sometimes legally, and as an excellence of the work itself—attention to the needs and concerns of another, often to the exclusion of one's own.[83]

The interest of the dependency worker remains attached to that of her charge, even as it exists in tension with that of the charge. The freedom of the dependency worker to shape her goals and give expression to her desires is limited not only by the goals and desires of other autonomous beings like herself. Her freedom is more fundamentally constrained by the internalized needs and aspirations of others who depend on her.

A woman's social and economic class—and sometimes her race, ethnicity, or sexuality—is a determinant of the form and severity of the economic dependency that results from the gender-based nature of most dependency work. Heterosexual, white, middle-class women generally become economically dependent on their husbands, even when the woman contributes financially to the household. Resorting to economically exploitative work, but having a kin and community network that permits the sharing of dependency work, is more typical among poorer women, especially women of color.[84] Where even low-paying work is not an option or needs to be supplemented by state welfare provisions, the state itself has, at times, taken on many of the powers of the patriarchal provider: dispensing financial rewards and punishments and controlling the woman's sexual activity, access to her children, her reproductive choices, etc.[85] Given strictures against homoerotic activity, the lesbian woman who is a dependency worker is vulnerable to economic sanction when she attempts to fill the role of provider. She has often lost the support of traditional kin, although she may gain support of other women within women-centered communities who will share her dependency work. She has few rights and little protection if she assumes the role of dependency worker for an ill partner or her partner's children.

Accompanying most forms of economic dependency is a debilitating psychological, political and social dependency as well. These can be called *secondary* or *derived dependencies*.[86] A fuller discussion of such secondary dependencies requires that we look at the *cooperative conflicts* in which they are often situated. Dependency on men or on patriarchical structures has seemed far more inevitable than it is. Female dependency takes on the appearance of a generalized inferiority, but at the same time comes to be a mark of femininity granted to women of a valorized class and denied to or granted grudgingly to women of lower social and economic standing.

Dependency Work in "Cooperative Conflicts"

Cooperative Conflicts—The Provider

I have spoken as if relationships of dependency are self-contained, as if their success or failure hinges on the good will of the dependency worker and the charge. Yet for the relationship to be effective in fulfilling its purpose, the dependency worker must have access to those resources required for the maintenance and well-being of both her charge and herself.

Where the sphere of economic productivity is concentrated outside the home, the nuclear family has been the favored "social technology."[87] One adult, call that individual *the provider*, participates in a public economy and is designated *head of household*—a term fundamentally gendered as reflected in the use of the nomenclature *female-headed household* which is never used when the woman is the major income earner in a two-adult heterosexual home. A second adult is occupied primarily (though rarely exclusively) with the dependency needs of the children, as well as with the dependency needs of disabled and elderly kin.[88]

Such families, then, are cooperative arrangements in which we find conflicting needs as well as cooperative aims. Amartya Sen (1989) calls these *cooperative conflicts*.[89] Within a cooperative conflict the participants can be thought of as parties in a bargaining situation. But cooperative conflicts are distinguished by the role of subjective factors, especially the participants' self-perceptions and their perceptions of the other participant's contribution to the cooperative arrangement. Subjective factors in cooperative conflicts are determinative even when assessing the bargaining situation. Even where the contribution of the two partners is equal, if it is not *perceived* as equal by either one of the participants, the outcome will be less favorable to the partner whose contribution is thought less valuable. For the relationship to continue, the less favored participant must be willing to tolerate a more conflictual situation—and one that is unfair by objective standards—than the more favored participant. Such tends to be the condition of the dependency worker within the cooperative conflict of family organization.

Breakdown Positions and Inequality in Cooperative Conflicts

Within the nuclear family, the familial dependency worker stands in a relation of cooperative conflict with other nondependents who offer access to necessary resources obtainable only outside the family unit. Because the dependency worker needs the cooperation of another to obtain the resources necessary to sustain both herself and her charge, she will tolerate a worse situation than her partner before permitting the arrangement to break down. She is in a *worse breakdown position*.

By virtue of her moral and emotional commitment to her charge and by dint of the ease with which her substance is grafted on to another (and the internalization of that vulnerability into a condition of her psychological makeup), in a relation of cooperative conflict, the dependency worker is exceedingly vulnerable to exploitation, to domination by the one upon whom she depends for support. The vulnerability of the familial dependency worker arises out of the necessity to have access to external resources over which she has limited control.[90] Nonetheless, because subjective factors can play a role as crucial as objective ones in cooperative conflicts, when the self-understanding of the dependency worker includes a need and desire to placate and please the person who takes the social position of the provider, even the independently wealthy woman who serves the dependency needs of her children can so position herself that she accepts a worse breakdown point. This is probably because, as Sen notes, "The nature of the family organization requires that these conflicts be molded in a general format of cooperation, with conflicts treated as aberrations or deviant behavior" (1989, 146). The potential for exploitation, domination and conflict are masked when the experiential need for cooperation is as strong as it is within families.

Where the family is part of a putatively egalitarian society, the real inequality of power within the family between familial dependency worker and provider also gets masked. (Note, in principle, this inequality need not presuppose gender inequality, although in fact, it is most often aligned with gender inequality.) The tendency is to view the partners in the cooperative conflict as occupying complementary, but equal roles. When one accepts the premise of equality, a cooperative arrangement benefiting only one party looks like one that could not have been freely chosen, and hence must have been coerced. Or else it is simply not seen for what it is. The inequality between adult members of a family, within a society that purports equality, is as antithetical to the ideology of the family as is the intrinsic presence of conflict in what is regarded as an inherently cooperative arrangement. Yet what Sen's analysis of the cooperative conflict reveals, especially when combined with the phenomenology of dependency work, is that the relation between the familial dependency worker and the provider is inherently unequal, even when the contributions of the participants are presumably valued as complementary and equal. This inequality easily lends itself to the injustice of domination.

We see then that within those social technologies whose design includes meeting dependents' needs, there are two sorts of inequalities: the inequality of capacity between the dependent charge and the dependency worker; and the inequality of power between both members of the dependency relation and the third party. For the sake of simplicity, we have called this third party "the provider." Nevertheless, we recognize that this person or persons may be responsible only for the availability of *some* of the external resources, and may, at times, not actually *provide* resources but only *control* the flow of resources to and within the household.[91] The social esteem and control over resources enjoyed by the best established professions ensure a large measure of autonomy to the professional whose work may well demand that they put the interests of another first. In the case of the dependency worker, the provider's control of resources combines with a general social devaluation of the work of dependency to thwart the possibility of a comparable autonomy for the dependency worker. To speak of this diminished autonomy is another way of speaking of the dependency worker's unequal relation to the provider.

The inequality between the dependency worker and the provider may presuppose some moral hierarchy, whereby those who care for others are viewed as morally lacking in some sense or as having virtues, that are morally inferior to those who do not do such work. Such a position was held by Aristotle. A person who would do dependency work and would suffer the diminished autonomy we described was viewed by Aristotle as the same person whose soul was defective in ways characteristic of a slave or a woman. Only the free male was thought morally capable of controlling the resources in the family economy and only he was granted the possibility of being a fully realized moral agent. But the inequality is found even when there is no such moral hierarchy. Nor does the hierarchy depend upon, although it is aggravated by, an acknowledged social inequality, for example a gender or racial hierarchy, between the dependency worker and the provider. The inequality arises out of the objective and subjective factors that make the exit options for the dependency worker less viable than those available to the provider.

Let us recall Bernard Williams's (1973) three-fold analysis of equality: the assertion of a common humanity, the claim to equal moral capacities, and the claim to equal opportunity. When we turn to the relation between dependency worker and provider, we see that although asserting any of these claims to equality for the dependency worker can restore a measure of equality into the relation between dependency worker and provider, none of these re-establishes a perfect equality. As long as the dependency worker must rely on a provider to meet: 1) her own needs; 2) the needs of her charge (which in the self-understanding of the dependency worker gets taken up as—even as they stand in tension with—her own needs); and 3) the resources required to sustain the dependency relation, the bargaining position of the dependency worker will be *worse* than that of the provider. The inequality in power between dependency worker and provider is an inequality *of situation*.[92] To be in a worse bargaining position is to be unequally situated vis-à-vis someone who has direct power over you. Any inequality of power can too easily become a relation of domination.

The dependent also experiences an inequality. The inequality is one *of capacity*, vis-à-vis both the dependency worker and those who are "independent." The inequality of capacity may or may not be something about which anything can be done. While efforts are required to make the dependent as capable as feasible, protections for the dependent—in the form of legislation, for example—need to be in place. One remains, however, at the mercy of the moral fiber of those who have the greater power. Inequalities of situation can have more structural remedies that protect the vulnerable and that reduce the possibility for exploitation and abuse. We will explore these in subsequent chapters.

Secondary Dependency and Equality for Dependency Workers

To lack certain sorts of capacities, those essential to surviving and maintaining oneself, is to be dependent in my sense. To be in a worse bargaining position is to be in a state of *secondary dependency*,[93] the state of dependency of the dependency worker herself. The dependency worker's perceptions of two factors play a crucial role in her determination of what she will tolerate in a cooperative conflict: first, her perception of her access to the external resources necessary to maintain herself, the dependent, and the relation; and second, the importance of sustaining the relation for her self-understanding as a morally and socially worthy person.

Since both subjective and objective factors figure in the evaluation of one's breakdown point, perceptions of social as well as economic equality are important determinants. When dependency work is done by a specifiable social group, the vulnerability of the dependency worker will be a function not only of her individual situation, but also of the status of her social group. Woman are especially vulnerable as dependency workers in situations where dependency workers are mostly women and women are not accorded moral equality (Williams's second sense of equality). They are less vulnerable when they are at least accorded moral equality.

The sort of equality made available through a purported equality of opportunity, however, can have a more ambiguous consequence where dependency work is done by an identifiable social group, such as women. On the one hand, the dependency worker can know that her social identity per se ought not to preclude her entrance into the competitive arena. On the other hand, her energies are channeled into the preservation and fruition of another. Her own needs, desires, and aspirations (in so far as these stand apart from the needs, desires and aspirations of those for whom she cares) are set aside, deferred, or obliterated, as are the exercise of those capacities needed to enter the free competition for the benefits of social cooperation. This handicapping feature creates her secondary dependency, her dependence on a provider.

A conception of society as constituted by autonomous self-interested individuals, equally situated so as to engage in the free competition for social goods, eclipses these secondary dependencies. This obfuscation can *worsen* the breakdown position of the dependency worker, for the social conditions do not accommodate dependency workers who wish to exit from an arrangement of cooperative conflict nearing the breakdown point. Social policy is not directed at the needs of dependency workers who step outside of the cooperative conflictual arrangements. And the public arena—the purported site of equality of opportunity—is ill-suited to meet the special conditions which would make it possible for the dependency worker to enter as an equal.

The ideology of the workplace and the public space—that we are a society of equals—is in tension with the conception of the worker as part of a mutual reliance system in which dependencies are provided for. The paycheck goes to an individual, the provider, and then only at this individual's behest is it handed over to those within the unit of dependency worker and charges. Susan Okin (1989) recognizing the vulnerability and the worse off exit options of the dependent homemaker, suggests that the provider's paycheck be split between homemaker and provider, as it is issued by the employer. Okin's suggestion has wonderful rhetorical value, but its practical help is less certain. If the provider remarries, does his check then get split three ways? Does the new homemaker only get one-half of one-half of the provider's check, and if so why should she be made so vulnerable to his previous obligations? Within an intact marriage, if half the paycheck were issued to the homemaker, could one insure that she would have control over those funds or that the provider would pay his fair share of the upkeep of the household and the expenses of additional dependents.[94] Within a marriage, a woman remains in a relatively powerless position vis-à-vis her male provider who has an arsenal of potential weapons to use against a wife who goes against his wishes. Diana Meyers points out that what is required to see the deficiency of this plan is an empathetic understanding of the traditional woman: "The traditional woman believes that her husband is the head of the household and that her proper role is that of helpmeet. A symbolic paycheck will not change her values and consequently will not make her an equal partner in her marriage" (Meyers 1994, 25).

The ideology of equality relies on a vision of autonomous individuals who stand outside relations of dependency. Yet we see that when families fracture, the fissure is rarely between dependency worker and charges, but between that dependency unit and the provider.[95] The autonomous individual is the provider, not the dependency worker who sees herself foremost as a custodian of a dependent's well-being—a self-perception well-warranted in the social arrangement in which she dwells. The ideology of equality of opportunity presumes that autonomous individuals are players in a competition for the social goods—a competition that takes place on a playing field, which, if not level, then is one in which the unevenness is uniformly distributed. Those who enter spheres where this ideology holds sway, while still remaining in charge of dependents, enter a race with one leg tied to a drag. Yet this goes unacknowledged, and so the dependency worker is not given the handicap she needs to function as an equal.

Knowing that one is supposed to be accorded equality while the handicapping conditions which push that equality out of reach go unmentioned, leads to a predicament well described by Sandra Bartky:

> It is itself psychologically oppressive to both believe and at the same time not to believe that one is inferior—in other words to believe a contradiction. . . . [O]ne can only make sense of that contradiction in two ways. First, while accepting in some formal sense the proposition that "all men are created equal," . . . I may [inconsistently] live out my membership in my sex or race in *shame*; . . . Or, somewhat more consistently, . . . I may locate the cause squarely within myself—a character flaw, an 'inferiority complex,' or a neurosis (Bartky 1990, 30).

This oppression is an outcome of the failure to succeed within the competitive world to which equal opportunity was to give entry. An equality that could serve the reality of dependency is one that looks for measures that treat the dependency worker as solicitously (with regard to her needs—especially when these result from her dependency work) as the dependency worker is expected to treat her charge. That is, it is an equality that recognizes that the dependency worker, too, is some mother's child. A condition for such equality is to have a principled understanding of the moral obligations incurred by need and by the dependency relationship. That will be the topic of the following chapter.

2

Vulnerability and the Moral Nature of Dependency Relations

There is every reason to react with alarm to the prospect of a world filled with self-actualizing persons pulling their own strings, capable of guiltlessly saying "no" to anyone about anything, and freely choosing when to begin and end all their relationships. It is hard to see how, in such a world, children could be raised, the sick or disturbed could be cared for, or people could know each other through their lives and grow old together (Scheman 1983, 240).

In the previous chapter, I developed features of dependency work and its pragmatic conditions that place dependency workers in positions of inequality and make them vulnerable to domination and exploitation. Not only its pragmatic conditions, but also its moral demands make this a labor in which, by virtue of caring for someone who is dependent, the dependency worker herself becomes vulnerable. At the nexus of these relationships of dependency is a moral responsibility. Because the dependency worker is herself uniquely situated to harm or benefit her charge, the work itself carries a heavy moral load. Intuitively, we can see that whatever else the dependency worker responds to, she responds to a moral claim on the part of her charge for her attention, good will, and sincere efforts.

In most accounts, moral claims within relationships are made by individuals who are equals, who can both make and discharge these claims. The inequalities in the relationships both with respect to her charge and to her provider constrain a dependency worker's ability to make moral claims on her own behalf. Wherever the equality of parties is presumed in the society at large, her circumstances, the obligation to one who is vulnerable to her actions on the one hand, and her lack of power, leave her handicapped. She is presumed to be an equal, but cannot function as

49

an equal. Her situation can only be rectified when those who stand outside the relationship of dependence understand it to be their moral obligation to extend themselves to the dependency worker, as she extends herself to her charge. The moral features of dependency work, then, include both the moral responsibilities of the dependency worker to her charge, and the moral obligation of those who stand outside of the dependency relation to support such a relation.

That neither the relation of the dependency worker to the charge, nor the relation of the dependency worker to a provider is a relation of equality has two important consequences for the present discussion. First, it means that any moral theory adequate to dependency concerns cannot presuppose either an equality of situation or capacity of the parties in a relationship. Second, it poses the question of whether the failure of policies of equality to improve the lives of women who tend to be the dependency workers is not related to these unequal situations—situations that often define women's lives and opportunities.[96] If we can establish the relation between the inadequacy of equality-based public policy and these relations of inequality, then we need to ask whether equality, in its traditional formulations, can successfully provide the guiding progressive objective for women. If not, can we develop an account of equality that reaches into the inequalities of these relations and that accommodates the concerns raised by attention to dependency work? The claim made earlier is that by missing the importance of dependency, the conception of society as constituted by free and equal autonomous agents poorly serves the needs of dependency workers. Is there a conception of social arrangements that sees the relationship between dependent and caregiver as central to equality itself? Although it may seem paradoxical, I claim that grasping the moral nature of the relation between unequals in a dependency relation will bring us closer to a new assessment of equality itself. The proposal is that rather than an equality based on properties that adhere to individuals, we develop an equality wherein the condition of its possibility is the inevitability of human interdependence: The interdependence which is featured both literally and metaphorically in the aphorism that we are all some mother's child.

In this chapter, I take on the first concern, leaving the second for the remainder of the book. The challenge, for the view I am promoting, is to develop a moral theory which, while recognizing some fundamental moral parity[97] of all, nonetheless recognizes and addresses inequalities of situation, capacities, and relationships. Such a theory will be pertinent to and will help delineate moral features in the dependency relation. The aim of this chapter and this book is not to provide a full-blown account of such a theory. The project of doing so is part of the work that feminist scholars have begun in developing an "ethic of care." Here I will focus on questions of vulnerability and moral responsibility pertinent to the vulnerability of dependency. To do so I need to focus attention on: 1) the nature of the moral self; 2) the nature of moral claims within a relationship of dependency; and 3) the moral demands on those who stand outside the relationship but who are necessary to sustaining these relations.

The Transparent Self of the Dependency Worker

The demands of dependency work favor a self accommodating to the wants of another; that is, a self that defers or brackets its own needs in order to provide for another's. Within the past decade or so, feminists have attempted to characterize a *feminine* sense of self—a self fashioned by a set of relationships and constraints imposed on (or chosen by) women within patriarchal societies. This construction of the self has been variously conceived as a *self-in-relationship*,[98] a *soluble self*,[99] and a *giving self*.[100] Each expression is useful in highlighting a different aspect of this self. I will want to add the idea of a *transparent self*—a self through whom the needs of another are discerned, a self that, when it looks to gauge its own needs, sees first the needs of another.

Such a self may seem too servile to be the autonomous[101] agent of moral actions. Many feminists have argued that to miss the significance of the relational self is to miss a whole dimension of moral life. Furthermore, recent feminist writings extol distinctive features of a self that is relational and giving. Its permeable ego boundaries, many have argued, facilitate not only caretaking responsibilities, but also deep friendships, intimate relations, a less exploitative relation to the natural world, an epistemological stance distinctive to women *and* a form of moral decision making that has inherent value.

Other feminists have disputed this valorization of the "feminine self." They argue against what they take to be the political liability of developing a relational or giving self. My concern here is not to enter the debate about the superiority or inferiority—moral or otherwise—of this "feminine" self. My concern is to consider the moral requirements of the self of the dependency worker in a dependency relation. We will see that this self contrasts with the self represented as participating as an equal in the social relations of liberal political theory. Whether or not it is desirable to be a relational, giving self, my argument rests on the moral requirements of dependency work that make such a self indispensable. As dependency work, in turn, is an indispensable feature of any human society, every society must count on certain persons adopting such a moral self. In focussing on the requirements of the self of the dependency worker, my concern is not only with the responsiveness of a giving self, and not only with the lack of separation experienced by the soluble self. I want to think about the extent to which this self does not allow its own needs to obscure its perception of another's needs nor to have its own needs offer a resistance to its response to another.

This is what I propose with the idea of a transparent self: The perception of and response to another's needs are neither blocked out nor refracted through our own needs. Of course, no self is ever truly transparent in this sense, but such transparency is a benchmark for the self-conception of the dependency worker qua dependency worker. It is a regulatory ideal for the dependency worker qua dependency worker. It is an altruistic ideal. But while altruism is often seen as morally supererogatory, this ideal is *required* of the labor I have called dependency work.

Where the vulnerability of the charge is absolute, such as that of an infant, an interference with the transparency of self can have dire consequences. An infant's caregiver who is more attuned to her own needs than to those of her charge can fail to notice—or can disregard—important, even life-threatening needs. It is neither capricious nor misogynist nor disrespectful of individual rights when we insist that individuals who mother[102] infants or young children defer their own desires, and even needs, to meet those of their dependent child. The child who awakes in the night, hungry, sick, or terrified, has the claim of the attention of her caregiver, even if that caregiver is herself exhausted and unwilling to be awakened. I will shortly discuss the basis of that claim. For now I want simply to point to the intuitions that prioritize the needs of the dependent over the needs of the dependency worker. The degree to which this prioritization is absolute diminishes as the dependency of the charge diminishes. As a child gets older, as a sick person recovers, as a disabled person mends or acquires self-reliant tools and skills, the dependency worker gains a measure of relief from the overbearing nature of the other's needs. The self of the dependency worker retains a transparency to the needs of the charge to the degree that the charge must depend on her.[103]

The transparency of this self is placed in stark contrast to the self of the liberal tradition of rights and utilities. The self of the liberal tradition is a rationally self-interested agency, rather than an agency in the service of the interests of another. This is not to say that altruism is merely irrational and goes entirely unrecognized in this tradition. But the claim has been that altruistic actions, actions benefiting another at the expense of oneself that do not fall within our contractual obligations, are supererogatory. In any case, acting in the interests of another presents a *problem*: "The problem ... is not how the interests of others can motivate us to some specific policy of altruistic conduct, but how they can motivate us at all," writes Thomas Nagel (1970, 79). As a matter of course, dependency work requires actions often deemed supererogatory when the actor is the autonomous self of liberal theory. Unlike the self of the participant in the Rawlsian original position, the transparent self of the dependency worker is neither moderately self-interested nor disinterested. It is often passionately interested—but the interest is vested in the well-being of another.

Moral Obligations of Dependency Workers and an Ethics of Care

Just as the selves in dependency relationships are not the selves of contracting parties, neither can ties between a dependency worker and her charge be represented as contractual relations. Ties of affection and concern bind dependency worker and her charge. The ties are not between generalizable others, but between non-fungible concrete others.[104] The relations and moral obligations between the parties are not the general obligations we bear to another person, whoever they may be, but special relations. In the case of special relations, we have obligations that are particular to the individual in that relationship. Unlike obligations incurred in special relations spoken of in traditional voluntaristic moral theories, they may not be voluntarily assumed. They are rarely the consequences of an explicit agreement—some performative utterance such as "I promise to ..." Frequently they involve obligations with no discrete endpoint. These special relations and their attendant obligations do not fit easily within a moral theory that understands justice as the primary virtue. When a parent saves her own child first, is she being unjust or is she meeting her parental responsibility?[105] When a parent, indifferent to a child's wishes, refuses her an innocent pleasure, is it a matter of rights or is it a failure of response? Yet, justice is not a virtue to be ignored in asymmetric relations.[106]

The character of the moral self, the asymmetry of the relationship, the partiality of its participants, and its nonvoluntary nature make the moral demands of the dependency relationship more amenable to an ethic of care than to a rights-based or an utilitarian-based morality. An ethic of care regards the moral subject as inherently relational. It understands moral reasoning to be contextual and responsive rather than a calculus performed on rights or utilities. And an ethic of care centers not on impartial judgments, but on judgments partial to participants within a caring relation. While a long history attaches to the moral claims in an ethic where the first virtue is justice, the *source* of moral claims in an ethic of care has not been made sufficiently explicit.[107] What are the moral claims of a relational subject? On what normative grounds can we accept contextual reasoning and responsiveness as bases for moral judgments? And how can the partiality exhibited in a caring relation, which might not even have been voluntarily assumed, have a moral character—especially when obligations that are not self-assumed and partiality have so often been the mark of heteronomy, i.e., of actions which fail to express our moral essence?

In what follows, the reader may object that I address myself only to those obligations that attach themselves to dependency workers with respect to their charge. I do not speak of obligations of the charge to the dependency worker. That is not because I think none exist. In the limiting case of a wholly dependent being, however, it makes no sense to speak about the obligation of the charge to the dependency worker. I begin with the most helpless charge so that we can glean certain moral features of the dependency relationship. Ultimately I am interested in addressing the obligations that are owed the dependency worker. Some of the obligations owed the dependency worker arise out of the moral obligations that devolve on the dependency worker to care for the charge. By beginning with the most helpless charge, we see how grave these obligations may be, how much they exact from the dependency worker, and how the charge, at least in the limiting case, cannot reciprocate the care or concern the dependency worker devotes to her. This is not to say that even the most dependent person does not reciprocate in some way—through love and affection perhaps. Nonetheless, the obligation to redress the "cost" that duties of dependency work exact from the dependency worker must fall on those outside the relationship itself. Of course, the responsibilities and costs of dependency work for the caregiver are graduated, and hang in part on the degree of the dependency. Where the charge is able to respond morally to the dependency worker, she too has an obligation. But the nature and extent of that obligation can be bracketed for the purposes of this discussion.

The "Vulnerability Model"

Justificatory ground for a relation of care can be located in Robert Goodin's work *Protecting the Vulnerable*. Although Goodin's concern is not specifically with an ethic of care, he sees the moral claim for special relations as situated in the vulnerability of another to our actions. In other words, while his own aim is not a foundation for an ethic of care, the point at which he situates the moral claims of special relations shares the moral ground of an ethic of care.

Goodin contrasts a Vulnerability Model of special relations to the Voluntaristic Model, whose paradigm is the promise. In the case of the promise, I assume a special obligation to another when I give my word to do that which I promised. Although the obligation is to a particular other, the form of the obligation is perfectly general: I would have that obligation to whomsoever I made that promise. The obligation is also self-assumed. Because I made such a promise out of my own free choice, and because I would expect anyone freely incurring such an obligation to honor their promises, I assume the obligation to fulfill my promise.

On the Vulnerability Model, the moral basis of special relations between individuals arises from the vulnerability of one party to the actions of another. The needs of another call forth a moral obligation on our part when we are in a special position vis-à-vis that other to meet those needs. We can call such obligations *vulnerability-responsive obligations*. Goodin argues that all special relations, business relations, relations between a professional and a client or patient, family relations, friendships, benefactor-beneficiary relations, even promises and contractual relations, are better described on the Vulnerability Model.[108]

Goodin's model can be described in strikingly relational terms. The moral claim is a claim upon *me* only if I am so situated as to be able to answer the need. It is a moral claim upon me, only if the other is vulnerable to *my* actions. What is striking about this model is that the moral claim arises not by virtue of the properties of an individual—construed as rights, needs, or interests—but out of a *relationship* between one in need and one who is situated to meet the need.[109] Given the earlier discussion of dependency relations, we see immediately how the vulnerability model speaks directly to the moral claim the dependent has upon the dependency worker. The dependency worker is positioned so as to be *the* individual best situated, or exclusively situated to meet the needs of the dependent.

Who Can Oblige Whom by Their Vulnerability?

The vulnerability model is not without difficulties. On the one hand, it is open to the charge of making our obligations too general and so obliging us to more than is reasonable. If, for example, a distant admirer declares his love for you and claims to be unable to live unless you extend yourself in some way, it is not at all clear that you have an obligation to that person. But the vulnerability model, on first blush, appears to put the power of obliging you into the hands of whosoever wishes to exercise that power. Upon further thought, the model can be charged with unreasonably limiting our responsibility. If our responsibility arises from being in a unique position to meet the need of another, then it seems we have no obligation to meet any needs which could as well be met by anyone else. Goodin's principles of individual and group responsibility (see Goodin 1985, 118, 136, 139) make our obligation to another depend upon the degree to which the vulnerable party can be affected by our actions. The principles are meant to delimit the sphere and scope of vulnerability-responsive obligations. Assigning a degree of responsibility resolves some of the difficulty but not all. The distant admirer can threaten suicide by your neglect and therefore the degree to which the vulnerable party can be affected is very great indeed. But it is less intuitively clear that this distant lover should have the power to thus oblige you in the first place. It also seems clear that to take the vulnerability model as the sole way in which we become obligated makes it odd that I should have any obligation to persons who simply do not need me to benefit them. And yet, I may well feel an obligation to a kin member, even when there is virtually nothing that I might do that another kin could not do equally well. Nor does it explain why I may feel a stronger obligation to kin than a non-kin who may be at least as vulnerable to my actions.

Two responses are possible to this last objection—and neither is satisfactory. On the one hand, one may reply that such a sense of obligation is simply a parochialism that the vulnerability model is intended to address. One of the attractions of this model is the result that obligations to kin are not to be preferred to those of other individuals who may be more vulnerable to your actions. However, it is not at all clear that we can just discard such conventions. A great deal relies on the historical and cultural circumstances and practices that determine our relationships to others in our community. On the other hand, one could argue that kinship defines a relationship in which kin are already vulnerable to the actions of each other. Much depends on the degrees of vulnerability, which must be weighed in each circumstance. But then the vulnerability model would just be begging the question of moral responsibility, for we can give whatever weight we choose to affinitive relations, and invoking vulnerability adds little to our considerations.

To resolve these various quandaries, we need first to acknowledge that who is responsible for whom is often a matter of absolute judgment and less a matter of degree; second, to accept that responsibility in special relations arises in multiple ways;[110] and third, to recognize that obligations, however formed, arise in a set of cultural practices. Many of the most binding relations and responsibilities arise out of a confluence of different practices and different obliging conditions. A relationship is set within a number of cultural determinations establishing who meets whose needs—modulated, necessarily, by exigencies not foreseen in the culturally established conventions. If I encounter a bleeding stranger and there is no one else around, then the fact of my being there creates a unique relation that calls forth an obligation on my part to do something to help the stranger. If, however, my child is hungry, then while there are many others around who can feed the child, the presumption is that *I* am responsible to see that she gets fed. As long as I am able to fulfill that obligation, it falls upon me to do so. Alternatively I can assign the responsibility to another to fulfil an obligation on my behalf—but the ultimate responsibility remains mine. It is an obligation that arises out of the relationship between parent and child.[111]

Most pertinent for our purposes, however, is that in the case of dependency work, a relationship is already given—either by familial ties, friendship, or the obligations of employment. These bases of the dependency relationship legitimate the situation whereby the charge is vulnerable to the actions of the dependency worker. The charge, unlike the distant admirer, is in a position that legitimates her obliging the dependency worker. The charge is vulnerable. Familial ties, friendships, and certain paid employment serve as socially acknowledged justifications for the charge being vulnerable to the actions of this particular individual—her dependency worker.

The Legitimacy of Needs in Vulnerability-Responsive Obligations

The vulnerability model has not only to solve the problem of who gets to oblige whom by their vulnerability, it also has to question what sort of needs legitimately impose obligations. Neither what is construed as need nor what is understood as an appropriate response can go unexamined. While the need of the hungry infant for food unquestionably calls for a response to provide food, the appropriate response to an alcoholic's need for drink is less clear.[112]

A person accustomed to riches and servants all her life may experience these as needs of such urgency that their absence is intolerable. Toni Morrison, in her novel *Song of Solomon*, explores the effect of such a need in a story told by Circe, the only remaining servant of Miss Butler, the daughter of a formerly wealthy but highly exploitative family. Miss Butler, whose wealth was eventually dissipated, commits suicide rather than face total destitution. A midwife as well as a servant, Circe helped birth Miss Butler and Miss Butler's mother before her. She remains on the estate after her mistress's death, tending to the dogs and presiding over the total decay of the former mansion. "The last few years we ate out of the garden," recounts Circe. "Finally she [Miss Butler] couldn't take it anymore. The thought of having no help, no money—well, she couldn't take that. She had to let everything go." In response to an interlocutor who mistakes Circe's abiding relationship to her mistress for a reciprocal and enduring loyalty, Circe exclaims, "I said she killed herself rather than do the work I'd been doing all my life! ... Do you hear me? She saw the work I did all her days and *died*, you hear me, *died* rather than live like me." Circe stays on, not out of a misplaced loyalty, but out of a commitment to see all her masters' beloved property—"They loved it. Stole for it, lied for it, killed for it"—undergo a material decadence commensurate with the moral decadence that formerly sustained it.

While there may well be fundamental, primary needs, needs without which no individual could survive, needs that would have a prima facie moral claim to response, all other needs are identifiable only within certain practices. The extent to which such needs have a moral weight depends upon a moral evaluation of the practice, as well as the urgency of the need as understood within that practice. A critical understanding of needs requires not only a sensitivity to the neediness of another and an understanding of how another may be vulnerable to one's own actions, but also a knowledge of when fulfilling those needs would morally diminish oneself or the other. Within a relation of dependency, false needs can be generated either by the charge or by societal expectations on the dependency worker. The critically assessed practices in which dependency work takes place offer a means by which to formulate a critical discourse about needs. Circe's understanding that her mistress's needs are predicated on the devaluation of her own person—that Miss Butler would rather die than lead the life that she, Circe, has lived—offers her a critical perspective of the practices in which she engaged as a dependency worker. These practices themselves originated in a set of false needs, diminishing the dependency worker and rendering the one for whom she labored hopelessly, but unnecessarily, vulnerable. Circe, a woman who had done dependency work both in the primary and extended senses, understood well the difference between a need to which a response was moral and a need that can be met only by diminishing oneself.

Limiting How *One Becomes Obliged in the Vulnerability Model*

Circe, a slave in the Butler household for the better part of her life, was in the unique position to meet her mistress's need only because of a practice that unjustly allocated responsibilities to her. Even after she was freed, she continued to be the one to whose actions her mistress, having become so dependent upon her during slavery, was vulnerable. Is the question of *how* someone comes to be in a position where another is vulnerable to their actions relevant to the moral warrant of the vulnerability-responsive obligation? Goodin claims it is never relevant. He writes:

> [T]he existing allocation of responsibilities, whatever its initial basis, should now be treated as a "social fact." Whether or not the existing allocation of responsibilities itself has any moral warrant, it has made some people vulnerable to others; and that fact, if no other, provides a moral warrant for discharging those responsibilities. The pragmatic "ought" ... attaches to the vulnerabilities ... And ... stays attached until and unless responsibilities—and the expectations and vulnerabilities surrounding them—are redefined (Goodin 1985, 125).

However, the justice of Goodin's position is questionable, and the "pragmatic ought" he invoked may be at odds with a "moral ought" that proscribes *self-demeaning behavior* or one that puts us at unjustifiable risk. Goodin does insist that we are always vulnerable to our own actions, and therefore have obligations to ourselves as well. Is this response adequate to Circe's problem? First, the appeal to an obligation to ourselves cannot help much here since responding to the vulnerability of a dependent other will often put us at risk. Still we expect to bracket our own interests if they conflict with those of a vulnerable dependent for whom we are caring. Second, we can say that responding to the needs of another unjustly thrust upon us is, in itself, demeaning. It requires that we place a lower value on ourselves than on those who would unjustly demand a response from us making us vulnerable to their needs or those of another. This, however, would hold in all cases where the pragmatic ought is in conflict with a moral obligation that arises out of a just allocation of responsibilities. If then, our obligations to ourselves trump the obligations to others in cases of unjust allocations of responsibility, there is no pragmatic ought and I have no quarrel with Goodin.

Appeal to obligations to ourselves then either defeat the pragmatic ought or conflict with the other demands of the vulnerability model. If Goodin insists on the pragmatic ought, so that an unjust allocation of responsibilities nonetheless obliges us, then he must agree that it can do so even in the face of coercive conditions. This is both counterintuitive and an undesirable feature in a moral theory. It seems more reasonable to insist that the injustice trumps any moral obligation induced by the vulnerability of the one-in-need to the actions of the coerced person.[113] Perhaps this is why even many opponents of abortion tend to agree that a pregnancy caused by a rape is legitimately aborted. A slave coerced into caring for an ailing master would be thought justifiable if she took the occasion of his incapacity as an opportunity to escape.

Nonetheless, if we are to judge from some accounts of slavery, not all slaves, in fact, viewed the moral situation in such stark terms. Margaret Walker's novel of the lives of slaves during the Civil War, *Jubilee*, invokes the reckonings of Jim, a house slave in the Dutton home who accompanied the plantation heir to the front lines. He contemplates what he is to do with his mortally wounded young master:

> "Marster Johnny dying and he can't get home by hisself. I'll carry him home to his Maw where he can die in peace, but I sho ain't staying there." If Jim had been a field hand, such a delicate conflict would not have disturbed him. He would have felt no ties to the Dutton household, but he had nursed the old man and he had watched the children grow. Contemptuous as he was of Big Missy he was nevertheless tied to a strange code of honor, duty, and noblesse oblige which he could not have explained. So he was taking Johnny home (Walker 1967, 184).

Judith Jarvis Thomson's notorious argument for the permissibility of abortion is worth considering here. Thomson (1971) contends that granting the personhood of a fetus does not preclude a woman's right to an abortion. In her famous analogy, she likens an unintended pregnancy to a scenario in which a hospital patient awakens from an operation only to find himself attached by tubes to a famous violinist whose life is temporarily sustained by the hookup. Thomson's point is that it cannot be unjust for the recruited party to refuse the obligation to aid the violinist no matter how vulnerable the violinist is to such a refusal, since the association was not undertaken voluntarily. To insist that the hospital patient stay hooked up to the violinist would be coercive and unjust. Similarly, goes the argument, the pregnant woman who is not voluntarily assuming the association with the fetus is under no obligation to lend her body to the fetus's development.

Although I do not dispute the right of a woman to have an abortion, nor do I wish to have my remarks so interpreted, the argument from voluntarism is troubling here. Surely there are many obligations that appear to have the force of the moral, yet do not follow from voluntarily assumed associations: obligations to parents, to neighbors, to strangers in need whom we happen upon. Thomson, it is worth noting, argues that it is only the moral virtue of justice which is contravened when the demand is made that we assume the life support of the violinist. A less exacting moral virtue such as moral decency—less exacting in what it insists upon before an obligation is posited—would urge that there is an obligation to sustain the violinist, at least as long as the cost to oneself is not too great.

The intuitions that are called upon to sustain Thomson's distinction here between the demands of justice and the demands of moral decency, however, are problematic. Many would argue that the demands of justice bear heavily on filial responsibilities, for instance.[114] Thomson's example of a person who is *kidnapped* in order to be the source of another's life-sustaining treatment is so effective, I propose, because kidnapping is a particularly compelling form of coercion (even if it is not "blood and gore" violence). If kidnapped, few would think that they have any sort of obligation to meet the needs of the one on whose behalf the kidnapping was done. Clearly coercive situations, situations in which one is *forced* to come to the aid of another, seem not only to be unjust, but the injustice also can be sufficient cause to cancel any moral obligation to respond as one might otherwise in the face of need. In Thomson's example an individual becomes the unique person to satisfy the need by virtue of the coercion. Once hooked up to another person's body, the other individual is so much more vulnerable to your refusal than he might have been before. If one were in fact the only person who could satisfy the need—if, for example, some rare blood type in combination with a particular set of antibodies were required and only one person was identified with these—the one in need would, I believe, have a great deal of moral suasion over the one capable of helping. But here, too, *someone* must determine if the moral claim of one life is greater than that of another.

Voluntarism has a great deal of appeal because we tend to think that the person called upon to help must make the decision that she wishes to forego her interest for another's sake. But a previous relationship between these two persons can alter those intuitions. If the person called upon to make the sacrifice of time, energy, money or even life itself is a mother or father, voluntarism has less appeal. We expect the parent to be willing to make the sacrifice. Contrary to Goodin, then, our intuitions about whose needs we have obligations to respond to partly depends on how or why we find ourselves in the position to meet those needs. Contrary to the voluntarist, however, voluntarily undertaken obligations are not the only source of obligations in relationships.

Thomson might agree that voluntarily undertaken obligations are not the only source of obligations in relationships. Nevertheless, she would want to argue, they are the source of all obligations we incur that pertain to justice. Think, however, of an encounter between a well-fed person with plenty of food and a starving person. Would we not want to say that a refusal to give the hungry person food is a matter of injustice and not just indecency? Here the vulnerability model seems to issue obligations that are matters of justice. The appropriate moral distinctions are not between what is just and what is decent, but between conditions which, when they place a person in a "privileged" position to respond to need, are either morally benign or morally unacceptable. Where these positions are voluntarily chosen, it is both a matter of justice and decency that we honor such obligations. Where these positions are coerced, then such obligations have no moral standing. Most common and interesting situations, however, are those which are neither coerced (either at all or in an obvious sense), nor voluntarily chosen.[115]

There is a sufficiently large class of such responsibilities and obligations. These noncoerced *yet not voluntarily chosen* associations fill our lives. They range from the most intimate familial relations to those of fellow citizen and fellow traveler. Duties incurred by these associations arise out of a whole network of expectations, bonds, and responsibilities, most of whose validity we do not question, even if we question some specific obligations they impose. This is to say that just because coerced responsibilities do not carry a moral warrant does not mean we can only admit obligations voluntarily assumed—even if we limit moral considerations to justice. By virtue of our acceptance of these nonvoluntary, but noncoerced relationships (whether formed by longstanding convention or mere happenstance), we question our capacity for acting justly and well. We question the kind of person we are[116] when we fail to meet a primary need, when we are uniquely situated to meet that need.

The "Coercion Problem"

The voluntaristic model offers a consistent reason for refusing a duty imposed through coercion, even if it cannot account for the intuition that it is unjust to refuse aid in an unchosen, but noncoercive situation. On the voluntaristic model, no one can legitimately exercise any claims against us unless we can aver to *some* consensual arrangement, hence neither the violinist in Thomson's analogy—nor an unwanted fetus has any claims against us.[117] We suggested that there were frequent instances of relations to others, non-voluntary but not coerced, in which many would think it unjust not to offer the needed assistance. The vulnerability model accounts for these intuitions. The switch to a vulnerability model, however, raises a different concern.

I have resisted Goodin's insistence that the moral warrant of an antecedent allocation of responsibilities is irrelevant to the moral warrant for carrying out vulnerability-responsive obligations. In arguing against Goodin's pragmatic ought, we needed to evoke a conception of justice—a justice that pertains to how "the existing allocation of responsibilities itself" came to be. We have argued that in special relationships, obligations (even obligations demanded by justice) can arise—whether or not the relationships are voluntary—just as long as they are not coerced. But we argued against any moral warrant of obligations within a relationship that is coerced by appealing to the injustice of such coercion. If justice, as it pertains to the institutions and practices through which special relationships arise, always requires some consensual, voluntaristic basis, then the vulnerability model faces a genuine difficulty. Either it must accept Goodin's pragmatic ought—and so cannot accept that coerced obligations carry no moral weight—or it cannot get off the ground.

Arguably, the theory that most comprehensively provides justification for such institutions and practices is social contract theory. Social contract theory, however, is a voluntaristic theory, in which social institutions derive their legitimacy from the voluntary agreement of an association of equally situated and empowered parties.

The voluntarism of social contract theory assumes individuals who act out of an elevated self-interest, who are rational and mutually disinterested, and who are equally situated to engage in moral interactions with each other.[118] The suitability of such a concept is what is at stake in this book. Such a view, I have claimed, fails to take into account the circumstance that some individuals will always be dependent, does not explain the moral commitment of those who care for dependents, and employs an unhelpful conception of equality. We hoped to find a more suitable basis for an ethic of care (an ethic that applies to dependency relations) in the Vulnerability Model proposed by Goodin. To again resort to a Voluntaristic Model to ground our obligations to vulnerable dependents undoes our efforts.

This difficulty leads us to what I call the *coercion problem* of the vulnerability model. The coercion problem is this: Either we reject Goodin's pragmatic ought, but find that we must rely on voluntarism after all, or we accept Goodin's pragmatic ought and accept that dependency relationships formed by coercing the dependency worker to take on these obligations have a moral warrant. Neither option is attractive to a feminist position with respect to dependency. Granting that a vulnerability model without Goodin's pragmatic ought must accept voluntarism also means granting that even the vulnerability model (the moral model best suited to dependency relations) must begin with the premise that the dependency critique disputes: that society is appropriately or ideally thought to be an association of those equally situated and empowered. Accepting the pragmatic ought, however, deflects from the urgency to see how often those responsibilities have unfairly been allocated to women. Women, and others who have done dependency work because of coercive conditions or without adequate compensation, have too long simply accepted these unfair allocations as social facts, thereby colluding with an oppressive and exploitative situation. Challenging the justice of the social facts is precisely what feminists must do, but accepting the pragmatic ought leaves no place from which to challenge unfair allocations, without, once again, resorting to the voluntarism that undercuts the validity of the vulnerability model. Is there a way out of the coercion problem? Is there room for a notion of justice within a vulnerability model?

With the coercion problem, our focus is not on how the person who is in the position to address the vulnerabilities of another behaves with respect to her responsibilities, but on what obligations others have to that person. The problem, as we have repeatedly indicated, is especially acute for those dealing with what we have called primary needs, since those with such needs make very compelling demands—ones that are met in relationships of dependency and that are potentially very costly to the dependency worker. Both the ground of the dependency workers' obligation to care and the obligations to the dependency worker need to be clarified. The coercion problem needs to be seen in the context of what is owed to those who meet the needs of others, most especially dependent others. To solve the problem of coercion, then, we need to shift the inquiry, deferring a resolution until we understand more generally what are the moral obligations to the dependency worker.

Moral Obligations to the Dependency Worker

We have said that dependency relations, especially in the primary sense we are privileging here, begin with the needs of a charge who is vulnerable, whose needs are legitimate, and who may stand in a prior relation to the person assuming the role of dependency worker. Because the dependency worker is charged with the welfare of her charge, the latter becomes vulnerable to the actions of the dependency worker. The vulnerability model gives us a basis for understanding the moral pull of being in a relation with another who is vulnerable to one's actions. It must be said that an individual has an unqualified obligation to assume the responsibilities of dependency work when the following conditions are met: 1) the needs are basic; 2) the vulnerability is extensive; and 3) the prior relation, which puts a particular individual into position of having to assume such a vulnerability-responsive obligation, has a moral warrant. Furthermore, this obligation has to be assumed even when there is a substantial cost to the dependency worker's own interests and projects. This is what every mother and every father who gets up at four o'clock in the morning to tend to a sick child knows so well.

What about the obligations owed to the dependency worker? Who is to care for the caregiver? How are her needs to be recognized? To the extent that the dependency worker is vulnerable to the actions of the charge, the charge is obliged to behave in ways that address those vulnerabilities. Not only is the charge vulnerable to the actions of the dependency worker, but the dependency worker may also be vulnerable to the actions of the charge. The elder-care worker who tends to a frail elderly man may be vulnerable to sexual abuse, economic exploitation, and poor treatment. The vulnerability is aggravated where the dependency worker is poor, a woman, a person of color, an immigrant, and so forth. Again, here the vulnerability model is just right. The charge may not have chosen her dependency worker or may not even want one, but she has an obligation to understand the extent to which the dependency worker may be vulnerable to her actions and act so as to avoid harm.

The response of the charge can also provide deep fulfillment to the dependency worker. The loving gaze and laughter of a child with profound cognitive disabilities can offer a special joy to her attendant, even if the child is unable to utter a "thank you." How vulnerable the dependency worker is to the actions of the charge is, in part, a function of what actions the charge is capable of. The newborn infant who is not yet capable of much, or a person with profound mental and physical impairments who is able to control very few of her actions clearly cannot be held responsible for vulnerabilities imposed by her. But now the circle of the dependency obligations must expand to include the vulnerability of the dependency worker, which is itself a consequence of her deferred interests as well as needs pertaining to her affective bond to her charge and her concern for her charge's well-being.

First and foremost, the obligation owed to a person who must defer her own interests and projects is that her responsibilities to another not be unjustly thrust upon her. To disregard such an obligation is to treat her as someone of lesser moral worth than either the person she cares for or those who placed her in the obliging position. It seems as if in decrying the injustice of being *compelled* to care, we have made an appeal to equality, a basic moral parity. Here we begin our thoughts of equality from the relationship of dependency.

Connection-Based Equality

If we start not with individuals in their separateness, but in their connectedness, we can read their demands for equality through these connections. If we can see each individual nested within relationships of care, we can envision relationships that embrace the needs of each. This leads us to an alternative understanding of equality.

The equality that begins with the interests of an independent self and is extended to others by virtue of an elevated self-interest is an individual-based equality. (See Chapter One, page 28). This is the equality registered in the equal right of each to form his or her own conception of the good and to compete for the resources needed to attain that good. It is the equality which is based upon the recognition of each person's individuality and independence—each one's own conception of one's own good—and the individually held rights and powers.[119]

The alternative conception that I propose—the equality claimed in the assertion that we are all some mother's child—is instead a connection-based equality. This alternative equality assumes a fundamental need for relationship, and it gives rise to a distinctive set of claims. The claims generated by a connection-based equality derives not from the rights we hold as independent individuals, but from what is due us by virtue of our connection to those with whom we have had and are likely to have relations of care and dependency. They are claims made not necessarily on our own behalf alone, and they are made not necessarily by those to whom they are due. Such claims are *entitlements* first to a relationship in which one can be cared for if and when appropriate, and second to a socially supported situation in which one can give care without the caregiving becoming a liability to one's own well-being. The last is an entitlement that goes beyond, and has different properties than, the entitlement to the care itself.

Family leave policies are a fine example of entitlements characteristic of this concept of equality.[120] The worker who claims an entitlement to a family leave not only claims it on her own behalf—for the release time from work—but primarily claims it for the sake of the dependent who receives the benefit, the care and attention made possible by the release time. Furthermore, this is often a claim that the dependent cannot make on her own behalf. In the case of the dependent who cannot voice the legitimate demand to have her needs attended to, a dependency worker must make the claim on the dependent's part—and the claim includes the time and resources of the dependency worker to attend to the needs of her charge. Furthermore, a claim based on a connection-based equality is a claim to have the need attended to by one genuinely, perhaps uniquely, concerned with the well-being of the dependent. That sort of claim is really what justifies and lies behind the moral soundness of a family leave policy.

"What Goes Round, Comes Round"—Reciprocity-in-Connection

Connection-based equality is not characterized by reciprocity in the standard sense. In standard relationships of parity, reciprocity requires that efforts I exert on your behalf will be met by some equivalent exertion on your part, immediately, at some specified time in the future, or when the need arises. I expect my act to be reciprocated by the same individual to whom I directed my action. The reciprocity has the nature of an exchange—it is an *exchange reciprocity*. Connection-based equality eschews this exchange reciprocity for another sort, one based on different kinds of expectations.

In studies indicating that women, whether employed or not, provide more hours of care and more care of every sort than do men, the sociologist Naomi Gerstel found that the expectations of others that they will give care was among the reasons the subjects gave for the time spent caring. But their willingness to respond to these expectations was based on an understanding of reciprocity characteristic of a connection-based equality. A fifty-year-old lawyer voiced a typical response:

> Well, my mother may be a pain sometimes but she is very frail now and needs me. She *expects* me to help her. And you know, she took care of her mother. So I have to help her. Nobody else will (Gerstel 1991, 18).[121]

Her mother's expectation is one that she accepts: Since her mother gave care to her mother, her mother is now owed care. And as the care her mother's mother received was meted out by the daughter, so that daughter now deserves care from her own daughter. Significantly, the reciprocation is based *not* on the care her mother gave her daughter and which she now expects her daughter to return.[122] That would turn the mother's care for her daughter into a sort of advance payment for later care—a maneuver typical of exchange reciprocity. The daughter instead invokes a set of nested obligations. The fulfillment of those obligations is now her responsibility and her's uniquely. If she does not do the caring, "no one else will."

Within the African-American community, Gerstel found that "especially women, but also men spend far more time helping people they know, especially kin, and volunteering than do whites" (1991, 20). She explains this finding in terms of a greater commitment of African-Americans to community life than that of similarly situated whites. Gerstel cites the words of one African-American woman who was justifying the large number of hours she spends on caregiving: "Well, what goes round comes round" (Gerstel 1991, 20). This chain of obligations linking members of a community creates a sense of reciprocity between those who give and those who receive that raises the expectation that when one is in the position to give care, one will, and when that person is in need another who is suitably situated to give care will respond. It is a reciprocity of those who see their equality in their connection with, and obligation toward, others.

Such reciprocity depends upon a linked and nested set of social relations, sometimes reciprocal in the standard sense, but not always. In Chapter Four, this connection-based reciprocity is brought to bear on the concept of social cooperation. Standard notions of social cooperation tend to invoke what I have here called exchange-based reciprocity. In dependency relations, however, the dependent is seldom in a position to reciprocate in kind. Reciprocation from the charge may never be possible. The dependency worker is entitled not to a reciprocity from the charge herself, but to a relationship that sustains her as she sustains her charge. Connection-based equality yields a nested set of reciprocal relations and obligations. It is the social cooperation that depends on these nested relationships and obligations that I call *doulia*—a term that improvises on the name of a postpartum caregiver (a *doula*) who assists the new mother as the mother cares for the infant. Just as the *doula* gives care to the one who cares for the dependent infant, the direction of the obligation in connection-based reciprocity goes from those in position to discharge the obligations to those to whom they are relevantly connected.

The Dependency Worker as Some Mother's Child

The maxim that "we are all some mother's child" supplies not only a notion of equality through connection, but also something substantial about the treatment each one is warranted to receive by virtue of the connection. To assert that "I, too, am a mother's child" is to assert that I am due treatment compatible with or analogous to the treatment a mother renders to a child. To be recognized as a mother's child is to be treated in a fashion that is compatible with or analogous to maternal practice: It is to be deemed worthy of such treatment. This worthiness is inalienable.

Our own behavior can render us less worthy, so that the full treatment as a mother's child may be justifiably overridden by other societal needs, but it can never be fully relinquished. The case of inalienable rights is analogous. There are some rights, such as the freedom to move about unhindered or the right to vote, which we maintain only if we are citizens in good standing—criminal behavior strips us of these rights, at least temporarily. But there are certain rights no one may be deprived of—we not only feed, clothe, house, give medical treatment to convicted criminals, but we also allow even the most vicious to have visitation rights. This indicates the societal recognition that nothing can take from an individual his or her worthiness for a certain amount of care and connection.

That nothing can fully alienate the responsibility of others to recognize us as some mother's child resides in that feature of human existence that demands connection as a fundamental condition for human survival. No one can survive and become a member of the human community without the interest of some mothering person(s) who has provided a degree of a preservative love, a concern in fostering the individual's growth, and a training for social acceptability.[123] When we respect an individual as some mother's child, we honor the efforts of that mothering person and symbolically of all mothering persons. When we do not, not only are rights belonging to the abused individual violated, but the efforts of the mothering persons are dishonored. The sanctity of the relation that makes possible all human connection is violated. The importance of human connection *per se* is thereby disavowed.

A connection-based equality depends on grasping an analogy: The relation between a needy child and the mother who tends to those needs is analogous to the mother's own neediness and those who are in a position to meet those needs. The maternal relation becomes a paradigm, an analogue, for social relations in which vulnerability is central. It is important to emphasize that I am talking about an *analogical* move. I am not suggesting that everyone be treated as a mother treats a child. That would constitute a maternalism as objectionable as paternalism. The role of analogical thinking seems crucial to the concept of equality-in-connection. The procedure by which we go from one situation to another is not a procedure of generalization or universalization, nor is it a deduction from a general rule. It is instead a process of analogical extension.

We have looked at the moral nature both of the self and of the relationship in the case of dependency work, but we still need to provide a critical understanding of the moral nature of the response called for by the relationship itself. The response must not only be possible but must be considered in light of the prior relationship between the individuals, the prior commitment of care, and the tensions between the needs of the charge and the condition of vulnerability in which the dependency worker is placed when meeting those needs. Connection-based equality, which is grounded in our understanding of ourselves as inherently related to others, can serve as a guide to thinking and even to policy.

If we think of each person as some mother's child, then we consider what is owed to a mother's child by virtue of its being vulnerable to the extent that the child is dependent upon the mother for its well-being. We need then to think analogically: Who stands in the position of the mother, who stands in the position of the child and what would be the analogue of the maternal practice?[124] The maternal paradigm is extended analogically to whatever situation we may be in where we *need* to be cared for—where our survival, our flourishing and our well-being as social creatures depend on the extension of another's care, concern, and connection to us. When I respond to the vulnerabilities of another, when I as a dependency worker tend to my charge, this concept of equality requires that it be remembered that I, too, am some mother's child. However my needs may be deferred, they cannot be permitted to languish. For the dependency worker to meet her responsibilities to another, it must be the responsibility of the larger social order to provide a structure whereby she, too, may be treated as a mother's child. Otherwise, she is both treated unequally and hindered in meeting her obligations to her charge.

Connection-based equality, partly justified by the vulnerability model, at the same time marks a limit to the morally acceptable sacrifice on the part of the caregiver or dependency worker—even without questioning the legitimacy of the needs of the vulnerable. A connection-based equality calls upon those within the nested set of social relations to support the dependency worker sufficiently, so that she is not made unduly vulnerable as she answers to the vulnerability of another. Just as the one-in-need is to be assisted and cared for, social relations must be arranged to meet her needs—especially, but not exclusively, those needs and vulnerabilities that result from the other-directed nature of her toils.

We can deduce other consequences from a connection-based equality that takes maternal practice as a paradigm for moral relations between two individuals who are not equally situated from the perspective of an individual-based equality. Some consequences will be further considered in the later chapters when we discuss policy proposals emanating from a connection-based equality and a public concept of *doulia*.

Maternal practice—providing for children—requires that we provide caring institutions while recognizing that the work itself often demands the commitment of a self transparent to the needs of the charge. The recognition of equality inherent in the understanding that we all are some mother's child—or connection-based equality—has implications for responses appropriate to the requirements of dependency work. Dependency work makes moral claims not only on the dependency worker, but also on the larger society. It falls upon the larger social order to permit the flourishing and preservation of dependency relations by providing for the dependency worker without creating the secondary dependency so debilitating to women today.

The vulnerability model is the one that best accords with the moral claims of the dependent on the dependency worker and of the dependency worker on those whose actions she becomes vulnerable to by virtue of this work. Goodin has argued that the vulnerability model is fundamental for all moral claims of special relationships. We have interpreted this model as fundamentally relational, or one in which the moral claim arises out of the relationships themselves. If these views are correct, then dependency relations are *the* paradigmatic moral relations.[125]

Revisiting the Coercion Problem

We are now in a position to justify limiting the moral responsibility for another when that responsibility is not the result of voluntarism but of a coerced special relation. A mother, acting in a manner compatible with the norms of maternal practice, does not force her child to sacrifice the child's own well-being for another's benefit. Such coercion is not commensurate with a maternal practice that remains true to the well-being of the child. At the extreme of coercion is the experience of the slave. It is no coincidence that the lament of the slave goes: "Sometimes I feel like a motherless child."

If we take the maternal relation as a paradigm of a connection-based equality, we see that when someone takes on the care of another we cannot ignore the fact that the dependency worker is also some mother's child. Working from the analogy of a maternal practice, we see that vulnerability-responsive obligations, which fall upon one by virtue of a coerced situation, cannot, under this conception, become morally binding. Coercion should no more be directed at the caregiver, than at the cared for, given that the caregiver is also a mother's child. This is not to say that a caregiver or dependency worker whose labor is coerced is incapable of providing care to another consistent with maternal practice. Empirical evidence tells us that the coerced dependency worker is capable of providing care consistent with maternal practice. But it is the moral status of her situation that is at issue. The individual coerced into doing dependency work is not being treated in a manner that is consistent with a conception of her as some mother's child. The presumptive obligations of a person so coerced are cancelled because that coercion is not consistent with a paradigm derived from an analogy with maternal practice. An ethic that makes maternal practice a paradigm with this normative force can no more countenance coercion than can a justice-based voluntaristic ethic. And yet the sanction does not presuppose that obligations take their moral force from their status as self-assumed obligations.

We are now in a position to resolve the coercion problem, a problem that appeared to undo the vulnerability model, which is otherwise well suited to the moral conditions of the dependency relationship. Within a moral framework that is voluntaristic there is no problem with coerced responsibilities, for as Thomson's arguments demonstrate, within a voluntaristic framework, it is against such coercion that moral obligation gets defined. But if moral obligation arises when the well-being of one party is vulnerable to the actions of another, then a relation resulting from a coerced situation seems no less able to generate morally binding obligations. Hence Goodin's pragmatic ought.

Goodin's pragmatic ought, however, provides a moral warrant to relationships of dependency—in both the primary sense and the extended sense—that are intuitively unjust. To think that the slave Jim was under a moral obligation to return his master to his home rather than take the opportunity to gain his freedom seems counterintuitive.[126] Here we appeal to justice. This is precisely Thomson's strategy in the arguments defending the right of one to unhook oneself from the violinist, or to abort an undesired pregnancy. Thomson's argument relies heavily on the fact that, when we are hooked up to the violinist against our consent or find ourselves host to an uninvited fetus, we have had no say in the arrangement. In such situations, she contends, justice does not demand that the one vulnerable to our actions has any claim on us, although moral decency may. My response has been that it is not the nonvoluntary nature of this arrangement that vitiates the moral claim of the one dependent on our actions, but its coercion. The argument that justice requires the association to be voluntary is rooted on a mistaken view of social arrangements and an individual-based equality. This view holds that to get at moral obligation we need to start with individuals equally situated and determine how they come together and interact in morally justifiable ways. Whatever determines how this is possible becomes the defining character of moral relationships. Here voluntarism plays a crucial role. Instead the picture that results when we focus on dependency compels us to start with persons firstly connected through relationships of dependency, and then take the moral commitments needed for such relationships as prior to all subsequent moral relationships. But these relationships are often nonvoluntary, and therefore whether or not a relationship is voluntary fails to play the vital role in establishing moral obligations.

Furthermore, if dependency relations form the first model for moral relationships, then the vulnerability model with its emphasis on the response to need is the appropriate one for moral relations—but need is not solely a property of the dependent. The dependency worker is also a person with needs. The mother who feeds her child also needs to eat. The echo of the dinnertime remark returns: My mother is also a mother's child. Just as well-done dependency work requires that the dependency worker not act coercively toward the charge—coercion, like domination is exercised for benefit of someone other than the one upon whom it is imposed—so, too, an equality that begins with caring relationships can give no moral warrant to actions or relationships that are coerced. The proscription against coercion and domination inheres in the moral vision that begins with relationships no less than one that begins with individuals. We can have a vulnerability model without giving a moral warrant to a coercive allocation of responsibilities; we can have a vulnerability model without Goodin's pragmatic ought. But we need the vulnerability model to be situated in a moral, social, and political theory that repudiates the notion that the founding obligations of a social order are derived from the voluntary association of equally situated and empowered individuals. This view is developed further in the next two chapters.

RAWLS BASIC IDEAS   KITTAY ATTACKS THESE PTS.

CONCEPTION OF THE PERSON

  - LIMITED (DEEPLY MALE)

BACKGROUND CONDITIONS

  - REASONABLE PLURALISM

  - SCARCITY

KITTAY'S ARGUMENT:

IF YOU CHANGE THE CONCEPTION OF JUSTICE IT WILL EFFECT THE ORIGINAL
POSITION WHICH IN TERN CHANGES POLICE OF JUSTICE
                            POJ

JUSTICE   VS.   CARE

(MALE)   (FEMALE)   3 PEOPLE CONNECTED TOGETHER

INDIVIDUAL   RELATED

ATOMISTIC   ~~RESPONSIBLE~~

           ~~REL~~ SHARED

RULES   IDENTITY

RIGHTS   RESPONSIVE

             RESPONSIBLE

AUTONOMY

  - DEPENDANCY WORKER (ANYONE WHO CARES FOR OTHERS)

      ✓ NOT AN AUTONOMOUS CHOICE

      · NOT MAXIMIZING OUTCOMES

      - WOMEN

      ✓ ECONOMICALLY LOWER CLASS

      - ETHNIC

NON-FUNGIBLE

  - GOOD OR SERVICE CANNOT BE TURNED INTO A MARKET COMODITY

  - NO-ONE CAN CARE FOR YOU LIKE YOUR MOM

  - NO MARKET SOLUTIONS FOR CARE

RAWLS ON CARE GIVING - RIGHT OR | @ PERSONAL GOOD?
                      JUSTICE | CONCEPTION OF THE GOOD
                              | INFANCY / SENIORS (NOT CITIZENS)

Part 2

Political Liberalism and Human Dependency

"That all men are created free and equal."

That's a hard mystery of Jefferson's.
What did he mean? Of course the easy way
Is to decide it simply isn't true.
It may not be. I heard a fellow say so.
But never mind, the Welshman got it planted
Where it will trouble us a thousand years.
Each age will have to reconsider it.
—Robert Frost, "The Black Cottage"

Dependency as a Criterion of Adequacy

The idea that the founding obligations of a social order are derived from the voluntary association of equally situated and empowered individuals is explicit in social contract theory. Until the publication of John Rawls's *Theory of Justice,* utilitarianism dominated political theory. Rawls revived social contract theory, providing a comprehensive systematic social and political theory and arguing that the principles of justice themselves rested on an implicit social contract. In so doing, Rawls created one of the most powerful and cogent theories of a liberal, democratic egalitarianism.

The view that within a just society *all* persons should be treated as free and equal is shared by different theories within the liberal tradition. The inclusiveness of the *all* has been extended to the formerly disenfranchised, for example, women and black men. The *all* presumes also to include persons with special needs who are dependent upon others in basic ways, that is to say, children, the disabled and the frail elderly. In order to include persons with the special needs of dependents in the community of equal citizens, however, these needs require special consideration. The dependence of dependent persons obligates dependency workers in ways that situate them unequally with respect to others who are not similarly obligated. What I deem the *dependency critique*[127] calls attention to the neglect of dependency and the consequences of that omission in theories of equality and social justice. In the following two chapters I bring the dependency critique to bear on the political theory of Rawls.

Rawls, the most distinguished contemporary representative of the liberal view, defines the political in terms articulated by traditional Western philosophies. For all of its comprehensiveness and power Rawls's theory, like those that have come before it, fails to attend to the fact of human dependency and the consequences of this dependency on social organization. He joins those who have omitted responsibility for dependents from, or relegated it to the periphery of, the political.[128] The presumption has been that these responsibilities belong to citizens' private, rather than public, concerns—a dichotomy that appears reasonable only by virtue of the neglect of dependency in delineating the political. The particular situation of those who care for dependents becomes invisible in the political domain—the domain in which parties are to be reckoned as equals. The liberal ideal of equality casts its light in this public domain and so fails to illuminate the nether world of human dependency.

I throw the spotlight on *inevitable dependencies*, those times in our lives when we are utterly dependent, because inequities in the organization and distribution of dependency work—and its impact on the possibility of equality for all—are most evident when dependency is a feature of our human condition rather than a consequence of socially prescribed roles, privileges, or distribution policies.[129] Previously, I have delineated a number of features that in the lesser forms of dependency are separable, but in utter dependency are inexorably linked. First, the dependent requires care and caring persons to meet fundamental needs for survival and basic thriving. Second, while in the condition of dependency, the dependent is unable to reciprocate the benefits received.[130] And third, the intervention of another is crucial to assure that the needs of the dependent are met and that the interests of the dependent are recognized in a social context.[131] Dependency, so understood, underscores not only the limitations of an individual's capability, but also the necessary labor of a dependency worker.

The point of the dependency critique is to show that, as long as the bounds of justice are drawn within reciprocal relations among free and equal persons, dependents will continue to remain disenfranchised, and dependency workers who are otherwise fully capable and cooperating members of society will continue to share varying degrees of the dependents' disenfranchisement.

Rawls may be said to address these concerns indirectly, either in his presupposition that the needs of dependents are met in the nonpolitical domestic domain, or in his concern for "the least well off," but he does not deal with them directly. Most importantly, Rawls does not consider these concerns as central to the political aim of his theory. Especially as he refines the political focus of his work in *Political Liberalism*, concerns of this sort are excluded. The exclusion is not trivial, nor is it Rawls's alone.

Because dependency strongly affects our status as equal citizens (that is, as persons who, as equals, share the benefits and burdens of social cooperation), and because it affects all of us at one time or another, it is not an issue that can be set aside, much less avoided. Its consequences for social organization cannot be deferred until other traditional questions about the structure of society have been settled without distorting the character of a just social order. Dependency must be faced from the beginning of any project in egalitarian theory that hopes to include *all* persons within its scope.

Theories which do not consider dependency at their heart may be based on the concept of persons as moral equals, but they will result in a society in which the claim to equal moral worth cannot be realized for *all*. In this chapter and the one that follows, I argue that to construct a theory of the political that excludes dependency concerns can be maintained only by the exploitation of those who do dependency work or by the neglect of the concerns of the dependents.

My argument features the work of John Rawls both because of his unequaled influence in contemporary political theory, and because of his evident interest in creating a theory sympathetic to the welfare of women and others that have been excluded from the political domain. In *Political Liberalism* Rawls, addressing his feminist commentators,[132] opines (optimistically) that "alleged difficulties in discussing problems of gender and the family can be overcome" (1992, xxix). He defends his theory's dependence on a "few main and enduring classical problems" (1992, xxix) of political philosophy, and especially the conception of the person it borrows from a long tradition in which the political actor was understood to be male. His own conception, he assures his readers, is merely a "device of representation" and not a characterization of persons in a full sense. Rawls clearly intends to include women within the scope of his theory. I contend that he cannot succeed because the theory effectively excludes as equal citizens two classes of persons whom Rawls did not intend to exclude: those who are dependent upon others, and those who attend to their needs. The contingent fact that women are, by and large, the dependency workers means that the theoretical formulations of Rawls's theory of justice effectively disadvantage women. I contend, but do not show here, that many of the criticisms applied to Rawls pertain (*ceteris paribus*) to other theories of liberalism.

The Role of Equality and Equality's Presuppositions

Equality, along with liberty, forms one of the two pillars on which liberal political theory is erected; and, appropriately, equality is at the core of Rawls's theory. Equal divisions of the benefits and burdens of social cooperation serve as a benchmark for "justice as fairness" (Rawls 1992, 282). Equality plays its role both at the start of theorizing (all persons are moral equals) and at its conclusion (social organization is to result in political liberties enjoyed equally by all and in fair economic distribution, with equal opportunity advantaging the least well-off).[133]

Rawls proposes principles of justice intended to govern the basic structures of a well-ordered society, principles which, he argues, would be chosen by reasonable and rational persons under certain specified conditions—conditions simulated in the *original position*. In Rawls's constructivism,[134] the original position (henceforth referred to as OP) is a hypothetical position from which representatives of citizens in a well-ordered society choose the principles of justice that they want their basic social structures (that is, their laws and institutions) to embody. The participants in the OP are all modeled on equal and free moral persons, who are rational and mutually disinterested. They know general facts about human nature and society but are ignorant of their own station in life, their "conceptions of the good," and "their special psychological propensities" (1971, 11). This *veil of ignorance* over participants in the OP should ensure that the choice of principles is unaffected by knowledge of one's own place in society, one's own vision of the good, or one's particular psychological proclivities; it should guarantee that parties choose principles impartially and, therefore, fairly. Parties in the OP are representatives of mutually disinterested *rational* agents concerned primarily with their own well-being. The constraints of the OP reflect fair terms of social cooperation to which rational persons could agree.

In *Kantian Constructivism in Moral Theory: The Dewey Lectures 1980*, Rawls exhibits the methodology and the foundational concepts of *A Theory of Justice* in what he calls "model-conceptions" (1980, 520).

The OP mediates between the "model-conceptions" of a *well-ordered society* and of a *moral person*, modeling the "way in which the citizens in a well-ordered society, viewed as moral persons, would ideally select first principles of justice for their society" (1980, 520). Answering criticisms addressed to his model-conceptions, Rawls in his later works[135] adds that thinking of ourselves as participants in the OP is analogous to "role-playing" (1992, 27).[136] Thus the OP and the model conceptions are meant "to show how the idea of society as a fair system of social cooperation can be unfolded so as to find principles specifying the basic rights and liberties and the forms of equality most appropriate to those cooperating, once they are regarded as citizens, as free and equal persons" (1992, 27).

My claim is that those within relations of dependency fall outside the conceptual perimeters of Rawls's egalitarianism. I shall trace the conceptual shape of this exclusion in Rawls through an analysis of the five presuppositions standing behind the concept of equality as we find it in Rawls's constructivism, and through a consideration of the principles selected in the OP in light of this analysis. I argue that the two principles of justice cannot accommodate the objections of the dependency critique unless Rawls's foundational assumptions are altered. In pointing to omissions in this theory, I contemplate ways in which the Rawlsian position could be amended. Whether the suggestions put forward suffice to make the theory amenable to dependency concerns without introducing new incoherencies for the theory is a question I leave for Rawlsians. My aim is neither to reform Rawls's political theory, nor to say that it cannot be reformed. Rather, I offer the arguments of the dependency critique as a criterion of adequacy, one applicable to *any* political theory claiming to be egalitarian.

The Arguments in Outline

"Equal justice," writes Rawls, "is owed to those who have the capacity to take part in and to act in accordance with the public understanding of the initial situation" (1971, 505). The moral equality of all members of a well-ordered society is represented in the model-conception of the person. In the *Dewey Lectures*, he writes, "The representation for equality is an easy matter: we simply describe all the parties in the same way and situate them equally, that is, symmetrically with respect to one another. Everyone has the same rights and powers in the procedure for reaching agreement" (1980, 550). "Equality" in this passage means the identity of members with respect to certain salient features: their rights and their powers in the procedure for reaching agreement. It also means that the parties are equally situated with respect to one another.[137] Representing equality here seems unproblematic. But, I wish to argue, what makes it an "easy matter" is that so much has been presumed already. Let us see if we can make the presumptions evident.

First, Rawls, borrowing from Hume, identifies the "circumstances of justice." These are preconditions for justice in a society, and include facts that are known and recognized by the free and equal persons who constitute society. The circumstances of justice set the parameters for all subsequent considerations.

Second, when Rawls provides the sense in which citizens in a well-ordered society are equal moral persons, he starts with an "idealization" of citizens in a well-ordered society—that "all citizens are fully cooperating members of society *over the course of a complete life*" (emphasis mine, 1980, 546).

For Rawls this means that no one has particularly taxing or costly needs to fulfill, such as unusual medical requirements. In *Political Liberalism*, Rawls writes, "The normal range [of functioning] is specified as follows: Since the fundamental problem of justice concerns the relations among those who are full and active participants in society, and directly or indirectly associated together over the course of a whole life, it is reasonable to *assume that everyone has physical needs and psychological capacities within some normal range. Thus the problem of special health care and how to treat the mentally defective are set.* If we can work out a viable theory for the normal range, we can attempt to handle these other cases later" (emphasis mine 1992, 272 n.10). That is, the case has initially to be made for the "normal" situation and then modified to include important but unusual considerations such as special medical requirements.[138]

Third, as everyone is equally capable of understanding and complying with the principles of justice (to a certain minimal degree) and equally capable of honoring them, and insofar as each person is free, that is, is a "self-originating" or "self-authenticating source of valid claims,"[139] each views him- or herself as worthy of being represented in a procedure by which the principles of justice are determined. An equality with respect first to a sense of justice and second to freedom as being a self-authenticating source of valid claims establishes the grounds for the claim to equal worth.

Fourth, the realization of equality assumes a common measure. But insofar as each person forms her or his own conception of the good, Rawls proposes an index comprised of those goods all persons require given the two moral powers of a person: an ability to form and revise one's conception of one's own good and a sense of justice. The possession of the two moral powers is itself a feature of the modeling of the parties as equals.[140]

And fifth, the representation of the parties as equals turns on a conception of social cooperation. The equality of those representing citizens requires that persons possess the two moral powers and have normal capacities because these are the only requirements for establishing fair terms of social cooperation.[141]

Rawls's account, by his own insistence, is an idealization. Still, he acknowledges that it must take into account "an appropriate conception of the person that general facts about human nature and society allow" (1980, 534). Rawls's idealization, unfortunately, neglects certain scarcely acknowledged facts bearing on "an appropriate conception of the person" which are of the utmost importance in social organization, namely, facts of human dependency. The question then arises whether, given the Rawlsian idealization, the equality of citizens applies to those individuals who are dependent either in the primary sense or in the derived sense, even in a fully compliant well-ordered society. In the following two chapters I will interrogate these five presuppositions:

(i)   The *circumstances of justice* that determine a well-ordered society's conceptual perimeters.

(ii) The norm appealed to and projected into the idealization that "all citizens are fully cooperating members of society over the course of a complete life."

(iii) The *conception of free persons* as those who think of themselves as "self-originating sources of valid claims."

(iv) The *moral powers of a person* relevant to justice as (1) a sense of justice and (2) a conception of one's own good; and list of *primary goods* based on these moral powers that serves as index for interpersonal comparisons of well-being.

(v)   The *conception of social cooperation* that supposes equality between those in cooperative arrangements.

I will show that in each of these assumptions dependency concerns are omitted. In this way, I demonstrate that dependency concerns are absent in the concepts which figure crucially in Rawls's theory, concepts that contribute to the model-conception of the person and the well-ordered society in which equality is realized. In Chapter Three, I begin, as does Rawls, by considering *the circumstances of justice*. I then look at how the model conception of the person is drawn in its idealizations, first in the *norm* that "all citizens are *fully cooperating* members of society over the course of a complete life" and second in the understanding of persons as free, insofar as they are "self-originating sources of valid claims." The specific conception of moral persons, their needs and their interaction in an ideal social order will be treated in Chapter Four, where I will look first at the *defining features of a moral person* and the *index of primary goods* and second at the notion of *social cooperation*. Examining these will allow us to see how conceptions of social goods and social cooperation need to be rethought if a social organization is to be responsive to dependency concerns. The argument concerning Rawls concludes with an examination of the principles of justice chosen in the original position and with the finding that they are unable to yield the egalitarian concerns that motivate the theory.

3

The Presuppositions of Equality

The Circumstances of Justice for a Well-Ordered Society

Dependency as Both an Objective and a Subjective Circumstance of Justice

The general facts about human nature and society that constrain the conception of the person and of the well-ordered society constitute the most fundamental presuppositions for the conception of equality and justice evoked in Rawls's scheme. The most general of these facts are encapsulated in what Rawls, invoking Hume, calls the *circumstances of justice*. These are either objective or subjective (Rawls 1971, 126–27; Rawls 1980, 536). Because each is so basic, the fact that Rawls overlooks an important circumstance has serious consequences for the whole theory.

The objective circumstance of dependency is familiar to us all. In complex societies nearly two decades are required to train individuals to be "fully cooperating members of society," and in all societies approximately ten childhood years are spent in nearly total dependence on an adult. As we live longer, a greater portion of our lives is led in a state of frail old age when, once again, we cannot be fully cooperating members of society.[142] Despite advanced medical care, serious disabling conditions strike as much as ten percent of the population of the United States. Surely, one would think, such a fundamental feature of our lives would be included among the circumstances of justice.

Similarly, we are familiar with dependency in its subjective forms: that is, as it affects our needs and desires. We have the need and desire both to be cared for and to care (or have someone care) for those who are important to us. Having these desires satisfied and these needs met are part of any conception of the good (see Chapter Four). By contrast,

not everyone's conception of the good will include doing what is necessary to take care of these needs and desires. A just distribution of the
burdens and responsibilities attached to meeting these needs is required
in the same way that adjudicating between differing conceptions of the
good is required of a just form of social cooperation. Furthermore the
subjective conditions resulting from inevitable human dependencies, like
the fact of differing conceptions of the good, are at the heart of considerations that propel us into social and political associations.

The Absence of Dependency in the "Circumstances of Justice"

From the *Dewey Lectures* onward, Rawls speaks only of the objective
circumstance of moderate scarcity, that is, the condition in which natural
resources are neither so abundant that distributive problems do not arise
nor so scarce that cooperative arrangements cannot be realized. With
respect to the subjective circumstances of justice, Rawls speaks primarily
of the condition that "persons and associations have contrary conceptions of the good as well as of how to realize them" (1980, 536).

But even under conditions of affluence, there are important questions
to raise with respect to the distribution of resources devoted to meeting
dependency needs, and the distribution of the burdens and responsibilities of dependency work. Distributive questions with respect to dependency needs are not traceable to circumstances of justice concerning
moderate scarcity. Yet nowhere in Rawls's work is human dependency
explicitly cited among the circumstances of justice.

In the earlier works, we can find allusions to dependency concerns in
two passages. First, Rawls (1971, 127) includes the equal vulnerability of
all to attack and to being hindered by the united force of the others in
the more complete enumeration of objective circumstances. This vulnerability, however, should not be confused with the vulnerability of
dependency. Rawls speaks of an *equal* vulnerability—e.g., the equal vulnerability to attack. Vulnerability originating in dependency is not a
condition in which all are *equally* vulnerable, but one in which some are
especially vulnerable. The unequal vulnerability of the dependent and,
secondarily, of the dependent's caregiver is an inequality in starting positions, which, if left unaddressed, is injected into the political situation.

Second, and more promising, is a passage in which Rawls says it is
"essential . . . that each person in the original position should care about
the well-being of some of those in the next generation . . . [and that] for
anyone in the next generation, there is someone who cares about him in
the present generation" (1971, 129). The remarks are provoked by the
worry that if the generations are mutually disinterested, then there is no

impetus to prevent the depletion of resources for future generations. This leads Rawls to propose a "motivational assumption" that will generate a "just savings principle" (1971, 285). He proposes that the parties to the OP represent generational lines and that they be heads of households, thereby securing the interests of subsequent generations.

Although Rawls speaks of each person in the OP caring about the welfare of some in the next, the concern is with a scarcity of resources across generations, not the care of dependents. Even as he talks about a member of each generation "caring about" one in the next, he urges us not to presuppose extensive ties of natural sentiment.[143]

Dependency and Heads of Households

Rawls does not introduce representation by heads of households to solve problems arising from dependency, and in *Political Liberalism* Rawls abandons the idea altogether. Might this device, nonetheless, be helpful in considering the circumstance of dependency, by having household heads represent the interests of dependents and familial caregivers?

In real politics, having one's own interests represented by someone who is differently situated is always a risky matter. Abigail Adams thought herself *represented* by her husband, but in the constitutional assembly, composed only of male heads of households, no one seemed to have heeded her call to "remember the Ladies."[144] But the OP posits a hypothetical representation: Why not just stipulate that those represented are represented faithfully?

The difficulty with such hypothetical representation in the Rawlsian framework has been pointed to first by Jane English (1977) and later by Susan Okin (1989b). Using heads of households as representatives means that, although the family is one of the basic structures of society, justice cannot be said to pertain *within* it—a difficulty for gender equality among those who share a household.[145] If parties to the OP already have a determined social position relative to the family, they will not choose the principles of justice in ignorance of their social position. And in the framework of Rawlsian constructivism, only principles that we choose in ignorance of our social position will issue in fair principles with respect to the basic institutions. Since Rawls does want to say that the family is a basic institution, and since justice should then pertain to it, the parties cannot be heads of households.

Okin's suggestion is that individuals, not heads of households, should be representatives. Our question then is whether the parties representing individuals will represent the interests of both dependents and caregivers. If human dependency counts among the general facts to which representatives in the OP have epistemic access, then they know that when the veil is lifted they may find themselves dependent or having to care for dependents. If the representatives are individuals instead of household heads, then they should be considering such contingencies in choosing their principles.

Although the theory allows an individual in the OP to imagine her or himself to be a dependent or a dependency worker, the construction of the OP does not guarantee that the principles of justice chosen will reflect the concerns of either. While the Rawlsian construct allows for the possibility that a representative *may* imagine himself or herself as a dependent or having responsibility for a dependent's care, it does not necessitate that a representative *will* do so when choosing the principles for a well-ordered society. Dependents do not form an obvious constituency within the Rawlsian construct.[146] Surely, some persons, envisioning themselves as having dependency responsibilities, may choose to adopt other-directed interests as their own. But this makes the representation of these dependents a contingent matter and not one integral to the procedure of determining the principles of justice (see page 87ff).

If we insist, instead, that the parties represent generational lines,[147] we face still another predicament. If the rational choices of individual parties modeled in the OP (along with the other conditions stipulated of the OP) sufficed, there would be no need for any additional motivational assumptions, such as the one securing resources for future generations. The motivational assumption is necessary just because we may find too few in any one generation willing take responsibility for those in the next, if we must rely on individual voluntary decisions to assure that everyone in a future generation will have someone who cares about his or her interest.[148] The choice not to take on such responsibility is neither irrational nor unreasonable[149] and accords with our reflective judgments, as the social acceptance of remaining childless shows.[150] To mandate such a responsibility could be seen as a serious constraint on individual conceptions of the good. The "just savings principle" stands in lieu of a mandate that each person in a society care about another in the next generation. But if the mandate itself is an undue constraint on each person's conception of the good, why is the substitute more acceptable, since it requires that we refrain from the enjoyment of at least some of our resources for the sake of a future generation whose well-being may play no role in one's own conception of the good? Either Rawls's motivational assumption fails or it allows into his scheme principles that constitute an unpalatable constraint on each person's choice of the good.

Now if the supposition that each party in the OP is a head of household—which is still meant to avoid supposing extensive ties of natural sentiment—is too strong to accommodate certain rational and reasonable conceptions of the good, then it surely cannot be helpful in covering the requirements of dependents whose care requires a commitment stronger still than the preservation of resources for the future. Therefore, we are confronted with the problem that however we conceive of the parties in the OP, as representatives of individuals or as representatives of households (or generational lines), the representation of dependents and those caring for dependents is not assured by the construction of the OP. And this is so even if we include facts concerning dependency among those that parties in the OP would know while under the veil of ignorance.

Chronological Unfairness and Intergenerational Justice

Rawls (1992) revises his strategy to assure the just savings principle. Acknowledging a proposal previously suggested by English (1977), Rawls now maintains that "the parties can be required to agree to a savings principle subject to the further condition that they must want all *previous* generations to have followed it" (1992, 274). Thus the motivational assumption that "constrains the parties from refusing to make any savings at all" remains (1992, 274n. 12) and is captured by a form of reciprocity peculiar to the savings principle. Rawls had earlier noted:

> Normally this [reciprocity] principle applies when there is an exchange of advantages and each party gives something as a fair return to the other. But in the course of history no generation gives to the preceding generations, the benefits of whose saving it has received. In following the savings principle, each generation makes a contribution to later generations and receives from its predecessors (1971, 290).

It is a natural fact that "We can do something for posterity but posterity can do nothing for us" (1971, 291). This is "a kind of chronological unfairness since those who live later profit from the labor of their predecessors without paying the same price" (Herzen cited, 1971, 291); being unalterable, however, it is itself not a question of justice but a consideration that we have to acknowledge in fashioning the just society.

But the conditions of human development, disease, and decline are similarly unalterable, as are inherent demands of dependency work that prevent the dependency worker from functioning as an unencumbered independent agent. What is not unalterable is the level of support extended to the dependent and the dependency worker. If we need a just savings principle (however it is formulated) to guarantee that the well-being of future generations is not jeopardized, we need a similar principle to ensure that the well-being of dependents and their caregivers is not jeopardized, since the natural developmental process to which the first is addressed is mirrored within the life history of each individual as well, and if the first needs to be addressed by a theory of justice, so does the second.

If these considerations are to be addressed in a theory of justice, one would suppose that the conception of what it is to be a person must in some way reflect such elemental facts about human existence. However, as we will see in the following two sections, this is not the case in Rawls's construct. Instead, we are asked to begin our inquiry concerning the principles of justice with the idealization of a fully functioning person.

The Idealization That "All Citizens Are Fully Cooperating Members of Society"

Fully Cooperating Throughout a Life—The Strong Interpretation

Representing the equality of citizens in a well-ordered society, Rawls claims, requires the idealization that "all are capable of honoring the principles of justice and of being full participants in social cooperation *throughout* their lives" (emphasis mine, 1971, 546). Rawls presumes this to be an innocent idealization, greasing the wheels of the theoretical apparatus allowing us to pass over the few difficult cases, persons, for example, with "unusual and costly medical requirements." He justifies his exclusion of "hard cases" such as disabilities and special health needs by claiming that they are "morally irrelevant" and can "distract our moral perception by leading us to think of people distant from us whose fate arouses pity and anxiety" (Rawls 1975a, 96).

But this idealization is seriously misleading. Amartya Sen remarks that leaving out disabilities, or special health needs, or physical or mental defects "for fear of making a mistake, may guarantee that the *opposite* mistake will be made"[151] (Sen 1987, 157). The opposite mistake, I contend, is to put too much distance between the "normal functioning individual" and the person with special needs and disabilities. Not a single citizen approaches the ideal of full functioning *throughout* a lifetime. The idealization, in contrast, suggests that those who are not fully functioning are relatively few, and that consequences of special needs is brokered only in monetary terms.

Perhaps by pressing the phrase "*throughout* their lives" we have interpreted Rawls too strongly. This phrase suggests that full functioning at *every point* in a complete life is the requirement for equal citizenship. Rawls also uses the phrase "over the course of a complete life" (which survives the revision of the *Dewey Lectures* in *Political Liberalism*). A weaker requirement is to be a fully cooperating member of society at just those points when it would be reasonable to expect an individual to be fully functioning. That a certain portion of the population is dependent at any given time would not necessarily imply that those persons are not "equal," since they may well be equal *over* the course of the complete life.[152] While individuals are minors, or disabled, and so equal citizens only *in potentia*, their representatives in the OP are modeled as rational fully functioning parties, with equal powers and symmetrically situated.

Fully Cooperating Over a Lifetime—The Weak Interpretation

The weaker reading of the idealization of full functioning allows parties to come to the "bargaining table" of the OP with a knowledge that they are dependent—and may have to take on dependency responsibilities—at some time in their lives. Those whom the parties represent are dependent *in potentia* (and possibly dependency workers *in potentia*). Although as rational autonomous representatives (Rawls 1992, 316) they come to the bargaining table of the OP in full possession of their power, the dependent (at least) should be robustly represented by the party to the OP. Behind the veil of ignorance, we do not know if we are dependent or independent, dependency workers or unencumbered. It should be the case that either the nature of the representative, or the construction of the situation in which the representative deliberates, will allow the interests of the dependent and the dependency worker to be taken into account in choosing the principles of justice. I argued above that, although nothing in the construction of the OP prevents a representative in the hypothetical situation of the OP from thinking about her or himself as a dependent or a dependency worker, nothing assures it and so these concerns will not necessarily be represented. Only the least well-off is assured representation, and in Chapter Four I will argue that assimilating either the dependent or dependency worker to the position of the least well-off is neither warranted by the theory nor by our considered reflections.

However, *if* dependency is recognized as one of the circumstances of justice, then the dependent *is* represented as a fully functioning citizen in a period of dependency, such as early childhood. If I imagine myself as a party to the original position, I consider that I will have such periods of dependency and will want to choose my principles of justice in such a way that, while I am in this state, my interests are protected. Furthermore, since I will also think that, in all likelihood, I will not always be dependent, I will want principles capable of generating policies that balance my concerns during periods of dependency with those during periods of full functioning. In this way, the weak interpretation does allow for the concerns of the dependent to be included.

However, as long as nothing in the construction of the OP assures that any party to the OP will identify their conception of the good, or their rational self-interest, with one who meets the needs of a dependent, we have not yet solved the problem of representing the dependency worker. When citizens are idealized as fully functioning, there is no internal incoherence in a theory that does not ensure that parties to the OP represent dependency workers. The theory simply is not concerned with such needs nor with the justice or injustice of how dependency needs are met. But as such a theory has neglected dependency concerns, it is not true to those realities of human life that move us to seek social alliances. Once we stop ignoring dependency, then we are obliged to think of how dependency needs are met in a manner that is equitable to all.

Let us say, however, that as a representative in the OP who knows that we all have periods of dependency, I *do* consider that I may choose (or be called upon to take on) dependency work. What kind of bargaining position do I need with respect to the other parties? I will be situated symmetrically to the other parties only if they too have envisioned this as a possibility for themselves. They may have, but because nothing in the moral psychology that Rawls sketches for us assures that they will,[153] they may not have.

In Chapters One and Two we already explored some of the ways the dependency worker is not symmetrically situated vis-à-vis her charge and those who stand outside the dependency relationship but provide support for it. The party who represents the citizen who does dependency work is also not situated symmetrically to the parties representing citizens who do not do such work. The party representing the dependency worker knows that the dependency worker cannot think only about her own interests, but must also consider those of the dependent. As such, this party (assuming that the parties do represent individuals, not heads of households), is not situated symmetrically to those parties who need only consider the interests of the citizen they represent. Let us consider how this is played out in the OP.

The egalitarian benchmark that constrains the OP is that each counts as one in choosing the principles of justice. The idealization of citizens as fully functioning over the course of their lives is needed for this modeling of the parties because only then can we think of each citizen as counting for one in the distribution of both the benefits and the burdens of social cooperation. All representatives of such citizens in the OP go to the bargaining table knowing that, whether they are successful at a lucrative profession or whether they are street sweepers, they have an equal voice in the choice of the fundamental principles governing the basic structure because they are each fully capable of participating according to the terms of fair social cooperation.

Reflect on what happens during those periods when we are not fully functioning and are dependent. Being too disabled (temporarily) or being too young to cooperate fully in benefits and burdens is morally irrelevant. Those so incapacitated still must have rights. But then these rights are in need of protection by others whose powers are intact. The dependent, however, cannot assume the burdens and responsibilities of social cooperation while in the state of dependency, even though as a citizen he or she should be able to enjoy the benefits of social cooperation. A dependent can define the terms of political participation *only* to the extent that she can speak on her own behalf, can be heard as an independent voice (neither is generally the case for "underage" individuals), and can act on her own behalf (which is circumscribed by virtue of the dependency). As for the rest, she must depend on those responsible for her well-being. Another must hold the rights of the dependent in trust,[154] just as another must take on the care for the physical well-being of the dependent.

If we all took turns being dependent and dependency worker, we would repay the debt incurred during periods of dependency of benefits-received-without-burdens-assumed. But there is no reason to suppose such a state of affairs—that is not what is implied in the norm of all citizens being fully functioning over the course of a life. Therefore the burdens and responsibilities of the dependent, which are assumed by the dependency worker, make the interests of the dependency worker importantly different from those of the unencumbered and fully functioning citizen. Looking at the economy of social cooperation in terms of burdens and responsibilities, we see that the independent fully functioning citizen assumes the burdens and responsibilities of one, while the dependency worker assumes those of more than one, and the dependent those of less than one. If we look at that same economy in terms of benefits, we see the dependent still counting as one, as does the full functioning citizen. In contrast, however, if the dependency worker must also secure rights and benefits for her charge, even at the expense of her own rights and benefits, her own welfare comes to count for *less* than one.

If citizens who take on dependency work can be said to do so simply as one among many possible conceptions of the good, then they should accept the disadvantage along with the advantage of that individual's autonomous choice—as must all citizens who form a conception of the good, but taking on dependency work is not one choice of the good life among others. If none made such a choice, society could not continue beyond a single generation. Therefore this is a conception of the good which occupies a special place with respect to the welfare of society. Also, when one takes on dependency responsibilities, one becomes poorly situated in a system of social cooperation in which each counts as one (see Chapter Four).

Unless some device acknowledges the fact that some citizens will be disadvantaged even as they provide the labor needed to care for and reproduce other citizens, and provides a mechanism for equalizing the prospects of all, situating their representatives symmetrically to those of unencumbered citizens cannot do the job of fairly representing all. The veil of ignorance won't suffice as such a device, because it gets us only the reasonableness needed for social cooperation when all the rational agents represent free and equal citizens—but we will see, first, that dependency workers are not free in the requisite sense and, second, that the social cooperation in which dependents and dependency workers engage is not social cooperation among equals. That is why, at the very least, we need a motivational assumption akin to the just savings principle, but one that recognizes the role of dependency and care in the lives of each of us.

The symmetries that allow the rational party to simulate the commitments of a rational and reasonable person do not hold for conditions pertinent to the dependency relation, and fail even on the weaker interpretation of the norm of full functioning. Whether we say that we are fully cooperating members of society throughout our lives, or over the course of our lives, the idealization is questionable at best, or pernicious at worst. Its virtue springs from the Kantian position that autonomy is that feature of human existence that gives us our dignity. But it fosters a fiction that the incapacity to function as a fully cooperating societal member is an exception in human life, not a normal variation; that the dependency is normally too brief and episodic to concern political life, rather than constituted by periodic, and often prolonged, phases of our lives whose costs and burdens ought to be justly shared.

Autonomy in the sense of self-governance is surely of special importance, but these Kantian considerations must find their way into a more adequate representation of persons, one capable of acknowledging dependency as an obligatory limitation to self-governance. Neither the condition of the self-governing adult—the liberal Kantian model—nor the condition of a minor—the secular and religious authoritarian model—

ought to serve as the "normal" condition of persons when choosing the design of a social order. Instead the full range of human functioning[155] is the "normal" condition. Otherwise, representing dependents and their caregivers within the OP and within the well-ordered society becomes *a problem*; and the demands on those who care for them become a personal issue standing outside considerations of equality and justice.

The adoption of the norm that all are fully cooperating members over the course of a lifetime makes plausible the modeling of citizens in the well-ordered society as parties in the OP who are symmetrically situated. But between the idealization (of equal situation and equal powers) and the reality (of asymmetries of situation and inequalities of capability) lies the danger that dependents and dependency caregivers will fall into a worst-off position. The procedure of construction modeled by the OP "shows how the principles of justice follow from the principles of practical reason in union with conceptions of society and person" (Rawls 1992, 90). Although Rawls believes that the conception of the person he employs is itself an idea of practical reason (1992, 90), it is an idea inadequate to the fact of a human's vulnerability to dependency. To model the representative party on a norm of a fully functioning person is to skew the choice of principles in favor of those who can function independently and who are not responsible for assuming the care of those who cannot.

Free Persons Are "Self-Originating Sources of Valid Claims"

Equal persons in a well-ordered society must also be regarded as free. Our contemporary sensibility refuses to tolerate slavery, serfdom, or any similar bondage within a well-ordered society. Rawls contrasts the free citizen to the slave or bondsman. He depicts citizens in the well-ordered society as "self-*originating* sources of valid claims" (emphasis mine) in the *Dewey Lectures*, and as "self-*authenticating* sources of valid claims" (emphasis mine) in *Political Liberalism*.[156] Rawls also contrasts claims originating from ourselves with those derived from our social role, wherein we act for others upon whose rights and powers our own depend. In the next two sections, I will argue that being a "self-*authenticating* source of valid claims" is an inapt characterization of freedom for the dependency worker. But because it is an important feature of the freedom Rawls attributes to the "free and equal citizen," parties to the OP who are modeled on free persons (in this sense) do not represent the dependency worker.

Is the Dependency Worker a Self-Originator of Claims?

What should we say of the mother and her claim to, let us say, the right to education—not for herself, but for her child? Is hers a self-originating claim, or a claim derived from prior duties or obligations owed to society or to other persons, that is, one derived from or assigned to her particular social role? The parent who presses the claim on behalf of the child also sees it—appropriately, I believe—as in her own interest.[157] A caring and responsible parent is one whose self-respect is bound up with the care she attempts to provide and the opportunities she attempts to make available to her children. Therefore, the claims she makes on their behalf are reasonably experienced as self-originating claims, although they are claims made on behalf of another within the context of a social role.

The dependency worker whose relation to the charge is more distant, and so whose own well-being is less intimately tied to her charge, may nonetheless make claims on the other's behalf—claims that exceed the dependency worker's prescribed duties. When her claims (in contrast to the mother's) go beyond prescribed duties, the *specific* claims cannot be said to originate in her social role, even if, in general, her claims on behalf of her charge derive from her social role. Thus, *both* for the mother (who, in making claims for her child, remains within her socially defined role but experiences those claims as her own) and for the other dependency worker who does not so closely identify her good with that of her charge (yet whose claims on behalf of her charge will exceed her specified responsibility), freedom is as bound up with claims that originate from others as it is with those which originate independently.[158]

It is important to stress here that a thick involvement of the dependency worker in the welfare of her charge is generally not, as it is so often portrayed, a neurotic, compensatory action on the part of an individual who has no hope of being a person in her own right. Because dependency work is so often conducted under oppressive conditions, it is easy to miss the fact that deep involvement is a normal and necessary part of good dependency work—while overinvolvement and self-abnegation may not even be good caregiving. A feverish child who wakes in the middle of the night has a claim on her caregiver's attention, even if the caregiver is very tired or even ill (see also note 162 below). Whether a dependency worker presses for a child's educational opportunities, or ignores her own fatigue to care for the ill child, her actions are good caring and not, generally speaking, neurotic overidentification or self-abnegating self-sacrifice. Caring about the welfare of persons for whom you are responsible and for whom you care is entailed in normal and *effective* caring. The failure of much institutionalized care-taking is traceable to the difficulty of evoking this thick involvement on the part of the caregiver; that is, the caregivers, so often, *don't care*.

The dependency worker cannot be said to be a self-originating source of claims, at least not in the terms suggested in the *Dewey Lectures*. Any retort that it is only the dependency worker, qua dependency worker, who fails to be a self-originating source of claims (since these claims issue from her as she fills a particular social role) fails to recognize an important difference between dependency work and most other forms of labor. Because of the moral demands of the work (see Chapter Two), the dependency workers' moral selves cannot easily be peeled from their social roles. Therefore freedom that demands a view of oneself as a self-originator of valid claims is not a freedom applicable to the situation of the dependency worker.

Of course, Rawls's is a normative and not a descriptive, theory. Slaves, too, would not count among the free individuals who have an equal claim to the fruits of social cooperation, since they also are not self-originating sources of valid claims. But in a well-ordered society all should be treated as free and equal, and slavery would be impermissible.

Perhaps we should ban dependency work if it demands a psychology in which the dependency worker's self-worth is more a function of another's accomplishments and welfare than her own. Some jobs, such as coal mining, do seem inherently oppressive. One may argue that no wage can compensate for the diminution in well-being that a coal miner must suffer, and that justice demands abolishing coal mining. Dependency work has another character, and justice could never demand that we abolish it. We cannot eliminate dependency work, nor would we want to. If, as Rawls writes, the members of a well-ordered society are to "view their common polity as extending backward and forward in time over generations" (1980, 536), and the course of human development inevitably requires that some persons care for dependents, we cannot tell the dependency worker to abandon her concern for the well-being of her charge, even though this constraint renders her freedom—construed as the self-origination of valid claims—an empty abstraction.

The restraint on freedom that dependency work shares with slavery has tainted this form of labor, especially in modern times where freedom as the self-origination of valid claims has been so highly prized. Only by naturalizing dependency work (e.g., women are *naturally* better with children, the sick, the elderly) have ideologues made their constraints on freedom palatable to a modern sensibility.[159] By so naturalizing the labor, the coercion required for the *modern* woman to engage in dependency work has been covered with sentimentality (see Badinter 1980).

There is not an inevitable tension between holding that dependency work is more important than most labor and holding that dependency work can be oppressive and ought not to be foisted on anyone. If dependency work appears oppressive, it is because the norm of freedom is shaped without attention to the role of dependency in our lives. If it is oppressive, it is so because it exists within a social setting that fails to foster the well-being of dependency workers and their charges. This is not to say that dependency work cannot be intensely rewarding. Not only *can* it be, but under favorable conditions it *is* rewarding. But when we highlight this sense of freedom, we are less likely to see this labor as the vital, fulfilling, humanizing work it is.

Is the Dependency Worker a Self-Authenticator of Claims?

The criticism launched here is against an individualistic view of citizens and their representatives in the OP. And the formulation in the *Dewey Lectures* may be most susceptible to such a reading.[160] Earlier, Rawls had explicitly warned against construing the self-interestedness of the participants of the OP as interested only in their selfish pursuits: "There is no inconsistency, then, in supposing that once the veil of ignorance is removed, the parties find that they have ties of sentiment and affection, and want to advance the interests of others and to see their ends attained" (1972, 129). Thus the parties in the OP may represent the wants and interests of others (and when the parties are heads of families they presumably do), and self-originating claims need not be self-interested. For example, if I want whatever *J* wants, and although the content of my wants is determined not by me but by *J*, the claim is self-originating if *my* want is to want what *J* wants. This is a noncoerced, other-linked, second-order wanting. One voicing such a want is less like the slave and more like the churches, or voluntary agencies, who press claims on behalf of others.[161]

This wanting can be assumed in a variety of ways, not all of which have the same moral standing or the same moral consequences. We need to distinguish between two kinds of relations based on noncoerced, other-linked wanting. In one, if we exit we do so without jeopardizing the vital interests of those in the relationship. In the other, we do not have such an exit option. Labor regulations prohibiting certain workers from striking because others are vitally dependent upon them recognize this distinction.

The dependency worker—especially one who is unpaid and whose responsibilities are familial—rarely has a morally acceptable option of exiting from her relation to the dependent. Even when she no longer wants to want what her charge wants, she feels morally obliged to continue assuming the other's interests. At best, the daily hour-to-hour responsibilities can be given over to a paid dependency worker. But the paid substitute's obligation becomes morally (even legally) as compelling until the paid dependency worker is herself relieved. For example, in group homes for the retarded, as in facilities providing twenty-four-hour caregiving, workers are mandated to work overtime if their replacements fail to show up and must remain on duty until relieved. Clearly, the interests of a paid dependency worker in such a situation *must* be subservient to those of her charges, whether or not she wants to subordinate her interests to theirs.

Ordinarily for a contracted period of time or amount of work, all workers must subordinate their own wants in a work situation. For a dependency worker, mandated overtime, unlike the hours for which she contracted, is work-time controlled—both legally and morally—by the needs of a dependent. The worker does not have the option to leave because she has a better paying job awaiting her after hours, or because she doesn't need the extra pay, or because she just doesn't want to work anymore. Although the dependency worker either need not or does not sort out self-interested preferences and non-self-interested preferences, when there is a conflict she may be so situated that the moral, and sometimes legal, obligation falls upon her to favor the non-self-interested preferences.[162]

Perhaps the disparity between the demands of dependency work and the status of the individual as a self-originator of valid claims are not irreconcilable. When Rawls's (1972) portrayed the party in the OP as the head of a generational line, that party, like the dependency worker, would in a less-than-voluntary-yet-not-coerced manner assume the responsibility of representing the claims of third parties and be morally compelled to protect the interests of the members of the household under the same constraints-of-exit options as the dependency worker. And the representatives of generational lines or heads of household would similarly be morally obliged to balance their self-interest against the interests of those they represent, and may even have to prefer the interests of third parties over and above their own. The Rawlsian thereby reminds us that only the mutual disinterestedness of the parties—not the mutual disinterestedness between the individuals of the society—is important for the OP.

Although the notion of generational lines has dropped out, the notion of a self-originator of valid claims used in the *Dewey Lectures* has been replaced with the idea that parties are "self-authenticating" sources of valid claims. The revision seems to address some communitarian and feminist objections to a metaphysical conception of a person which is highly individualist—a problem aggravated when we drop the idea of parties as representing generational lines or heads of households. By altering his formulation to "self-authenticating," Rawls allows himself to state: "Claims that citizens regard as founded on duties and obligations based on their conception of the good and the moral doctrine they affirm in their own life are also, for our purposes here, to be counted as self-authenticating" (1992, 32).

This new formulation opens a space for an expanded notion of "self"-interest, compatible with the interest of the dependency worker. The mother who insists on the child's right to an education may not be acting on a self-originating claim, but she surely is acting on a self-authenticating one. The particular claims she makes as a dependency worker may be self-authenticating in this sense. This solution is only partial, for it returns us to the vagaries of the relatively arbitrary choices individuals make about their work and their conception of the good, and to the uncertainty of whether or not their representatives in the OP will choose principles that will take care of dependency needs in a just and equitable fashion, as judged by our considered reflections (see pp. 85–87 above). Without the assurance that dependency concerns will be handled equitably, we still have to question the self-authenticating nature of the choice to be a dependency worker.

If dependency work were well-paid, and had a high status, or received some other social recognition, we could conclude that the constraint of freedom and its other demands explained the sufficient supply of dependency workers. The disparity, however, between the rewards offered in the labor market and the vital interest to have good dependency care makes it clear that market forces have not been relied upon to supply adequate dependency work. Indeed, a clear-eyed look at the nearly universal twin features of female caregiving and female subordination indicates: 1) that a certain class of persons has been subjected to and socialized to develop the character traits and the volitional structure needed for dependency work;[163] 2) that certain sexual behaviors commensurate with forming attachments, being submissive to another's will, and so forth have been made compulsory for women (see Rich 1978); and 3) that poor women and women of color have been forced into paid employment as dependency workers by the scanty financial resources and limited employment opportunities available to them, and middle-class women have been forced out of paid employment not commensurate with their (largely unpaid) duties as dependency workers. It has not merely "happened" that women have consistently "chosen" to make dependency relations and dependency work central to their vision of the good life, while men have chosen a wider variety of options.[164] Because care of dependents is non-optional in any society, some societal measures are inescapably taken to meet the inevitable need for care. If the means by which a society distributes responsibility for dependency work is not guided by principles of justice, then coercive measures—often in the guise of tradition and custom, sometimes in the guise of merely apparent voluntary life choices—are the predictable response.

The contention that dependency work is freely chosen and results in self-authenticating, if not self-originating claims, pushes the problem of distributing dependency work back into the realm of the private—into private choice and so outside the purview of public demands of justice. The consequence is that many claims are presumed to be self-authenticated when they are really heteronomous. The dependency worker who fits this description will be no more a self-authenticating source of valid claims than she is a self-originating source of valid claims.

The self-origination of claims may be an inapt characterization of the dependency worker's freedom in any society. But a well-ordered society that is not yet a society in which a principle of care, *doulia*, is operative is also not one in which dependency workers can be said to be self-authenticating sources of valid claims. The dependency worker would not yet be among the free citizens of such a putatively well-ordered state. If only those who are equals and free in the Rawlsian sense are eligible to participate in social cooperation, then dependency workers can not be included among the "free" individuals who have an equal claim to the fruits of social cooperation.

4

The Benefits and Burdens
of Social Cooperation

Justice, in the egalitarian liberal tradition that Rawls exemplifies, should provide principles that fairly distribute the benefits and burdens of social cooperation among free and equal persons given the circumstances of justice. In Chapter Three we probed Rawls's conceptions of the circumstances of justice and the norms that pertain to a conception of persons as free and equal. In this chapter we continue to ask about the inclusion of dependency concerns in the elemental concepts needed to provide a well-ordered society—one in which justice is provided for all. Here we focus on the concepts that determine what are seen as benefits and burdens: the notions of social goods and the idea of social cooperation.

The Two Powers of a Moral Person and the Index of Primary Goods

The Omission of Care as a Primary Good

Social cooperation, as Rawls understands it, is achievable among persons conceived as having certain moral capacities, a sense of justice and a conception of their own good. Presupposing "various general facts about human wants and abilities, their characteristic phases and requirements of nurture, relations of social interdependence, and much else" (1992, 307), Rawls generates an index of *primary goods*, goods that presume the possession of the two moral powers and that serve as a basis for making comparative assessments of interpersonal well-being.

The list of primary goods has remained unaltered since *A Theory of Justice*:

(i) The basic liberties (freedom of thought and liberty of conscience) . . .

(ii) Freedom of movement and free choice of occupation against a background of diverse opportunities . . . as well as [the ability] to give effect to a decision to revise and change them . . .

(iii) Powers and prerogatives of offices and positions of responsibility . . .

(iv) Income and wealth . . .

(v) The social bases of self-respect . . . (Rawls 1980, 526).[165]

Without questioning the merit of such a gauge as a measure for interpersonal well-being,[166] I want to ask: Does this list adequately address needs of dependents[167] and those who care for them?

The question presumes that the two moral powers Rawls attributes to citizens are the only ones relevant to persons as citizens. The list of goods is supposed to be motivated by a conception of moral persons as ones possessing a sense of justice and the capacity to form and revise a rational life-plan. Assuming that those in dependency relations count as citizens, assessing the adequacy of the list requires asking whether these moral powers suffice as the moral powers of citizens in a society that takes dependency needs seriously.

An ethic reflecting concern for dependents and those who care for them demands, first, a sense of attachment to others; second, an empathetic attention to their needs;[168] and third, a responsiveness to the needs of another. As we pointed out in Chapter Two, such an ethic goes well beyond duties traditionally assigned to justice, but in the context of caring relations they are not supererogatory. To fulfill these duties requires the cultivation of capacities which, while not required by justice traditionally conceived, are required by a state which recognizes that taking dependency seriously is a requirement of justice.

Neither of Rawls's two moral powers requires such concern nor yields such an ethic. First, for some the good shall include attachments of sentiment leading them to cultivate capacities to care for others. Still, this remains a private matter requiring no responsibility on the part of the society at large and no assurance that dependents can be cared for without extracting undue sacrifices from those upon whom the responsibilities fall.[169] Second, unlike the ability to form and revise a conception of one's own good, a sense of justice is necessarily an other-directed moral power. Although it is one that involves reciprocity, it says nothing about an empathetic attention to the needs of another who may be incapable of reciprocating. Thus, the moral capacities for care are never invoked in the moral capacity of justice as construed in Rawlsian constructivism.[170]

A construction adequate to meeting dependency needs justly would (CHANGE) expand the list of moral powers and amend the list of primary goods.[171] (CoP?) The moral powers of the person should include not only (1) a sense of justice (construed in the more narrow sense that Rawls suggests) and (2) a capacity to pursue a conception of the good, but also (3) a *capacity* to respond to vulnerability with care.[172] Neither (1) nor (2) addresses citizens as they may be vulnerable to the dependencies of age or illness or disability or as they may have to care for others in that state of dependency. Although justice and caring have often been seen as distinct, even opposing, virtues, the arguments put forward in this book press for a different view.[173] A justice which does not incorporate the need to respond to vulnerability with care is incomplete, and a social order which ignores care will itself fail to be just.

Care as a Primary Good Issuing From the Moral Power to Care

Rawls's list of primary goods neglects the goods that issue from a commitment to care. If the list were to reflect such a commitment, then we would find represented: 1) the understanding that we will be cared for if we become dependent; 2) the support we require if we have to take on the work of caring for a dependent; and 3) the assurance that if we become dependent, someone will take on the job of caring for those who are dependent upon us. We can possess basic liberties, freedom of movement and choice of occupation, the powers and prerogatives of public office, even income and wealth, without the assurance that we will be cared for if we become dependent; that when we are called upon to do the work of caring for a dependent, we will be adequately supported in our undertaking; and that, as we focus our energies and attention on another, we do not thereby lose the ability to care for ourselves.

Must these concerns be reflected in a list of *primary goods?* That is, are these goods basic for any individual who is capable of fashioning a conception of the good for herself and needed whatever one's life plan happens to be? And, if they are, are they also among those needs "relevant in questions of justice?" (Rawls 1982, 172).[174]

The answer to both queries is "yes." Regardless of how we fashion our conception of the good, we would want to be cared for when we are dependent and would want to be adequately supported if we find ourselves having to be responsible for the care of a dependent. Moreover if the failure to secure these conditions impairs the capability of those most vulnerable to dependency and dependency work to participate as equals in an otherwise well-ordered society, then these conditions are indeed relevant to questions of justice. Therefore the good *both to be cared for in a responsive dependency relation if and when one is unable to care for oneself, and to meet the dependency needs of others without incurring undue sacrifices oneself* is a primary good in the Rawlsian sense because it is a good of citizens as citizens pursue their own conception of the good and exercise their moral faculties of justice and care.[175]

Furthermore, like all the other primary goods, such a good has a bearing on the social bases of self-respect for the members of the well-ordered society. Patricia Williams (1991) cites a passage from Marguerite Duras's *The Lover*:

> We're united in a fundamental shame at having to live. It's here we are at the heart of our common fate, the fate that [we] are our mother's children, the children of a candid creature murdered by society. We're on the side of society which has reduced her to despair. Because of what's been done to our mother, so amiable, so trusting, we hate life, we hate ourselves. (Duras 1985, quoted in Williams 1991, 55).

To the extent that we grow into a relatively safe and secure adulthood in consequence of care secured through the sacrifice of another, a sacrifice that can never be adequately restored, we carry with us a shame that diminishes self-respect. We are diminished in this way as long as we live in a society in which care can be had only through such a sacrifice.

If women, through their maternal roles, have been the sacrificial lambs, they have also been the ones who have recognized care as a primary good and have engaged in political struggle when their ability to care has been undermined. Historian Temma Kaplan (1982) documents that the political participation of women in diverse nations, cultures, and historical periods is tied to circumstances rendering women unable to give care to their families. By their willingness to engage in political struggle to ensure their ability to care for their families, women, at least, have contended that being able to care for others is a primary social good. The political nature of these struggles is consistent with Rawls's conception of self-respect, which is contingent not only on how the individual conducts herself privately, but on "the public features of basic social institutions" and "publicly expected (and normally honored) ways of conduct" (1992, 319).

The Public Conception of Social Cooperation

Dependency Concerns in Rawls's Conception of Social Cooperation

Social cooperation, for Rawls, is more than "simply ... coordinated social activity efficiently organized and guided by publicly recognized rules to achieve some overall end" (1992, 300). Indeed, it also demands "fair terms of cooperation" among citizens. These are terms citizens can accept not only because they are *rational* (in that they satisfy each person's view of their rational advantage), but also because they are *reasonable* (in that they recognize and accept that not all people have the same ends when engaging in social interaction).

Dependency concerns, if they are both reasonable and rational, ought to be, but are not now, included within the features of a well-ordered society reflected in the public conception of social cooperation.[176] That demands for the care of dependents are reasonable can quickly be established. What is reasonable (in Rawlsian terms) is to recognize that the interests of others need to be considered along with our own. Since any society into which we are born and in which we expect to remain for the duration of our lives contains both those whose capacities make them (comparatively speaking) "fully functional" and those who are dependent and so unable to realize either capacity independently, the interests of both need consideration. Furthermore, unless a human society exists under especially hard conditions, we think it reasonable and right that humans care for those in a weakened or impaired condition. Thus it is reasonable to expect that a well-ordered society is one that attends to the needs of dependents, and whatever else that necessitates.

Are dependency concerns also rational? That is to say, does it accord with each individual's self-interest to choose principles that would include such concerns among the terms of social cooperation? Because, even if we are fully functioning at the time we choose our principles of justice, we have at one time been dependent and may again find ourselves dependent, or we may find ourselves with dependents. In these circumstances, we would want to know that the means are available by which we can either be properly cared for or have resources available and help available to do an adequate job caring for the needs of those dependent upon us.

Yet these concerns are scarcely acknowledged in Rawls's writings. In some, he states that the theory of justice as fairness needs to be extended to cover "what we may call *normal* health care" (emphasis mine, 1992, 21), thus extending the theory to cover some dependency concerns. But the daily care of infants and young children, prolonged periods of dependency (e.g., frail old age), and health care that exceeds the bounds of the "normal" are either not "health care" or not "normal."[177]

Rawls expresses the hope that his theory could extend not only to normal health care but to other questions as well. Perhaps he would acknowledge that dependency issues are numbered among those other questions. Rawls's notion of social cooperation, I want to insist, excludes a great number of these concerns from consideration as *political* matters on systematic grounds.

We see this especially in the way in which social cooperation is characterized, not only in the later work, but already in *A Theory of Justice*:

> The main idea is that when a number of persons engage in a mutually advantageous cooperative venture according to rules, and thus restrict their liberty in ways necessary to yield advantages for all, those who have submitted to the restrictions have a right to a similar acquiescence on the part of those who have benefited from their submission (Rawls 1971, 112).

And in *Political Liberalism*, Rawls writes, "Those who can take part in social cooperation over a complete life, and who are willing to honor the appropriate fair terms of agreement are regarded as equal citizens" (1992, 302).

It would surely be unreasonable to expect those so disabled that they are permanently dependent to similarly reciprocate care or in any relevant sense "restrict their liberty in ways necessary to yield advantages to all" (Rawls 1972, 112).

They would then fall outside the bounds of social cooperation, and in *Political Liberalism* Rawls seems willing to deny these persons *citizenship*.[178] Those who are only temporarily dependent—and that includes us all—presumably will be, or have been, in a position to reciprocate according to the fair terms of social cooperation. But even where the dependency is temporary, during their dependency they are rarely in such a position. And the moment to reciprocate may never come: A child may not reach maturity; an ill person may die or become permanently incapacitated; a now needy and elderly parent may never have been an adequate provider or nurturer. So unless the needs of their caregivers are to be met in some other form of reciprocity, the only available moral characterizations of the caregiver's function are either exploitation or supererogation.[179]

I have argued that, within the purview of a notion of social cooperation, dependency concerns *are* pertinent to political justice. First, because they are rational and reasonable considerations in choosing a conception of justice. Second, because a society that does not care for its dependents or that cares for them only by unfairly exploiting the labor of those who do the caring cannot be said to be well-ordered. And third, when we reorient our political insights to see the centrality of human relationships to our happiness and well-being, we recognize dependency needs as basic motivations for creating a social order. This means that we cannot limit our understanding of social cooperation to interactions between independent and fully functioning persons because it obscures or minimizes the social contributions of dependents—who, even in their neediness, contribute to the ongoing nature of human relationships— and of those who care for dependents.

Reciprocity and Doulia

The reciprocity and mutuality articulated in fair terms of cooperation apply to "all who cooperate." They must each "benefit, or share in common burdens, in some appropriate fashion judged by a suitable benchmark of comparison" (1992, 300). Because the relations of dependents and dependency workers to one another and to the larger society do not fit standard models of reciprocity, it is difficult to include dependency concerns within a conception of justice as fairness.

One might, therefore, construe the arguments above as defending the position that dependency concerns fall within political justice, but insist that this idea of justice is outside the bounds of *justice as fairness*. Rawls, who notes that justice as fairness may not be entirely coincident with political justice, remarks, "How deep a fault this is must wait until the case itself can be examined." He reminds us that political justice needs to be complemented by additional virtues (1992, 21). I suggest another possibility. We can reconceive fairness. By enlarging the concept of reciprocity, we return to some of the ideas expressed on pages 87–88, but now applied to relations in which not all are independent and fully functioning.

The need, then, is to expand the notion of reciprocity, and in so doing open a conceptual space for dependency concerns within social cooperation in a just society. To fix our ideas, we consider the situation of the postpartum mother caring for her infant. The extreme neediness of the infant, and the physiological trauma of giving birth create a special vulnerability for the mother. Some traditional cultures and religions mark this period of maternity: The mother is enjoined to care for her child while others attend to her needs and her other household and familial duties. Some assign a *doula*, a postpartum caregiver who assists the mother, and at times relieves her. In the United States today, where families are geographically dispersed and lack community support as well as adequate worker's leave policies, there is a fledgling effort to adopt the idea of a *doula*. Instead of the timeworn paid help—the "baby nurse," who displaces the mother by taking over care of the infant—the *doula* assists by caring for the mother as the mother attends to the child.[180] *Doula* originally meant slave or servant in Greek. It is intriguing to redirect the concept and signify instead a caregiver who cares for those who care for others. Rather than the notion of a servant fulfilling the function of a *doula*, we need a concept of interdependence that recognizes a relation—not precisely of reciprocity but of nested dependencies—linking those who help and those who require help to give aid to those who cannot help themselves. Extending the notion of the service performed by the *doula*, let us use the term *doulia* for an arrangement by which service is passed on so that those who become needy by virtue of tending to those in need can be cared for as well.[181] *Doulia* is part of an ethic that is captured in the colloquial phrase: "What goes round comes round."[182] If someone helps another in her need, someone, in turn, will help the helper when she is needy—whether the neediness derives from her position as caregiver or from circumstances that pertain to health or age. We can state a principle of *doulia: Just as we have required care to survive and thrive, so we need to provide conditions that allow others— including those who do the work of caring—to receive the care they need to survive and thrive.*

Since society is an association that persists through generations, an extended notion of "reciprocity" (a transitive—if you will—responsiveness to our dependence on others) is needed for justice between generations. As Rawls recognizes, the care we take to hand over a world that is not depleted is never reciprocated to us by those whom we benefit. Rather, the benefit we bestow on the next generation ought to be the benefit we would have wanted the previous generation to bestow on us. The resemblance between this extended notion of reciprocity and *doulia* is not accidental.[183] In both, we deal with human development and with its "chronological unfairness." Moreover, just as the gains and savings from a previous generation pass from us to the next generation, the care a mother bestows on her child calls for reciprocation from the adult child not only back to the parents, but also forward to a future generation.[184]

The *doula* who serves as our paradigm is engaged in private interactions. Rawls's concerns are limited to the public—to the basic structure of society. While the paradigm concerns domestic interactions, I am arguing for an analogical extension of the idea of *doulia* to the public domain. The caregiver has a responsibility to care for the dependent. The larger society seeks ways to attend to the well-being of the caregiver, thereby allowing the caregiver to fulfill responsibilities to the dependent without exploiting the labor and concern of the caregiver. This is a *public* conception of *doulia*. As human dependency is inevitably a circumstance of justice (one which marks our most profound attachments) and as care of a dependent morally obliges the dependency worker to give a certain priority to the welfare of her charge (see Chapter One), a public conception of *doulia* is needed to accomplish the tripartite goal of treating the dependency worker equitably, providing care for dependents, and respecting the dependency relations in which fundamental human attachments grow and thrive.

"Although a well-ordered society is divided and pluralistic, ... the public agreement on questions of political and social justice supports ties of civic friendship and secures the bonds of association" (Rawls 1980, 540). As potent as the bonds of association created by public agreement are, they are not as powerful as those created by caring relationships. These are bonds that tie individuals together into families, kin, and other intimate relations, bonds that allow individuals at different stages of life to withstand the forces that act upon them. These intimate bonds make civic order and civic friendship possible (Held 1987a).

The etymology of *doulia* as slavery is instructive as a contrast to the principle of care advocated here. While slavery is a morally impermissible form of service, dependency work is an inescapable one. While slavery under even the most favorable conditions is demeaning and dehumanizing, dependency work under the right conditions reaches into the core of our humanity. While slavery is the most debased of human relations, dependency work forms the most fundamental of social relations.

Principles of right and traditional notions of justice depend upon a prior and more fundamental principle and practice of care. Without practices based on an implicit principle of care, human beings would either not survive or they would survive very poorly—and surely would not thrive.[185] A political theory must attend to the well-being of dependents *and* of their caregivers, and also to the *relation* of caregiver and dependent upon which all other civic unions depend. A principle of care, then, must hold that: In order to grow, flourish, and survive or endure illness, disability and frailty, each individual requires a caring relationship with significant others who hold that individual's well-being as a primary responsibility and a primary good.

But for a society to attend to the need for care and to do so justly, it is not sufficient for the dependency worker alone to be caring. There must be principles that secure social institutions providing aid and support for dependency workers in their caring responsibilities. This requires the broadened conception of reciprocity (and a suitably modified sense of fairness *within* each generation) expressed in the concept of *doulia*. *Doulia*, so conceived, requires that the value of receiving care and giving care would be publicly acknowledged; that the burdens and cost incurred by doing the work of caring for dependents would not fall to the dependency worker alone (even when that dependency work is freely assumed); and that the commitment to preserving caring *relations* would be assumed by the society. A principle of *doulia* would mandate: first, a *social responsibility* (derived from political justice realized in social cooperation) for enabling dependency relations satisfactory to dependency worker and dependent alike; and second, social institutions that foster an attitude of caring and a respect for care by enabling caregivers to do the job of caretaking without becoming disadvantaged in the competition for the benefits of social cooperation.

The Rawlsian (and the liberal) account of a well-ordered society as characterized by the narrower notions of justice and of right, then, is either incomplete or inadequate. And this is so not for the reason communitarians have stressed, namely that, on the one hand, it purports more of a conception of the good life than it admits to, and, on the other hand, fails to provide enough of a guide to the good life to be fully satisfying. Rather, a society cannot be well-ordered—that is, one capable of sustaining its members and providing them with a basis for self-respect—if it fails to be a society in which care is publicly acknowledged as a good which the society as a whole bears a responsibility to provide in a manner that is just to all.

Rawls, speaking of the need to give priority to the basic liberties, points out that even when the political will does not yet exist to do what is required (as it might not in a society that is less than well-ordered), "part of the political task is to help fashion it" (Rawls 1992, 97). Likewise, if the political will to imbue citizens with sensitivity and a sense of priority for care does not yet exist, it is "part of the political task . . . to help fashion it."

Conclusion: The Principles of Justice and Dependency Concerns

Chapter Three and the previous sections of this chapter have shown that the model-conceptions omit dependency concerns and why this is a shortcoming for an egalitarian theory of justice. Can we now conclude that the presumably egalitarian suppositions do not yield sufficiently egalitarian outcomes? Ultimately, a definite answer rests on the capacity of the chosen principles to accommodate dependency concerns.

The principles of justice chosen by the parties to the OP are selected from a "short list" of principles drawn from traditional Western political thought—none of which consider the justice of dependency arrangements for dependency worker and dependent alike. Therefore no other principle on the short list is more likely to accommodate such concerns. For example, some of the argument on pages 89–93 not only run counter to contractarian assumptions, but also points to a difficulty with at least one form of utilitarianism: preference-satisfaction utilitarianism. Do the preferences of a mother for the goods pertaining to the well-being of a child count as the preferences of one individual, the concerned mother, or of two, mother and child? If they count for one only, then how are we to tally the preferences of the child? If they count for two, we violate the egalitarian principle that each one counts for just one. Few, if any, political theories have focused on the consequences of dependency and dependency work, because few, if any, political theories have seriously concerned themselves with the lives led by those persons (women) who have had to deal with inevitable dependencies.

Nonetheless, now that these concerns have been raised, we can use the notion of reflective equilibrium to "test" the adequacy of the principles that emerge. If the principles selected will yield an egalitarian outcome for dependents and dependency workers, it could render arguments in this chapter and the previous one superfluous. The first principle, the principle of equal liberties, is irrelevant to our concerns, although dependency concerns introduce a worry that those who do dependency work will not be guaranteed the fair value of political liberties. But I shall not take up this matter here. I proceed to demonstrate that the second principle, the difference principle, fails in the relevant respects.

Dependents and Dependency Workers as the Least Well-Off

The latest formulation of the difference principle states: "Social and economic inequalities are to satisfy two conditions: First, they are to be attached to positions and offices open to all under conditions of fair equality of opportunity; and second, they are to be to the greatest benefit of the least advantaged members of the society" (Rawls 1992, 6).

Dependency work, when done for pay, is poorly paid. Furthermore, it is largely gender-determined. If the second principle is to assure a fair distribution of goods to those in dependency relations, it must be interpreted so that: 1) the group that is least advantaged includes paid dependency workers; and that 2) fair equality of opportunity ensures against forms of sex discrimination that result in women being restricted to poorly paid or unpaid work. If fair equality of opportunity is realized, then the question is: Will distributive policies favoring the least well-off ensure adequately meeting needs of dependents and caregivers? I do not believe they will.

Fair equality of opportunity would mean that a woman who chooses dependency work as paid labor, even if the work is poorly paid, makes her choice unconstrained by gender discrimination. And if that choice puts her in the ranks of the least advantaged, she would know that justice requires distributive policies that would not favor any other group unless it ameliorates her condition. This is doubtless an improvement over today's situation. But is it good enough?

Paying workers so poorly that this indispensable contribution to the well-being and sociality of any society places the paid dependency worker in the least favored situation seems not to cohere with our reflective judgments of what is fair. The least favored situation, one would think, is the condition inhabited by those so poorly endowed that they simply cannot take advantage of fair equality of opportunity to better their condition. Moreover, is it reasonable to expect the dependency worker to continue to be sufficiently motivated to give the *caring* care critical to good dependency work, all the while assuming the status of the least well-off, when truly fair equality of opportunity is in the offing? Normally, some degree of coercion is present when dependency labor is had "on the cheap."

Perhaps then market forces will push up the monetary value of dependency work: If we want good day care for our children, then we will have to pay good money for it and both children and their caregivers will be well situated. So it may seem that we look only at paid dependency work. But much dependency work has always been done as unpaid labor, and because so much of this work involves affective bonds and is infused with social meaning, it is likely to remain so. Due to the importance of the affective bonds to the quality of care—*who* does the caring is frequently as important as the care itself—the dependency worker is nonfungible. (This is especially true when dependency work is familial and unpaid, but can be significant even when the dependency worker is paid.) I venture that, as long as dependency work continues to be unpaid and filled with social and affective significance, even fair equality of opportunity for all is unlikely to alter wages significantly because its value will not be assessed in market terms. Under the best scenario, assimilating the dependency worker to the least well-paid worker will make the dependency worker better off than she is now. But this solution does not reach into the situation of the unpaid dependency worker, nor does it touch the individual who has dependency care as a major responsibility along with wage work. The nonfungible nature of much dependency work vitiates much of the *freedom* assumed available for the caregiver under equality of opportunity, and constrains her, by ties of affection and sentiments of duty, to her charge.[186]

The Dependency Relation as a Social Position

A less Rawlsian option would be to count the position of the dependency worker, along with the positions of the citizen and the least advantaged, as a distinct social position (Rawls 1972, 95ff.). Although Rawls does not encourage us to multiply social positions, this strategy would ensure that no advantage in the distribution of goods can accrue to those better off than the dependency worker unless the inequality does benefit the dependency worker. However, given Rawls's two moral powers and his list of primary goods, there is no basis upon which to construct such a new social position. To create a special social position for the dependency worker would seem arbitrarily to favor one form of socially useful labor over others—and moreover a form of labor that a person would choose because it somehow fits with his own conception of the good life.

If, however, we add the capacity to give care to the other moral powers, and if we include goods related to our interdependence in states of vulnerability in the index of primary goods, we can make a case for adding the dependency worker and the dependent to the short list of social positions from which to consider issues of fairness and just distributions. For example, we can make a case for a paid employee who is in a dependency relation, and so has dependency responsibilities, to receive additional pay, benefits, time off, or services, which would enable her to support the dependency relation in a manner suitable to the situation. She could opt to pay another *adequately* to do all or some of the dependency work or to do the dependency work herself by virtue of the freed-up time and added support. This would be seen not as a privilege, but as what is properly due citizens of a just and caring society—enabling us each to be cared for without extracting an undue burden from those charged with our care. But if being cared for by one upon whom you depend and being able to give care to one who depends on you are not seen as primary goods, then there would be no reason for principles of justice to be chosen that would facilitate such policy making. To the extent that the difference principle is based (as it is) on a list of primary goods blind to dependency, it fails to accomplish this task.[187]

A Third Principle of Justice?

The social position of the citizen gives rise to the first principle of justice. The social position of the least advantaged gives rise to the difference principle with fair equality of opportunity. If we were to amend the theory of justice as fairness to include the social position of the participants in a dependency relation, it would most likely give rise to a third principle of justice. This principle, in contrast to the others, would not be based on our equal vulnerability, nor on our possession of rationality, a sense of justice, and a vision of our own good. Instead, it would be based on our unequal vulnerability in dependency, on our moral power to respond to others in need, and on the primacy of human relations to happiness and well-being. The principle of the social responsibility for care would read something like: *To each according to his or her need for care, from each according to his or her capacity for care, and such support from social institutions as to make available resources and opportunities to those providing care, so that all will be adequately attended in relations that are sustaining.*

I see no natural way of converting such a principle to either of Rawls's two principles of justice. Therefore, it still seems that the theory of justice as fairness, relying as it does on the suppositions outlined and contested above, fails to meet dependency concerns and so fails to sustain the egalitarian vision that purports to inform it.

1ST PRINCIPAL
1ST - EQUAL LIBERTIES

HUMAN NEEDED ABSTRACT TO ADJUST RAWLS' THEORY

Part 3

Some Mother's Child

Introduction

Public policy, particularly in most Western industrial nations and especially in the United States, presumes not to reach into the familial arrangements of dependency work (except in exceptional circumstances of neglect and abuse). This is consonant with the liberal distinction between the public and private domain, which is nowhere more pronounced than in the United States. Democratic welfare states have moved to address a number of dependency concerns, either in their efforts to move to a more sexually egalitarian model—as in Sweden, where sex equality is an explicit aim of some welfare policies—or to promote pronatalist policies—as in the case of France and Germany.

Public policy, particularly in the United States, directly addresses dependency concerns on at least three different occasions. The first is in welfare policy, particularly welfare policies intended to assist impoverished families (usually, though not exclusively, single-parent poor households). The second is in family and medical leave policies. The third concerns the rights of disabled persons. A call for policies dealing with childcare and eldercare are only now beginning to be heard in the United States, although other industrialized nations have made headway in these arenas.

In the next three chapters, I will concern myself both with policy issues and with the lived reality of dependency. The first chapter will discuss welfare policies impacting on poor women and their children, especially Aid to Families with Dependent Children (AFDC)—rescinded in 1996—and family and medical leave policies in the United States. In the following two chapters, my attention is on the care of the disabled. There is little in the way of policies to help families with the care of disabled family members, although we have an impressive piece of anti-discrimination legislation for the disabled. Public policy with respect to the care of persons dependent due to disability will be discussed in the wider context of the personal and social impact of disability on caregivers.

My discussion focuses on the United States, the nation that most completely realizes the emphasis on individualism that so easily occludes dependency concerns. Although it is the wealthiest and the one best able to meet the economic demands of caring for dependents, the United States is the most recalcitrant. A history of racism, a fierce market ideology, and an emphasis on individualism collude to make the United States resistant to the forces that have shaped the development of the welfare state in Europe, Australia, and New Zealand. Not only is the United States the case I know best, but in its approach to dependency concerns, it is either atavistic or the harbinger of things to come. Even as there are struggles in the U.S. to expand policies that concern dependency care, welfare policies in other nations are curtailing services, under the rubric of "restructuring the welfare state" in just those areas where dependency concerns are most pressing. Progressive forces in the U.S. are struggling to bring to this nation policies that are friendly to dependency concerns and that have been firmly in place in many other industrial nations. But at the same time, the cutbacks in the miserly welfare state that we know in the U.S. portend similar developments in the very nations that are models of the progressive welfare state.[188]

5

Policy and a Public Ethic of Care

Welfare De-Form

"Welfare," in the United States, has denoted something short of "well-being." The term, as it most frequently occurs in the context of the final decade of the twentieth century, has even been cut loose of a set of policies that characterize most forms of modern industrialized societies—the welfare state. While the welfare state retains some of the benevolence associated with "well-being" (formally, co-extensive with "welfare"), the term welfare reeks—of indigence, indignity, and social anomie. Yet this program, set in motion by the same Social Security Act that produced the popular program known simply as Social Security,[189] has been the mainstay of women who—for whatever reason—found themselves unable to both care and provide for themselves and their families. "Welfare as we know it" suffers from at least a double stigma: It is for the poor and it is for women. While most of the recipients of the now-defunct program Aid to Families with Dependent Children were children, 90 percent of the adults benefiting from the program, which we called welfare, were women. The new welfare program established under the Personal Responsibility and Work Opportunity Reconciliation Act of 1996, Temporary Assistance to Needy Families, similarly affects mostly women and their children. Clearly, welfare is not *only* a poverty issue, it is a *woman's* issue. And as poverty here, as elsewhere, is frequently associated with matters of race, welfare bears a triple stigma—it disproportionately affects women of color and their children.[190]

This welfare—*aid* to families with *dependent* children—has became so stigmatized that it was jettisoned in favor of a harsh policy insisting that women caring for children under conditions of dire poverty, with no other support available, are to sweep streets and take care of other

117

people's children, rather than tend to their own. And if within five years they cannot find paid unsubsidized employment, they and their families will simply be cut off from all aid. Yet, if one accepts the principle of doulia articulated and argued for in the previous chapter, welfare—aid to those with dependent children or dependent elderly or disabled or ailing persons—ought not to be a despised policy but a right issued forth from a principle of care and freely dispensed to all dependency workers.

Why is welfare so despised? Why has a nation as wealthy as the United States chosen to cast adrift poor women and their children rather than devote the one percent of the Federal budget and the two percent of state budgets needed to provide the stingy aid? Why was the Left unable to provide a convincing rhetoric to counter those on the Right who insisted that welfare must be "reformed"—a "reform" that amounted to its virtual dismantling? To answer these questions adequately would involve invoking complex sociological and political factors which lie outside my expertise. What I propose is to examine some of the rhetoric against and some of the justifications for welfare. This means, inevitably, looking also at the justifications for the welfare state that provide the theoretical ground for welfare for poor single-adult families. I will argue that grounds for the welfare state have harbored presuppositions which have left the gate open to attacks mounted against welfare, especially for solo mothers. I will end the discussion with a vision of what welfare based on a principle of *doulia* might look like.

"Welfare Is a Woman's Issue"[191]: *The Subtext of Welfare "Reform"*

The debate surrounding welfare in the United States has produced a strange cacophony of justifications and rebuttals of welfare and welfare reform. While the Right speaks of "family values," "unwed mothers," "family breakdown," and "teenage pregnancy," the Left responds with appeals to "structural unemployment," "creating jobs," and "ending poverty." "Welfare policies encourage dependency," the Right insists. "Provide jobs," answers the Left. "Provide values," the Right retorts. This appears to be a mismatch in call and response. Yet, these two stances, I hope to show, share certain philosophical underpinnings. Both positions, in different ways, assume a conception of the citizen based upon a male model of the "independent" wage earner. Both see the person on welfare as someone who can be incorporated as a full citizen only by fulfilling the role of the "independent" wage earner. That is, both models fail to take dependency relations to be a central feature of social organization and fail to understand dependency work within an adequate model of reciprocity. Thus neither questions a conception of social cooperation which presumes, but does not credit, women's unpaid labor as caregiver (Young 1995; Pateman 1989).

The Left and Right differ, however, in a crucial consideration. While the Left—and here I bracket the feminist position(s)—views the issue of welfare essentially as a question of how to deal with an *economic* problem, the problem of poverty, the Right views it as a *social* problem, the unconstrained behavior of women who refuse to be governed by either the rules of patriarchical marriage or a market economy. So while the nonfeminist Left sees in welfare an ungendered issue, the Right sees a gendered one.

Feminists, on the other hand, see welfare and the welfare state as a woman's issue: as patriarchal control over the lives of poor women, but also as an essential safety net for all women.[192] Paraphrasing Johnnie Tillmon, Kate Millet, in a recent talk[193] on welfare, remarked, "The Man walked out—he quit."[194] But poverty remains, and it is poverty with a woman's face.

That welfare affects largely women and their children should be sufficient to qualify it as a "women's issue." But if it were a contingent matter that the impact of welfare legislation was primarily felt by women (because it affects the poor and women are disproportionately the poor) then attacking poverty would be the way to relieve the need for welfare. However in the attacks by the Right on welfare a different agenda emerges. What we find is a stalwart defense of traditional arrangements of dependency work (although in a new guise), arrangements that have privileged men and that disadvantage those who assume these responsibilities. We find this agenda revealed in the very language of the legislation, in its proposals and in its predictable impact.

From its inception in the 104th Congress, the point of the most recent U.S. welfare reform legislation has been something other than the ending of poverty. The first welfare legislation passed by the House of the 104th Congress, *HR. 4,* "The Personal Responsibility Act" was slated as a bill "To restore the American family, reduce illegitimacy, control welfare spending and reduce welfare dependence."

If restoration of the American family has an innocent ring to those not influenced by feminist criticisms of the family, a closer look at the act proves more troubling. It is not only sexism, but racism that forms the subtext. The very first part of the bill is "Title 1—Reducing Illegitimacy." It begins:

It is the sense of the Congress that:

1) marriage is the foundation of a successful society;

2) marriage is an essential social institution which promotes the interests of children and society at large;

3) the negative consequences of an out-of-wedlock birth on child, the mother, and society are well documented as follows. . .

Title 1 lists questionable statistics on "illegitimacy" and its putative "ill effects," which are, curiously, disaggregated by race. What begins as a discussion on illegitimacy becomes one about "single parent mothers" and "teenage mothers" as if all single parent mothers were or started out as "out-of-wedlock mothers" and as if all women who give birth while still in their teens are not married to the fathers of their children. Neither implication is supported by empirical evidence. Instead it is the ideology of the deviance of solo motherhood and female teenage sexuality[195] that is being promulgated. Nowhere is any blame attached to men, and when men are represented as deviant (in particular, young black men engaged in crime), the cause of their misconduct is imputed to parenting by solo mothers. For example:

(O) the likelihood that a young black [sic] man will engage in criminal activities doubles if he is raised without a father and triples if he lives in a neighborhood with a high concentration of single parent families; and

(P) the greater the incidence of single parent families in a neighborhood, the higher the incidence of violent crime and burglary.

It concludes that

4) in light of this demonstration of the crisis in our Nation, the reduction of out-of-wedlock births is an important government interest and the policy contained in provisions of this title address the crisis. (Rep Shaw et al., 1995: Title 1)

With such an ideology dominant in the architects of "welfare reform," it is perhaps not surprising to find a prominent welfare official remark:

> Every time I see a bag lady on the street, I wonder, "Was that an AFDC mother who hit the menopause wall who can no longer reproduce and get money to support herself?" (Lawrence Townsend, a Riverside California welfare reform director [Williams 1995, 6]).

The misogyny sits before us denuded in this passage. And because the pictures of the "welfare queen" and the "bag lady" that media present are generally black or brown, the racism is only somewhat veiled.

The Right has seen the connection between a safety net and women's autonomy, but it has managed to produce a rhetoric that at once keeps the connection invisible and yet invokes the security of a longstanding institution, the patriarchal family. The campaign to "reform" welfare has billed itself as one intended to decrease women's dependency on welfare and to increase women's self-sufficiency, but by simultaneously withdrawing federal assistance for women who find themselves without male support, this legislation serves to discourage women from attempting to raise children without male support by threatening to pauperize those who persist. It thereby serves not to promote women's independence but to return women to the economic dependence on a man within a traditional marriage—whether or not she wants to, and whether or not the man is dependable. Within the traditional family, men retain patriarchal prerogatives. These carry the responsibilities, but also the power, that comes with the role of the provider. They are prerogatives that either came with class and race privilege or substituted for class and race privilege. Because these prerogatives are parasitic on playing the role of the provider, poor men from marginalized classes have less access to this power.[196] The alternative of single motherhood is made increasingly harsh—so harsh that women may find themselves unable to provide for their families and face the need to relinquish their children to foster care or adoption.

What we see is that the "fixes" that have been put into place through the political success of the Right not only adversely affect many women, they also threaten *feminist* gains. The rhetoric of welfare "reform" has resurrected the notion of "illegitimacy," an ugly idea steeped in sexual inequality signifying an attack on women who chose a reproductive life outside the only one acceptable institution for raising children.[197]

Indeed, financial rewards are promised to states that can reduce rates of out-of-wedlock births without increasing abortions, that is for reducing so-called "illegitimacy ratios." We can note that these ratios are calculated not only according to the procreative behavior of women on welfare, but of *all* the women in the State. Furthermore, this same legislation provides money[198] for "abstinence education," which teaches, among other things, that abstinence from sex outside marriage is the expected standard, that abstinence is the only way to avoid nonmarital pregnancy, sexually transmitted diseases and other associated health problems, and that nonmarital childbirth harms children, parents, and society.[199]

The new welfare legislation serves still another challenge to the reproductive rights of women, especially poor women who are most vulnerable to control. A number of states have implemented "family cap" laws which prevent women from receiving assistance for children who were born while the mother was receiving welfare benefits.[200] Also, the constriction of aid to solo mothers deeply affects women's exit options in abusive relationships.[201] Furthermore, welfare laws that insist that all persons, even those caring for small children, find paid employment makes a mockery of feminist demands for fulfilling and well-paying non-familial labor. To be *compelled* to leave your child in a stranger's care or with no care at all and to accept whatever work is offered is another form of subordination, not a liberation. Furthermore, it devalues the work women traditionally have done.

While the end of AFDC is a siren call to understand why "a war against poor women is a war against all women" (as the slogan of a feminist advocacy group, the Women's Committee of One Hundred, declares), it provides the occasion to reconsider the basis of welfare. Welfare policies that can serve women raising families without stigmatizing those in need are consonant with a just society in which equality can be extended to all. Women and whosoever undertakes dependency work must have access to such benefits. These policies, then, are necessary for the consolidation of feminist gains and for the achievement of equality and the full citizenship for women, especially in the context of modern industrial economies (Orloff 1993; Mink 1995; Young 1995; Sevenhuijsen 1996; Fraser 1997). If the political will does not exist to bring such policies about, it is, to borrow the words of John Rawls, "part of the political task . . . to help fashion it."

Justifications of Welfare

Traditional Justifications

To aid in fashioning the requisite political will, we need to be clearer about the justification for welfare, generally, and the justification for welfare targeted at the needs of women, in particular. The contemporary "Right/Left" debate reflects a number of different understandings of the bases for welfare and the welfare state by those who endorse it and by those who oppose it.

The welfare state, and especially its policies directed at the poor, are, by one account, based on the need to protect against failures of the market and to eliminate poverty. Within a market economy, the satisfaction of needs, the creation of needs, and the negotiation of what constitutes need is tied to one's participation in a relation of reciprocity between the production of wealth and its consumption. To participate in such a reciprocal relation is to be involved in social cooperation which is requisite for citizenship. This participation is marked first and foremost by labor that is compensated in wages or salaries.[202] It defines "independent." To stand outside these reciprocal arrangements reduces one to the status of dependent, and as someone dependent on an individual, a charity, or the state.[203]

But as even the earliest proponents of a market economy saw, a market economy in and of itself will not guarantee that all who can and want to work will be adequately employed. The dynamism of a capitalist economy produces great wealth, but also great poverty. Such poverty is morally unacceptable in the midst of wealth and is politically destabilizing. But efforts at redressing the inequity encounter what Donald Moon (1988) has called "Hegel's dilemma," a dilemma articulated and never resolved by the philosopher in his *Philosophy of Right*. For while the redistribution of wealth can mitigate the poverty, such redistribution (through cash transfers or the provision of goods and services in kind) may, on the one hand, undermine a citizen's sense of participation in the community and so undermine the citizen's sense of self-worth. If, on the other hand, the state steps in to create jobs, such action interferes with the autonomous functioning of the market, and so disrupts the machine that generates wealth.

The creation of the welfare state is a compromise between capitalism and democracy. Marmor, Mashaw and Harvey (1990) suggest that welfare policies take the form of one of the following: social insurance, residualism, behaviorism, and populism. Some of these policies skirt the offense to self-respect. Populist policies, such as progressive taxation or free public education, have as their goal redistribution in the service of community and equality. Social insurance policies are another compromise that avoids the offense to self-respect. These benefits are understood as "earned entitlements" intended to "protect citizens against the `predictable risks of modern life'" (Marmor, Mashaw and Harvey 1990, 27). Although redistribution is not the goal of social insurance policies, they too redistribute wealth, since what is received as a benefit by a participant normally exceeds what is paid in by that individual. The remaining two visions of welfare, residualism and behaviorism, are aimed at the poor. Residualism establishes a safety net—a floor beneath which individuals must not fall. Behaviorism attempts to alter the behavior of the poor. Behaviorism makes explicit the view that poverty is the fault of those who are impoverished. Residualism as practiced in the U.S. today makes the same assumption implicitly. While populist and social insurance policies avoid one horn of Hegel's dilemma, residualist and behaviorist policies do not spare their recipients a goring. The scar marks them as "dependent." And as Fraser and Gordon (1994) argue, dependency, which in preindustrial times was seen as a structural social feature, has in industrial society and still more strikingly in postindustrial society come to be seen as a characterological feature of the poor who rely on public assistance. Poverty itself comes to be viewed as a characterological flaw.

Welfare debates today are most often between residualists on the Left and behaviorists on the Right.[204] The Right, emphasizing the evils of dependency on state support, has pushed workfare, or work outside the home in exchange for benefits. The Left does not question the "debilitating effects of dependency" and does not dispute the premise that a job is preferable to a "hand-out." It insists that if there are persons who are employable but not employed, there is a need for job creation. That is what is implied in the question "Where are the jobs?" to which the welfare "dependents" are to turn in their newly forged (and forced) independence.

Supporters and foes alike nonetheless recognize that not *everyone* in a society is able to perform wage work, even if jobs are limitless. Individuals may lack the capacities required for employment, due to ill health, disabling conditions, or inadequate education or training.[205] Nor does any society expect *everyone* to work. Within most industrial societies, we exempt and even prohibit children from working and do not presume that those over a certain age will continue to work.[206]

Welfare policy initially assumed that solo mothers would not work outside the home. Aid to Dependent Children, the forerunner of AFDC, was, in the words of the 1937 Committee on Economic Security, "designed to release from the wage-earning role the person whose natural function is to give her children the physical and affectionate guardianship necessary not alone to keep them from falling into social misfortune, but more affirmatively to make them citizens capable of contributing to society" (Abramovitz 1996, 313). It was aimed precisely at those women who were *justifiably* not engaged in wage labor. ADC, like its predecessor Mother's Pensions, was supposed to be doled out to mothers—though only to "deserving" mothers, that is, widowed or abandoned mothers. The racial politics of the day saw to it that these deserving mothers be not of African descent.

The 1962 amendments to the Social Security Act stressed the twin goals of strengthening the family and family self-sufficiency. "For the first time in 1962, federal law permitted states to require adult recipients to work in exchange for benefits" (Abramovitz 1996, 333). These amendments, which altered the name of the federal welfare program from Aid to Dependent Children to Aid to *Families* with Dependent Children, also permitted two-parent families to receive assistance where the breadwinner was unemployed. Congress and welfare rules expressed general ambivalence about forcing mothers to find employment rather than care for their children, focusing work expectations on fathers as family providers. Once again, however, racism complicates the picture for, as Abramovitz points out, even as late as 1966, "Many states refused assistance to black women if their eligibility for AFDC interfered with local labor market demands" (1996, 333). Perhaps not coincidentally, we find the first pressures to institute workfare programs was when black mothers joined the ranks of ADC/AFDC.

Paradoxically, women's dependency on public assistance for support has, since 1962, coincided with women's entry into the workforce and their greater equality of opportunity. The shifting expectations and opportunities has altered significantly our understanding of mothers' dependency on state aid. The declarations of 1937 and the debates of 1962 are scarcely conceivable today when nearly half of the women with children of preschool age are in the workforce, and are employed at least part-time.

As systematic, formal barriers to social goods are removed, injustices that remain become less visible and those who are unable to take advantage of new opportunities are blamed for their own distress.[207] So while previous social policies attempted to distinguish "deserving" from "undeserving" poor women, the removal of obstacles to women's employment has opened the door to characterizing all unemployed poor women as undeserving. Nonetheless, not all poverty, even in postindustrial society, has been viewed as a character flaw. When the disabled are poor, we either fix the working environment to enable employment, or we look to supplemental income for those so disabled that they cannot maintain employment even with altered work environments. We do not say to them "work or lose benefits." When, in our recent past, the aged constituted the majority of the poor, our nation looked for solutions that were adapted to that population. The solution was not to force every able-bodied elderly person to get a job, but to provide old age insurance, to peg benefits to inflation, and to provide medical care for the elderly.

In reading the literature by men, and some women, one comes to wonder why, when *women* are poor, theorists and social scientists fail to ask if there are not particular causes of *women's* poverty.[208] Why are the conditions faced by women, especially those caring for dependents, not highlighted? There is a presumption that when it comes to getting jobs there is no gender inequity; that the joblessness of women is independent of the gender-related vulnerabilities they face at home, in the family and in the economic sphere. There is no talk of gendered wage inequity; of the gendering of familial caretaking responsibilities; of gendered susceptibility to spousal abuse and sexual abuse in the workplace.

The inattention to the gender issues behind women's poverty should be of special concern to feminists. Not only must feminists always be alert to analyses that ignore gender, but feminists must be aware that gains for some women may jeopardize other women, especially those least benefited by equal opportunity gains and reproductive rights legislation. For example, reproductive rights currently benefit least those women who are poorest, as they often lack the means to procure contraception or choose abortion. But they are held accountable for each pregnancy and birth as if they had the same choices the middle-class women do. Even feminist women will ask of poor women, "Why do they have children if they can't afford them?"[209] With respect to the expectation that even women with children will be employed, Linda Gordon points out, "The fact that most mothers today are employed . . . nurtures resentment against other mothers supported (if only you could call it 'support') by AFDC." (1995, 92). In particular, feminist successes (removing legal barriers to women's economic and political participation and achieving reproductive rights) have promoted a presumption of gender equality. This presumption has facilitated an analysis that ignores the gendered concerns of women who have turned to welfare to support their families. In another context, Naomi Zack (1995) warns, "You must dismount a tiger with great care." The efforts of some better situated women to dismount the tiger of patriarchy may well have left other women—less well situated—in mortal danger.

The Maternalist Justification of Welfare

As we have noted, at the inception of U.S. social policy, the poverty of women was thought to be distinctive. Feminist scholars have documented the influence of women in building the welfare state in the United States and in drafting the policy that was to become AFDC (Sapiro 1990; Gordon 1994; Nelson 1990; Fraser 1990). The story of how a welfare program initiated by women for women became the despised program we now call simply "welfare" is a fascinating, if depressing, one. At best, it is a story of a "progressive maternalism," which gained power through the efforts of well-educated upper and upper-middle-class women even before women had gained the vote. At worst, it is a story about how these same women, mostly white, used the social benefits conferred upon women to "Americanize" (and thus erase the native ethnic identities of Eastern and Southern European women), even at the cost of preventing those benefits from being extended to black women and non-European immigrants.

The progressive maternalists adopting a philosophy of "social housekeeping" saw their role as bringing maternal virtues into the public sphere. Along with establishing a Children's Bureau within the executive branch of government (the Sheppard-Towner Act and Mother's Pensions), they were also responsible for administrative rules, which monitored the mother's sexuality, reviewed the women's housekeeping standards, and intervened in feeding and rearing customs retained from the Old World. These policy makers were *maternalists* in that they wanted to bring women's values into the public sphere. But as the city housekeepers, the eyes of the well-meaning reformers were primarily directed at the end result—the child. They bypassed the mother as a citizen in her own right. Gwendolyn Mink writes: "The fruits of maternalist social policy research were policies designed to improve motherhood through cultural reform. The beneficiary of these policies was the child, the conduit her mother, the social goal the fully Americanized child" (1995, 27).[210]

The maternalists' feminist vision resonates with certain feminist visions today, especially those which are associated with the feminist morality of care.[211] Although there are doubtless many significant differences between the historical case and feminists today, the historical example alerts us to some of the dangers lurking in the otherwise worthwhile project of bringing women's value of care, of concern for children, and so forth, to the public arena. For how, and in what spirit, we try to import these values makes all the difference.

Welfare Justified by Dependency Considerations

Dependency Revisited

The question before us now is whether, and how, we can conceive of welfare in such a way that it addresses women's lives, particularly recognizing the extent to which women continue to carry the social burden of dependency work. How, that is, can we fashion policy that does not insist that all women must fit the Procrustean bed of the male wage worker, that recognizes the demise of the "family wage," and that recognizes the dependency of those for whom mothers care, but does so without reducing the mothers themselves to dependency and control? Another way to pose this question is to ask if we can conceive of social welfare policy that extends an equality of *social citizenship* to all women?[212] As feminists have argued, women's social citizenship requires social recognition and support for the caring labor done by women.[213] Can we develop policies that meet this goal?

To conceive and argue for policies that will advance the goal of a full and equal citizenship for women, we need to shift our attention on dependency away from the social, political, economic, and moral registers which Fraser and Gordon explicate. The other deployment of the term that gets lost but which is retrievable in the acronym AFDC—Aid to Families with *Dependent* Children—is the use that this book has stressed, namely, the "inevitable dependencies" (also see Fineman 1995) of human development, disease, disability and decline. To shift attention to those who are dependents in this sense is necessary if we are to consider the fate of the class of persons upon whom the dependent persons depend, those persons I have called dependency workers. These individuals who attend to the dependency needs of others (whether full-time or part-time, paid or familial) incur, I have argued, a secondary dependency. The dependency worker and her charge constitute the dependency relationship without which no human society is conceivable. In the solo mother and her children, we find the distillation of these founding social relationships.

Robert Goodin (1988) writes that the justification for the welfare state is, ultimately, an ethical one: to address the needs of dependents. His argument is that "those who depend on particular others for satisfaction of their basic needs are rendered, by that dependency, susceptible to exploitation by those upon whom they depend. It is the risk of exploitation of such dependencies that justifies public provision—and public provision of a distinctively welfare state form—of those basic needs" (Goodin 1988, 121). There is much to be said for an understanding of welfare as the protection of the vulnerable. The vulnerability in need of protection, however, is not only the dependent who is disadvantaged by age, illness or disability, but also the vulnerability of the dependency worker.[214] Furthermore, because the dependent requires not only the caretaking itself in order to thrive, but a relationship, and because the dependency worker, to be a caring worker, requires the recognition that only a genuine relationship provides, the relationship itself requires protection. Because of the incurred secondary dependency, an obligation devolves on the larger social order to support the dependency relationship and the individuals that constitute it. These are the considerations that enter into the public ethic of care I have called *doulia*, and these are the considerations from which we need to argue for welfare.

What I will be suggesting here is that the concept of *doulia* can serve as a justification for welfare extended to the solo mother, but that it is a justification that calls for a much broader implementation. Not only must welfare be extended to impoverished solo mothers, but it should be extended to all dependency workers on a model that moves away from residualism and approaches the universalistic models of social insurance and populism.

Conditions for the Derived Dependency of Dependency Workers

To make this argument, we need to establish the relation between the incurred dependency of the dependency worker and the welfare "dependency" which so exercises the critics of welfare. The latter is not the dependency of the children, but that of their mothers. But these two dependencies are linked through the secondary dependency of the dependency worker. We have already pointed to the moral and work-related requirements of the labor of dependency care that disadvantage the caregiver in the competition for the benefits of social cooperation. To these we can add some further considerations. Whenever caring for dependents is incompatible with producing the material support needed to sustain those in the relationship, and this is generally the case in more highly developed economies, the dependency worker, as well as those who depend on her, are in need of support. We need to add that the dependency worker is not only economically vulnerable, but is also less able to make her social and political voice heard, especially when it goes against the provider of the material support that helps to sustain her and her charge.[215]

Feminist research has established "that in all industrialized Western countries, welfare—tending to children, the elderly, the sick and disabled—is largely provided in private households by women without pay, rather than by states, markets and voluntary nonprofit organizations" (Orloff 1993, 313). That is, women not only do most of the dependency work, they do it without pay. Having dependents to care for means that without additional support, you cannot—given the structure of our contemporary industrial life and its economy—simultaneously provide the *means* to take care of them and do the caring for them (to use the useful distinction in the term "caring" that Joan Tronto [1993] has introduced). This also means that without additional support you cannot participate in the reciprocal arrangements of production and consumption, as defined within a market economy. The requirement for support then constitutes an additional condition of the derived dependency for dependency workers, especially those who do unpaid dependency work. The dependency of the unpaid dependency worker is derivative, not inevitable—it is structural, not characterological.

In previous chapters we have argued that even dependency workers who are paid incur a special vulnerability to derived dependency, because of the nature of dependency work and the consequent relation to the dependent. There are then three features of this labor—"love's labor"—that together are responsible for this vulnerability. First, because dependency work involves the charge of one who is in many important regards helpless without the caregiver, there is a moral obligation which transcends the bounds of most jobs. Second, because dependency work requires a responsiveness to needs, often an anticipation of needs, the fact is that when it is done well, it requires a significant degree of emotional attachment to the charge. As we pointed out earlier, whether we require care or want someone for whom we are responsible cared for, we want a caregiver who *cares*.[216] In addition, because the work of dependency care is "functionally diffuse" rather than "functionally specific," a caregiver does not have a fixed set of tasks, but has to address the individual's general state of well-being and do whatever is needed to assure that her charge's needs are met. Such responsibilities will often override the needs of the caregiver herself, except where meeting her own needs are crucial to meeting the needs of her charge.[217] Third, the demands of familial dependency work often conflict with the demands of market-based employment.

As Joel Handler has argued, regulatory models and legal rights that now govern citizen-state or citizen-citizen interactions serve poorly to adequately protect the dependent and to limit the obligations of, as well as properly compensate, dependency workers.[218] It is for these reasons that the dependency worker is liable to incur a dependency that has a character different from the dependency on economic and governmental structures to which all workers are subject.

Patriarchal family structures, we pointed out in Chapter One (see page 43), whether these be the nuclear family prevalent in industrial societies, or one of the many extended family forms in agrarian societies and peasant communities, have been responses to the requirement that dependency relations require support. And, as feminist critiques of the patriarchal family have shown, they are neither the only nor the best response. Not only is it the case that within these structures the dependency of the dependency worker is the condition of her vulnerability to exploitation, abuse and all the ills against which feminists have fought. In addition, dependency work is assigned by gender, not by skill or disposition. Patriarchal state support in the form of welfare has been the response to the solo mother in need in capitalist welfare states.[219] Again, it has been a poor response—better than none, but too little, too stigmatized, and too intrusive. The welfare repeal, or "reform," is no response at all. The demand that women on welfare "work" not only fails to value the unpaid dependency work of the women using welfare to support themselves and their children, but, by imposing on these women the model of the male breadwinner, it fails to recognize the dependency work of mothering. In the name of fostering a fictive "independence," it refuses to acknowledge the obligation of society to attend to relationships upon which all civic relationships depend. A society that refuses to

support this bond absolves itself from its most fundamental obligation—
its obligation to its founding possibility.

The Citizen and Social Goods

In Part Two, and especially in Chapter Four, we demonstrated the
omission of social goods that bear on the needs of dependency workers,
dependents, and the relations of dependency in the most influential contemporary theory of the just state, suggesting that this neglect arises out
of the venerable tradition which Rawls's work continues. Consider, once
again, the conception of the citizen as the free, independent, equal individual to whom rights attach. This is the citizen who enters freely into
exchanges with equals with a sense of justice, but also with a conception
of his own good. He both benefits from social cooperation with equals
and partakes of the burdens of such cooperation. The moral features of
the citizen (an ability to form and revise one's conception of one's own
good and a sense of justice) are those that contribute to political and
civic participation with equals and call for a set of social goods ("primary goods") necessary for their exercise. The "primary goods" serve as
an index for making comparative assessments of interpersonal well-
being. Omitted from Rawls's list, I argued in Chapter Four, are the
goods of dependency care and relationships of caring. These are just the
sort of social goods that are critical for women's social citizenship.

If we say that the moral capacity of the citizen includes a third moral
power, the capacity for responding to those in need with care, we can
insist on the additional social goods needed for its exercise. If we possess
basic liberties, freedom of movement and choice of occupation, and have
access to the powers and prerogatives of public office, as well as income
and wealth, then we can be said to possess the political and civil rights
of citizenship. But full social citizenship requires that if we are called
upon to care, we can fulfill these duties without losing our ability to care
for ourselves, and that in caring for another, the full burden of support
as well as care for the one dependent on us will not fall upon our shoulders alone. Without such assurance, we have not yet attained the powers
and capacities to function as free and equal citizens. These, then, are the
social goods all citizens, but particularly women, require for social citizenship. Before we discuss how these might translate into demands for
particular social policies, we need to consider whether an index of social
goods is the appropriate way to address the needs of dependency.

Amartya Sen has argued that goods or resources are not the appropriate indices of interpersonal comparisons of well-being.[220] The emphasis on goods, he argues, is a fetishism that prevents us from seeing that
the equality we strive for has to do less with the goods themselves than

with what we can *do* with them. It is our capability, our freedom of functioning, that we wish to equalize, not a bundle of resources. Sen's approach is more compatible with the dependency concerns I have argued for than the Rawlsian notion of primary goods. The set of primary goods is normalized for the ideal of the fully functioning citizen. The citizens of the well-ordered state that I envision are instead a non-normalized group whose starting points are not assumed to be the same. Where the initial conditions of individuals are different, indexing well-being to a set of goods is problematic at best. Individuals with different starting capabilities will be able to utilize resources differently. What we want to insure, claims Sen, is not merely that everyone has access to the same goods with fair equality of opportunity, but that we equalize each person's capability to function freely. With this in mind, let us have another look at the "goods" pertinent to dependency relationships: 1) the understanding that we will be cared for if we become dependent; 2) the support we require if we have to take on the work of caring for a dependent; and 3) the assurance that if we become dependent, someone will take on the job of caring for those who are dependent upon us. Instead of being thought of as "goods," these desiderata may just as well be thought of as "capabilities." The knowledge that adequate support will be there when we need it is a capability as well as a good. The goods invoked here are the *capability* to do the caring and *capabilities* that are made possible when we cannot care for ourselves. What I have proposed here is therefore compatible with a goods-based index, but better served by a capability-based measure of equality.[221]

The Principle of *Doulia* as a Justification for Welfare

Incorporating dependency and the dependency relation into social relations, I argued in Chapter Four, requires a concept of interdependence capable of recognizing "nested dependencies." Through a form of reciprocity I characterized as *doulia*, these nested dependencies link those who need help to those who help, and link the helpers to a set of supports. The equality concept inherent in the idea that we are all some mother's child utilizes such a notion of nested dependencies. This equality insists that our full functioning presumes our need for and ability to participate in relationships of dependency without sacrificing the needs of dependents or dependency workers.

As we look for a way to bring a care ethic into the public arena (the contemporary version of social housekeeping), we need both a conception of social goods, and a notion of social cooperation which acknowledges dependencies and the need for care, and which employs a notion of reciprocation appropriate to a situation where one member of the relation is incapable of reciprocating. This is the concept of *doulia,* the concept of social cooperation that derives from the Greek word for service: *Just as we have required care to survive and thrive, so we need to provide conditions that allow others—including those who do the work of caring—to receive the care they need to survive and thrive.* By extending the notion of service (rendered to the postpartum mother by the *doula* so that the mother can care for her child and yet be cared for herself) and by shifting from the private circumstance of postpartum care to a public conception of care, we think of the circles of reciprocity moving outward to the larger social structures of which we are a part and upon which we depend. The principle of *doulia* will then provide a basis for welfare. For just as the caregiver has a responsibility to care for the dependent, the larger society has an obligation to attend to the well-being of the caregiver. Only so can the caregiver fulfill responsibilities to the dependent without being subject to an exploitation some have called "compulsory altruism" (Taylor-Gooby 1991 cited in Orloff 1993).

If we agree that the care of dependents takes place within a dependency relation, then a principled ethical justification of welfare, and indeed of the welfare state, is to support dependency relations. The purpose of welfare needs to be at once to care for dependents and to mitigate the costs to dependency workers for their participation in the dependency relation. As we look at women's poverty and the social response to "welfare" from a perspective of the dependency relation, and we attempt to reconstruct our understanding of social goods and cooperation from this perspective, we get, I believe, an argument for welfare (as it pertains to women especially) that differs from both the anti-poverty (the residualist model) and the social control justification (the behaviorist model). To be politically viable, however, this welfare must not be restricted to the poor, but extended to cover dependency work and dependency workers more generally.

The Family and Medical Leave Act

Even as the rhetoric on the Right reaffirms that the patriarchal family is the only acceptable social institution in which dependents receive care, contemporary societies, particularly those with industrialized economies, have been confronted with vast increases in women's participation in the labor force. The altered expectations concerning women's entry into the public workplace has disrupted the longstanding (if exploitative) organization of that labor we have called dependency work. Whether women's increased participation in the labor market has resulted from aspirations for equal status or from changing economic circumstances, it has left many in a quandary of how to care for our children and our aging parents, our sick partners, and our disabled neighbors.

We have seen that with changed expectations surrounding women's employment, we have encountered a major upheaval in welfare policies directed at poor women heading families. Simultaneously, there has been a push for policies enabling workers, male as well as female, to take time out to have babies, care for sick children and family members, and care for themselves when ill. These family and medical leave policies have been aimed not at impoverished women, but at women situated well enough to contribute financially to the family income.

My arguments thus far have looked at the inadequate response to dependency concerns of poor women. I have argued that policies adequate to meeting the needs of poor women's dependency concerns will need to be based on a conception of *doulia*. Furthermore, I have hinted that policies based on *doulia* will cast the net wider than welfare's present coverage of indigent women and their children. Before examining what a welfare policy would look like if it were based on an extended conception of social goods and social cooperation (that is, if it were a welfare policy based on *doulia*), it will be instructive to see how a liberal social policy aimed at women—but not at the poorest women—fares with respect to dependency concerns.

Among industrialized nations, the United States, in spite of its early history of equal opportunity employment legislation, is especially primitive in its response to the conflicts between paid employment and familial unpaid dependency work. In 1993, the Family and Medical Leave Act, a national piece of legislation, provided for some parental leave and some leave time to take care of ailing family members. The Act is a rare piece of social policy in so far as it recognizes a public responsibility toward dependency care. In this section we will examine its positive contribution and shortcomings.

Reading the Family and Medical Leave Act

The Family and Medical Leave Act of 1993[222] (henceforth FMLA) is, in many ways, emblematic of the sort of legislation and social policy that is required to meet dependency needs of paid workers. It permits up to twelve workweeks of unpaid leave within any twelve-month period for one or more of the following reasons:

A) Because of the birth of a son or daughter of the employee and in order to care for such son or daughter.

B) Because of the placement of a son or daughter with the employee for adoption or foster care.

C) In order to care for the spouse, or son, daughter, or parent of the employee, if such spouse, son, daughter, or parent has a serious health condition.

D) Because of a serious health condition that makes the employee unable to perform the functions of the position of such employee. (Public Law 103-3—Feb. 5, 1993, 107 STAT. 9)

This law expressly recognizes the dependency relations that I have argued are so grievously ignored in much political theory. And it recognizes the importance of acknowledging some of the demands of dependency not only of the employee herself, but those of the individuals who depend on her. While the Family and Medical Leave Act is an immensely important piece of legislation, the law is relatively limited in its scope and in the real benefits it provides. Consequently, its contribution to fair equality for all is circumscribed. Its limitations are traceable to an ideology of reciprocity and equality that continues to push dependency concerns back into the domain of the private, that is, to a conception of dependency concerns that still fails to recognize the extent to which addressing these needs is a matter of the social cooperation required for a well-ordered and just society.[223]

Among the limitations of the Act are the following:

1) leave is unpaid

2) employers with less than 50 employees are exempt from the FLMA

3) the FLMA construes family in relatively traditional terms.

Let us look at the "Findings and Purposes" of the FMLA, and then return to consider if these bear on the limitations of the Act.

Let us first look at the "Findings." I cite these in full:

a) FINDING—Congress finds that—

1) the number of single-parent households and two-parent households in which the single parent or both parents work is increasing significantly;

2) it is important for the development of children and the family unit that fathers and mothers be able to participate in early childrearing and the care of family members who have serious health conditions;

3) the lack of employment policies to accommodate working parents can force individuals to choose between job security and parenting;

4) there is inadequate job security for employees who have serious health conditions that prevent them from working for temporary periods;

5) due to the nature of the roles of men and women in our society, the primary responsibility for family caretaking often falls on women, and such responsibility affects the working lives of women more than it affects the working lives of men; and

6) employment standards that apply to one gender only have serious potential for encouraging employers to discriminate against employees and applicants for employment who are that gender. (Public Law 103-3, 107 STAT 6–7)

First among the findings is that the number of single-parent households and two-parent households in which the parent(s) all work has significantly increased. The fact that this counts as a finding for a bill such as the FMLA is indicative of the way in which the breakdown of the sexual division of labor on the male side of the divide—expanding the paid labor force to include more women—is putting pressure on degenderizing the female side of the divide—the largely private and unpaid care for dependents. This is the first significant step in understanding that dependency concerns need to be a part of the public understanding of social cooperation—that decisions to undertake dependency care can not remain matters of private decision making with only private consequences, but belong within the public arena.

The second finding recognizes the nonfungibility of many dependency relations, for example, the need of a sick child to have a parent's attentions. But it also moves retrogressively in the direction of the privatization of dependency care. For it suggests that care of ill family members and early child rearing are important for "the development of children and the family unit" rather than for the general welfare of the nation and a feature of social cooperation.

The third finding points to the need for policies that avoid pitting job security against parenting demands. Both job security and parenting are regarded as matters that are important for the well-being of individuals. The law recognizes the importance of the state in assuring both goods to those individuals who may be torn between competing concerns—while it establishes a responsibility of public institutions to assure that individuals can fulfill dependency responsibilities as well as job-related duties—

and that the burden of dependency work must sit not solely on the shoulders of those who undertake these obligations. But how far does it go? Not very far. The leave is unpaid and the exemption for employers of less than fifty is not insignificant. Therefore it represents only a very limited acknowledgment of public responsibility to assure job security for workers who must provide dependency care.

It is here that a public conception of *doulia* needs to be brought into play—the particular reciprocity of *doulia*. More than "accommodation" is required. Accommodation presumes the situation of employment as it now is, rather than challenging concepts of what counts as part of the economy and fully recognizing the importance of restructuring employment conditions so that they are suitable to a society in which dependency concerns are included as matters of social justice and are not simply thought to be private responsibilities.

The fourth finding, addressing the inadequate job security for workers with serious or prolonged health conditions, is an acknowledgement of the vulnerability to dependency that is shared by all employees.

The fifth and sixth findings are of special interest for they acknowledge the gender specific nature of much dependency work, and the gender inequality that results within the male side of the sexual division of labor when there is insufficient support on the female side of the divide. The justification for the bill that can be garnered from findings five and six is an equality argument, an inference which is sustained by the 4th and 5th stated purposes of the bill (see below). But unless we reconstrue equality and political conceptions such as justice and social cooperation, and unless it becomes a public priority to refashion sensibilities accordingly, the FLMA leaves intact the gender-structured nature of dependency concerns, and while it helps to move these concerns into the public arena, it cannot move us sufficiently in the direction of understanding that dependency work cannot be privatized and genderized without justice and equality being violated.

Let us now look at the "Purposes" of the Act. I reproduce these in full:

b) PURPOSES—It is the purpose of this Act—

1) to balance the demands of the workplace with the needs of families, to promote the stability and economic security of families, and to promote national interests in preserving family integrity;

2) to entitle employees to take reasonable leave for medical reasons, for the birth or adoption of a child, and for the care of a child, spouse, or parent who has a serious health condition;

3) to accomplish the purposes described in paragraphs (1) and (2) in a manner that accommodates the legitimate interests of employers;

4) to accomplish the purposes described in paragraphs (1) and (2) in a manner that is consistent with the Equal Protection Clause of the Fourteenth Amendment, minimizes the potential for employment discrimination on the basis of sex by ensuring generally that leave is available for eligible medical reasons (including maternity-related disability) and for compelling family reasons, on a gender neutral basis; and

5) to promote the goal of equal employment opportunity for women and men, pursuant to such clause. (Public Law 103-3, 107 STAT 6–7)

The purposes of this act are to recognize "national interests in preserving family integrity." But *why* is it important to the national interest to preserve family integrity and what sort of structures will count as family? The purpose stated in (3) is to "accomplish the purposes described in (1) and (2) in a manner that accommodates the legitimate interests of employers." But then why should (1) and (2) not trump the interests of employers? And if they don't, what are the consequences?

In light of the reading of the "Findings and Purposes," let us consider what I have listed as the limitations of the Act.

First, the leave is unpaid—all twelve weeks of permissible leave time are unpaid. To take off from work to attend a sick child then remains a luxury, or a factor moving one closer to impoverishment. The United States is not only one of the last industrialized countries to have a family leave policy, it is also the only one in which the leave is entirely unpaid (See Olson 1998). One of the purported findings and purposes to which the act is addressed is the increase in the number of single parent households. But how many single parent employees can afford to be without pay for three months of the year? How are they supposed to put food on the table of a sick and needy person? One need not even argue that the full twelve weeks ought to be paid, but surely some of that time needs to be paid leave—by law, not merely by the good will of some employers who provide paid leave—if it is to have a substantial impact on the practices of single parent households—which now constitute one-fourth of all households.[224]

Second, employers with less than fifty employees are exempt from the family leave policy. But employees in companies with less than fifty employees make up a very large portion of the American workforce. In fact, they make up the *majority* of the workforce.[225] That means that a majority of paid employees in this country are not covered under the FLMA! What is clear, again, is that giving heed to dependency concerns is not viewed as a general responsibility. These can be trumped by the employer's needs—the benefits for employers are not thought to be only personal. The benefit to the employer is conceptualized as part of the economic well-being of the wider public. Meanwhile, little is put in place to substitute for the merely *personal* demand of the employee. Dependency care is not counted as part of the economic structure, for example. It does not figure into the Gross National Product.

Third, the FLMA construes family in relatively traditional terms. Although *parent* includes not only biological parents but any individuals who have stood *in loco parentis*, and the term "son or daughter" means "a biological, adopted or foster child, a stepchild, a legal ward, or a child of a parent standing in loco parentis," the term "spouse" is restricted to husband or wife, leaving out non-married adults who are co-habitating, gay and lesbian families, extended families and so forth. Contrast this with the "nurturance leave" proposed by feminist legal theorist Nadine Taub (1984-5), which argues for nurturance leaves for any adult members of a household. If the stress in our policies is to support dependency relations because the fabric of social structure is founded on the maintenance of such relations, then the relations themselves and not the social institutions in which they have traditionally been lodged ought to become the focus of our concern.

The decisions or situations from which these dependency relations result may appear to be private decisions between the parties involved—decisions between parties which do not devolve obligations on third parties. But there are some social institutions which appear to be formed by private decisions between the parties involved and which nonetheless induce obligations in third parties. Marriage is such an institution.[226] The private decision by me and another to be a married couple means that socially and legally certain actions are binding on my employer, my landlord, hospitals, insurance agencies, and the Internal Revenue Service. In an analogous fashion, the private decision to take on the work of dependency and form a dependency relation with a charge ought to induce third party obligations to support the dependency worker in his or her care for the charge. In the case of marriage, the binding obligations are part of a larger interest in society to maintain the institution of marriage. Recognition of its legal and social status means that two individuals are treated as if there is a connection between them. But a major reason to recognize such institutions is that they are the locus of the care and sustenance of dependents. The relation of dependency is morally and socially still more salient and fundamental, and so forms the very ground of this feature of the marriage relation. The social technology of the traditional family makes both dependency worker and charge vulnerable in a relation of (to use Sen's term) "cooperative conflict." The claim on third parties to support and help sustain the dependency relation, independent of a particular arrangement such as marriage, has morally the stronger force. This claim is realized in the public obligation to recognize caregiving within the arrangements of social cooperation through the principle of *doulia*. And the argument for *doulia* transcends the institution of marriage as traditionally understood as well as family arrangements sanctioned by traditional marriage and biological relation. Its basis is the undertaking of care, and responsibility for care, and the dependency to which the caregiver then becomes vulnerable.

Welfare Re-Formed: A Vision of Welfare Based on *Doulia*

Whether it targets impoverished unemployed women who have dependency demands and no other means of support, or women who participate in the labor force but who continue to have dependency work demands, social policy continues the fiction that the citizen is the healthy, autonomous adult who, as Rawls would have it, is "fully functioning" and for whom justice requires the reciprocity of those equally situated. Dependency is acknowledged only as a breach of this norm. Policies directed at dependency concerns are niggling and insufficient. How would this change if we took dependency seriously?

In the previous section we suggested that a family and medical leave act that was adequate to dependency concerns would first of all mandate a generous, paid leave and would broadly construe "family." In this section we approach this question by considering the needs of the women for whom the lack of a social responsibility of dependency concerns is perhaps more pressing than those women who could benefit from family and medical leave. We approach the question by imagining how to reconceive welfare. The concept of *doulia* itself, however, suggests that the dependency worker must be involved in what Fraser has called "the struggle over needs interpretation." The theorist and advocate must be careful not to follow the model of the invasive baby nurse rather than the assisting *doula*. Nonetheless because dependency work does partially deprive the dependency worker of political voice, interventions are crucial. With these caveats in mind, I would like to make a few observations about what basing welfare policies on a concept of *doulia* entails.[227] First, it entails that all dependency work, whether it is care for children, the ill, the aged or the disabled, must be recognized as social contributions which require reciprocation, not by the cared for but by a larger social circle in which the dependency relation is embedded; that the social goods and burdens to be distributed and shared must include the good of caring relations. There are a number of possible ways in which such goods and reciprocation can be recognized.

As we've already noted, the traditional family, with its breadwinner and caregiver, forms one such embedding nest, at least for the care of young children. Let us, for the moment, presume the viability of the traditional family—ignore for the moment the social forces which have hammered away at it and at the questionable justice of its gendered division of labor. Let us imagine a family form and an economy in which one breadwinner can produce income sufficient to support a spouse who does the domestic labor and caring work and a couple of children; and let us suppose that this family is not governed by traditional gender divisions of labor. The dependency worker cares for the dependents, and the breadwinner, "the private provider," supports the dependency relation with resources sufficient to maintain all. This is then a private arrangement which presumably calls upon no additional social supports and so is "self-sufficient."[228]

There are at least three problems with this resolution. The first is conceptual, the second is economic, and the third is ethical and a matter of justice. First, it is an obfuscation to think of such a structure as "self-sufficient." Although dependency work results in the dependency worker's derived dependency, all employment involves some dependency. The provider is dependent on an employer and still more significantly dependent on an economy in which certain skills, services, or products are marketable. The wage worker is him/herself in nested dependencies—dependent on an employer, who is dependent on a market and on a particular configuration of economic structures and forces, such as interest rates, global competition, etc. A private provider does not lend "self-sufficiency" to the dependence relation, because this self-sufficiency is a conceptual chimera in a capitalist economy. The appropriate contrast between a dependency worker and other workers is not between those who are self-reliant and those who are dependent, but between those whose labor results in some sorts of vulnerabilities rather than others.[229]

Second, an economically self-reliant provider/caregiver model requires a rate of compensation that makes it viable for a provider to support a family. The structural unemployment characteristic of modern capitalism, as we all know, insures that not all providers can find employment, especially employment adequate to support a family. The rates of poverty among families with two adults present indicate that, for large numbers of families, this goal is not achievable within the current economy.[230] The reality for most two-parent families today is a wife who both has primary responsibility for domestic work and dependency work, but who also holds down a job, often part-time, almost always not paying as well as her husband's. The pure provider/caregiver model has been hybridized. The change comes in part out of women's aspirations, and in part out of economic necessity since the average weekly inflation-adjusted earnings have declined by 19 percent since 1973.[231]

Dependency work and provision can be so divided that each of two partners engage in each of the two forms of labor and relationship. But more often, even the hybridized model follows many of the same structural features as the pure model.[232] The hybridized dependency worker continues to assume primary responsibility for dependents and remains largely (though not totally) dependent on the income of the hybridized breadwinner partner. If the marriage falls apart, the financial suffering falls largely to the one who bears the major responsibility for dependency work. It is often the demands of dependency work which prevent that partner from pursuing financially more advantageous situations.

Third, as we have argued in Chapter Two, the work of dependency care disadvantages the dependency worker with respect to her (or his) exit options if the relationship with the breadwinner becomes fragile. Orloff has argued that the social right which women need to demand is the capacity to form and sustain autonomous families. Only such a right would adequately address the vulnerability of the dependency worker. The dependency worker's vulnerability to the good graces of the private provider deprives women of the social citizenship which the welfare state affords the male worker by "decommodifying" his labor (Orloff 1993, 319). The consequences of her worse bargaining position in cooperative conflicts and of her economic dependency on an individual man are aggravated by woman's subordinate position in the larger society— that is, by the likelihood that she will receive a smaller paycheck, that she is susceptible to sexual intimidation on the job, and so forth. The injustices of intimate life, public injustices, and the gendering of dependency work, however, only aggravate a vulnerability that attaches itself to the work and relationship of dependency.

This means that a just reciprocation for dependency work cannot be based on the so-called private arrangement of the traditional breadwinner/caregiver model—or even the hybridized model. Instead I propose a socialization and a universalization of compensation for dependency work. Just as worker's compensation and unemployment insurance became programs that were universally[233] available to workers, with benefits rationalized and routinized (and extended without stigma), so must compensation for dependency work (Waerness 1987).

Imagine, for example, a payment for dependency work, suitably rationalized and routinized, which can be used to compensate a mother for her time caring for her child, or allow her to use the money to pay for daycare. Or to provide money for a son or daughter to care for an ailing parent, or to pay someone else to perform the service. The level of reciprocation, furthermore, must allow the dependency worker not only merely to survive, but to have the resources to care properly for the dependent as well as herself. This means considering what else a dependency worker requires: health coverage (which all workers and all dependents deserve); certain in-kind services or goods or monetary equivalent; and housing. But again, specifying these must be a work in which dependency workers are themselves engaged. Following Sen, the emphasis must be not on goods, per se, but on capabilities.[234]

The conception of *doulia* respects not only the nature of dependency relations, but also the caregiver as a dependency *worker*. Like other workers they need vacations, exit options, retraining when they are no longer needed at their employment. And like all work, dependency work must be de-gendered, in fact, not in name only. This suggests public programs of educating for dependency work—especially young boys and men.

But workers normally are accountable to those who pay their wages. One problem with having public support for dependency work may be that when the State pays for the labor of caring for one's own children, or one's aging parents, then the State can claim that it has the right to oversee the quality of work and the input of the worker. Such intrusion into the "private domain" runs counter to much liberal thought. Can we justifiably say to the State, "Be the 'public' provider, be the one who pays the dependency worker her salary, but then (except of course when the dependency worker violates the trust of her charge and begins to be abusive or negligent), stay out of the 'private' dependency relation?" Putting the matter this way may rely too much on the dichotomy of public and private that feminist theorists have urged us to reconsider. But state oversight of personal relations, except to protect against abuse and the perpetuation of sexist oppression, seems to run counter to most feminist liberatory goals as well.

I believe that the concept of social cooperation inherent in the concept of *doulia* offers a resolution to this dilemma. Ordinary concepts of reciprocation dictate that if I provide you with a product or a service, you compensate me for the product or the labor I poured into that product or service. Lines of accountability follow the lines of reciprocation. If you do not pay me, I do not receive the benefits for which I labored, and so I hold you accountable, and it is my right to do so. If you pay me but I do not deliver the goods, you do not receive the benefits for which I got paid, and you hold me accountable and again, it is your right to do so. There is no third party affected by the transaction, and each party is accountable to the other, except that the State may have a duty to insure that both parties honor their agreements. But the labor of the dependency worker flows to the dependent. If I do a good job as a dependency worker, the dependent is the beneficiary. I am accountable first and foremost to the direct beneficiary of my actions, that is, to my charge. Just as any other worker, I have a right to demand compensation for my labor. But because the dependent, virtually by definition, is not in a position to compensate, the compensation comes from another source: the provider. The right to demand that the work be well-done, however, is the right of the dependent. The duty of the State, whether it is a provider or not, is to be sure that the work is well done and that the dependency worker is compensated. The duty of the State is especially significant in the case of a party as vulnerable as the charge. The point is only that when a larger social structure is the provider, being such a provider is not the same as being the employer to whom a worker is responsible. Such a duty is not an open ticket to intrude upon the relationship or to regulate the life of the dependency worker. The duty of the public provider remains the duty of the state at present: to insure that a child is neither neglected nor abused nor denied provisions of a fundamental sort. Such a duty is consonant with the obligation of the state to protect its citizens against abuses from other citizens. Just as we do not want the "private relation" of spouses to be exempt, so we cannot want dependency relations to be exempt.

Adequate public support of dependency work, then, would significantly alter the dependency workers' bargaining position, making both them and their charges better able to respond to abuse within the family, and less subject to intrusive state regulation. Even the miserly AFDC program was primarily a boon to women with children escaping abusive relations. A welfare program that universalizes compensation for dependency work, whether or not another able adult was present in the home, would allow women to leave abusive relations without the stigma of current welfare participation.

Within our own society, dependency workers—paid or unpaid—are generally poorer than others. Paid dependency workers, such as child care workers, are the most poorly paid workers relative to their level of education and skill (Hartmann and Pearce 1989). In hospitals and nursing homes, orderlies and aides, those who do most of the hands-on dependency care of patients and clients, are the lowest paid staff. Female-headed households account for the poorest families in the U.S. *Doulia* requires that dependency work which is currently paid work be well-paid. It is not enough that women be able to have affordable child-care. We are not adhering to a principle of *doulia* when we exploit other women to care for our children.

And finally, a concept of *doulia* would be accepting of any family form in which dependency work is adequately realized. It would honor different familial forms of caring: a child caring for an elderly parent; a gay man caring for his partner with AIDS; a lesbian woman caring for her lover, and her lover's children, through a bout of breast cancer; a single parent household or a multiple adult household in which children are being raised. A concept of *doulia* only recognizes need, and the vulnerability arising from the responsiveness to need—not family form, forms of sexuality, gender, class, or race.[235]

Underlying the debate over AFDC has been the question of the visibility of and the social responsibility for the dependency work of women. By keeping the responsibility private, poor women will stay poor and those not poor will be impoverished if they try to raise families without support of a man. Dependency work is a category in which the interests of women of different races or classes can be turned against each other. White women benefit from the dependency work of women of color for example, and wealthy women benefit from the dependency work of poorer women. Glenn (1992) points to the difficulties that await an effort to unite women around issues of care. She writes:

> With the move into the labor force of all races and classes of women, it is tempting to think that we can find unity around the common problems of "working women." With that in mind, feminist policy makers have called for expanding services to assist employed mothers in such areas as child care and elderly care. We need to ask, Who is going to do the work? Who will benefit from increased services? The historical record suggests that it will be done by women of color . . . and that it will be middle-class women who will receive the services (1992, 36).

When she applies this scenario to the needs of employed middle-class women and to regulations insisting that women on welfare find employment, Glenn wryly points out that the apparent coincidence of interest disappears: at current wages, childcare work will not suffice to bring the welfare mother out of poverty, and if wages are raised, the middle-class woman will not be able to afford the less advantaged women's services. Feminism will come apart unless women speak and think together about how to forge policies that will benefit both sets of women and will lessen the increasing disparity between them.

The call for a concept of *doulia* and universal policies is not intended to smooth over these difficult issues between women with different interests and from different races and classes. Nor is it to reinstate universalism as if identity politics, postmodernism, and critical race theories didn't matter. But the call for universal policies is not universalism. Universal policies do not pretend that we are all alike in some designated characteristic. They only maintain that if anyone should have access to a given resource, everyone should have access to such a resource, because such a resource comes to us by virtue of our membership within a given community, often because it is believed that such a resource is needed for each to function as a full member of such a community. As I indicated earlier, universal policies have had their critics. They have been criticized as not sufficiently redistributive and as benefitting most those who need them least. But universal policies that are formed from the perspective of the least well-off and formed to serve their needs first are least likely to be deficient in this respect. A good example is provided by the case of disability. The ramps and modified sidewalks meant to serve the disabled, but available for all to use have benefited many populations for whom they were not envisioned, without diminishing their usefulness to the disabled.

The universal policies advocated on a conception of *doulia* derive from the need that women have to function as full citizens in a postindustrial world. To function free of vulnerability to exploitation due to paid or familial dependency work, and free to engage with the full resonance of their voices, women must have access to a universal provision that recognizes the indispensable role of dependency workers and the importance of their participation as full citizens.

6

"Not *My* Way, Sesha.
Your Way. Slowly."
A Personal Narrative

A Child Is Born

> The most important thing that happens when a child with disabilities is born is that a child is born (Ferguson and Asch 1989, 108).

The most important thing that happens when a woman becomes the mother of a child with disabilities is that she becomes the mother of a new child. When Sesha was born, I, along with Jeffrey, her father and my life-partner, fell madly in love with our baby. It was 1969. I was twenty-three, my husband twenty-five, and we were pioneers in the natural childbirth movement. I was reaping the benefits of being "awake and aware" (Lamaze 1956). Exhilarated by the vigorous labor of propelling my baby into the world, and amazed by the success of my own body's heaving, I now gazed into a little face emerging from me, a face wearing a pout that slowly became the heralding cry of the newborn infant. The nurses cleaned her off, handed her to me, and my Sesha melted into my arms. With her full head of black hair, her sweet funny infant's face, and her delicious temperament, this baby was the fulfillment of our dreams. We saw in her the perennial "perfect baby:" the exquisite miracle of a birth. It was December 23, and all the world was poised for Christmas. But we had our own Christmas, our own celebration of birth and the beauty, freshness, and promise of infancy. This birth, and each birth, unique and universal—common, even ordinary, and yet each time miraculous. Such were my reflections as I lay in a New York City hospital room watching the snow fall while bathing in the glory of a wanted, welcomed baby. Only the hospital wasn't conforming to my mood or my expectations. The staff was being either bureaucratic or inept. I had anticipated seeing my baby shortly after she had been wheeled out of the delivery room, and thought she would soon thereafter join me in my room. "Rooming-in" was an innovation, a concession to new women's voices, to women who wanted to breast-feed and to have their infants by their side, not in a nursery down the hall to be fed on a rigid four-hour schedule. I was to have my baby in my room after a twenty-four-hour observation period. But more than twenty-four hours had passed and no one had brought her in. Why? Could something be wrong? The nurses evaded my questions, and the doctors were nowhere to be found. Finally someone provided an explanation. Sesha had some jaundice ("common, nothing to worry about") and a cyanotic episode of no known origin (that is, she had briefly stopped breathing). She had been examined by a pediatrician, and she seemed fine. I could start nursing her and we could leave the hospital according to schedule. It was four months before anyone thought again about that episode.

As the months wore on, I slowly adjusted to motherhood, and Sesha helped make the adjustment easy. Jeffrey and I shared all aspects of parenting, except that I did the nursing. One wise nursing book, I no longer recall who wrote it, advised against a baby nurse for the nursing mother. Instead it urged that the father (grandmothers, friends, and paid help, if affordable) should help care for the mother and take over all tasks except the care and feeding of the nursing baby. This would allow her to regain her strength, and to nurse the baby in a rested condition and peaceful frame of mind. I was fortunate enough to be able to follow that advice. In fact, I recognized then and have come to believe still more deeply that this advice contained a profound principle: that to nurture a dependent being well, and without damaging the nurturer, requires that the nurturer herself be nurtured.[236] This advice embodied the egalitarian ideals of marriage and parenthood that I shared with my spouse.

So the two of us embraced our parenthood and were blissful with our new baby. Sesha didn't cry much, fell asleep at my breast at night, and by day slept and munched (though with less vigor than I had expected). While she slept a great deal, when awake Sesha had a wonderful wide-eyed questioning look that made us feel that she was very alert and taking in everything around her. At four months she was developing into a beautiful little baby, very cooperative and oh so sweet. Only she wasn't doing new "tricks." When friends and relatives would ask us what the little prodigy was up to, we'd have curiously little to report. But then, I wasn't interested in foolish competitions of how early my child did such and such. All potential sources of anxiety were water off a duck's back: I was the happy mama, content to be gliding through this new period of my life with duckling and mate in tow. Yet it was precisely at this fourth month that a swell of extraordinary proportions engulfed us and interrupted my blissful journey into motherhood.

At this time, friends with a baby approximately Sesha's age visited us, and we were disturbed by the significant difference in the development of these two infants. A physician friend indicated that I ought to visit a pediatric neurologist. (Our own pediatrician responded to my query of why Sesha, at four months, was still not picking up her head, by saying that she must have a heavier head than the average baby and that such a trait is generally inherited from one of the parents. He advised me to go home and measure my husband's head to see if he, too, had a large head. Like fools, my husband and I pulled out the tape measure and determined that, yes, my husband's head was somewhat large. What cowardice propelled this pediatrician to evade his responsibility to be forthright and refer us to a specialist?!) The neurologist we visited must have known then that Sesha was severely impaired, but he was breaking the news to us gradually—over a period that lasted nearly two years. In contrast to my pediatrician, this physician was being kind, not evasive. He did not try to falsely reassure us. His efforts to gently ease us into the realization of the extensive damage Sesha had sustained was nonetheless thwarted when, on his recommendation, we visited the star pediatric neurologist on the West Coast while on holiday.

Sesha was six months old, still as lovely and sweet and pliant as one might wish any baby to be. The handsome, well-tanned doctor examined our daughter briefly, and told us without any hesitation that she was and would always be profoundly retarded—at best severely and not profoundly retarded. His credentials as a physician who can correctly predict an outcome remains secure, but his understanding of how to approach parents with such harsh news, also an important skill for a physician, is quite another matter. The swell that had been threatening to engulf us for two months now crested, and we were smashed onto a rocky shore with all the force that nature could muster against us. Never will I forget how ill I was in that San Francisco hotel room—how my body convulsed against this indigestible morsel. My husband had to care for Sesha and me, even as he ached. This brutal, insensitive manner in confronting parents with such devastating news is one that I have heard recounted again and again. The stories differ. The pain of the prognosis is matched only by the anger at obtuse and insensitive doctors. In our own case, we had a near repeat performance when, just to be certain of his suspicions, our first and humane physician wanted still one more consultation. We thought that we had now visited the Inferno, and we were prepared to begin the arduous climb back up—to find some equilibrium, some way to live with this verdict. But on our encounter with the third pediatric neurologist we were again told outright—after a five-minute exam—that our daughter was severely to profoundly retarded and that we should consider having other children because "one rotten apple doesn't spoil the barrel." As I type these words nearly twenty-seven years later, I still wonder at the utter failure of human empathy in a physician—one whose specialty, no less, is neurological impairment.

Sesha would never live a normal life. It would be another year before we completed the tests, the evaluations, the questionings that confirmed those first predictions. We couldn't know or fully accept the extent of her impairment, but some things were clear. We knew it wasn't a degenerative disability and for that, we were grateful. But the worst fear was that her handicap involved her intellectual faculties. We, her parents, were intellectuals. I was committed to a life of the mind. Nothing mattered to me as much as to be able to reason, to reflect, to understand. This was the air I breathed. How was I to raise a daughter that would have no part of this? If my life took its meaning from thought, what kind of meaning would her life have? Yet throughout this time, it never even occurred to me to give Sesha up, to institutionalize her, to think of her in any other terms than my own beloved child. She was my daughter. I was her mother. That was fundamental. Her impairment in no way mitigated my love for her. If it had any impact on that love it was only to intensify it. She was so vulnerable. She would need so much protection and love from us to shelter her from the scorn of the world, from its dangers, from its indifference, from its failure to understand her and her humanity. We didn't yet realize how much she would teach us, but we already knew that we had learned something. That which we believed we valued, what we—I—thought was at the center of humanity, the capacity for thought, for reason, was not it, not it at all.

Portrait of Sesha at Twenty-Seven

> Ian's sense of humor is part of what makes him Ian, not part of what makes him retarded, even though his cognitive limitations have helped to shape that humor. [This] goes beyond a tolerance of difference ... to an appreciation of a child's individuality (Ferguson and Asch 1989, 112).

I am awakening and her babbling-brook giggles penetrate my semi-conscious state. Hands clapping. Sesha is listening to "The Sound of Music." Peggy, her caregiver of twenty-three years, has just walked in and Sesha can hardly contain her desire to throw her arms around Peggy and give Peggy her distinctive kiss—mouth open, top teeth lightly (and sometimes not so lightly) pressing on your cheek, her breath full of excitement and happiness, her arms around your neck (if you're lucky; if not, arms up, hands on hair, which caveman-like, she uses to pull your face to her mouth). Sesha's kisses are legendary (and if you're not on your toes, somewhat painful).

Sesha was almost twelve before she learned to kiss or to hug. These were major achievements. Sesha is now a young woman in chronological age. She has the physical aspect of a young teen. She's tall, slender, long-legged, with dark beautiful brown eyes, brown short wavy luxuriant hair, a shy smile, which she delivers with a lowered head, and a radiant laugh that will make her throw her head back in delight. Sesha has been beautiful from the day of her birth, through all her girlhood and now into her young adulthood. Her loveliness shines through a somewhat twisted body, the bridge that substitutes for her natural front teeth (lost in a fall at school), and her profound cognitive deficits. The first thing people remark when they meet Sesha, or see her photo, is how beautiful she is. I've always admired (without worshipping) physical beauty and so I delight in Sesha's loveliness. The smoothness of her skin, the brilliant light in her eyes, the softness of her breath, the tenderness of her spirit. Her spirit.

No, Sesha's loveliness is not skin deep. How to speak of it? How to describe it? Joy. The capacity for joy. The babbling-brook laughter at a musical joke. The starry-eyed far away look as she listens to Elvis crooning "Love Me Tender," the excitement of her entire soul as the voices blare out "Alle Menschen werden Brüder" in the choral ode of Beethoven's Ninth Symphony, and the pleasure of bestowing her kisses and receiving the caresses in turn. All variations and gradations of joy. Spinoza characterized joy as the increase in our power of self-preservation and by that standard, Sesha's is a very well-preserved self. Yet she is so limited. She cannot speak. She cannot even say "Mama"—though sometimes we think she says "Aylu" (our translation, "I love you"). She can only finger feed herself, despite the many efforts at teaching her to use utensils. She'll sometimes drink from a cup (and sometimes spill it all). She is "time trained" at toileting, which means that she is still in diapers. Although she began to walk at five, she no longer can walk independently—her scoliosis and seizures and we do not know what else have robbed her of this capacity—and is in a wheelchair. Her cerebral palsy is not severe, but it is there.

She has no measurable I.Q. As she was growing up she was called "developmentally delayed." But delay implies that she will one day develop the capacities that are slow in developing. The jury is no longer out. Most capacities she will not develop at all. Is she then a "vegetable?" The term is ludicrous when applied to Sesha because there is nothing vegetative about her. She is fully a human, not a vegetable. Given the scope and breadth of human possibilities and capacities, she occupies a limited spectrum, but she inhabits it fully because she has the most important faculties of all. The capacities for love and for happiness. These allow those of us who care for her, who love her, who have been entrusted with her well-being to form deep and abiding attachments to her. Sesha's coin and currency is love. That is what she wishes to receive and that is what she reciprocates in spades.

On the Very Possibility of Mothering and the Challenge of the Severely Disabled Child

My mother would help in the early days and months of Sesha's life. My mother is a warm affectionate woman. She miraculously survived the Holocaust, and survived it emotionally intact. She loves children and especially loves babies. As an only child, I alone could provide her with grandchildren, and Sesha was the first and only grandchild on both sides of the family. All the grandparents were thrilled with Sesha's birth, and deeply saddened at the news that there were suspicions of retardation. We thought that we would slowly introduce them to the idea that the prognosis was as dire as we knew it to be. In the meanwhile, my mother would baby sit Sesha when both Jeffrey and I were busy and would take her for the night when I had a paper to write for graduate school. We never brought the grandparents to the doctor's visits, hoping to spare them some of the pain we experienced at each visit, but once it could not be helped. It was on that fateful visit that my mother grasped the full extent of the trauma to Sesha's brain. (There is still no etiology of her impairments—the cyanotic incident may have been a cause or an effect of some other injury or underlying congenital problem.) Upon our return, my mother, in her inimitable and insistent fashion, urged me to place Sesha in an institution.

Of all the traumatic encounters in that first year and a half of Sesha's life, none, perhaps not even the realization that Sesha was retarded, was as painful as these words from the woman that I loved most in my life: The woman who had taught me what it was to be a mother, to love a child, to anticipate the joys of nursing, of holding and caring for another, of sacrificing for a child. My model of maternal love asking me to discard my child? Would she have banished me to an institution had I been "damaged?" Surely, she couldn't mean this. But, no, she *insisted*, with conviction, with surefooted rightness that I *had to* put this child out of my life. It made me crazy. I couldn't comprehend it. Only the images and stories of the Holocaust could reclaim for me my mother and her love. Only the knowledge that in those bitter times, a limp was a death warrant (to merely be associated with disability was a death warrant), could redeem my mother at this time in my life. Of course she was acting like a mother, as someone whose interest was my well-being. I see now that she thought this child would ruin my life, but she was unable to transcend her own maternity and project that quality onto me: To realize that the maternal love and concern she had for me, I had for Sesha. I remained in her eyes a child, a daughter and not a mother with her own daughter. She who had taught me that "she, too, was a mother's child" could not see that her child was also a mother. This was her failure to engage in analogical thinking.

But my fury and disappointment in her was also my own inability to understand her feelings using the analogy of my commitment to my child. Now I think back and wonder how much of my mother's response was attributable to fear of the unknown (and what was known but in different circumstances), how much was the result of the stigma attached to disability, and how much was resistance to the reality of my maternity? In time, my mother came to understand that we could build a good life with Sesha. She allowed herself to love Sesha with the fullness of a grandmother's love. And in time, I forgave my mother and came to appreciate how her intense, if misdirected, love for me fueled her stubborn insistence that we "put Sesha away."

This was 1970, and parents did institutionalize retarded children. And this all happened before the horrors of the New York State residential facility Willowbrook were exposed, although there had been exposés, if not as sensational and gripping as Willowbrook, still chilling enough to give anyone pause before committing their child to an institution. I cannot say what I might have thought if we did not have, as we did (through the good fortunes of family) ample resources to care for Sesha. The image I had of public institutions was that they were merely dumping grounds. No one whose material resources gave them a choice would opt for such putative "care." Private institutions were perhaps less dismal, but nonetheless sad affairs for families who for a variety of reasons, some financial, some psychological and emotional, could not see themselves facing the challenge of raising a mentally retarded child at home. But nowhere in my heart and mind did I find room for that alternative, and in this my husband and I were in complete accord.

It was simply impossible for me to part with my child. This is what I knew of mothering, mothering, at least, that is chosen. A child is born to you. This child is your charge—it is your sacred responsibility to love, nurture, and care for this child throughout your life. Is this "maternal instinct?" I don't know what those words mean. Do all women who become mothers believe thus? Clearly not. Is it then a cultural construct? If so, it is a belief constructed in many cultures, in many historical periods. Perhaps this commitment is rather the condition for the possibility of motherhood—realized differently in different cultures, under different conditions, and differently realized even by women within a single culture, or a single historical period. It may not be inspired by birth, but by adoption, but once a child is "your" child, at that moment you become its mother and the duty emerging from that bond is one of the most compelling of all duties. At that point you commit yourself to the well-being of one who is dependent upon you, whose survival, growth and development as a social being[237] is principally (if never solely) your responsibility.

The birth of a child with very significant impairments may test the limit of the commitment that I take to be the very condition for the possibility of mothering.[238] It may do so for some women, under some—adverse—circumstances. In my own understanding this felt conviction is so fundamental that it serves as a benchmark. The extent to which a woman cannot realize it (in the idiom appropriate to her own culture) because of adverse social, political or economic conditions, to that extent she faces an injustice. I take it then that the requirement to be able to mother, that is, to realize the condition for the possibility to mother, constitutes one of the "circumstances of justice."[239] So many women worldwide face daunting obstacles in choosing to mother a significantly impaired child. I would not judge another woman who makes a choice not to mother a disabled child. I had the moral luck to make a lucid moral choice. It was to abide by what was both a principled and a heartfelt conviction that I and her father would not leave her fate to a hoped-for kindness of strangers.

Mothering Distributed: The Work of Dependency Care

> Mothers perceive the mentally retarded child as more of a hardship in direct proportion to the child's incapacitation and helplessness (Wikler 1986, 184).

Sesha's expansive, affectionate nature is a gift. In comparison studies with autistic children, researchers have found that "the mother's ability and enthusiasm for functioning in the maternal caregiver role are adversely affected by the developmentally disabled child who is *not* affectionate and *not* demonstrative" (Wikler 1986, 184, author's emphasis). But researchers have also found (to no one's surprise I hope) that the greater the degree of "incapacitation and helplessness," the greater the burden the child poses. Taking care of Sesha, meeting her daily needs, her medical needs, interpreting her needs and desires, not over the span of twenty-seven months, but twenty-seven years, has posed a substantial challenge.

I never wanted to hire help to care for my child. I believed that with shared parenting it should be possible to care for a child and still pursue an additional life's work. I soon found that I was wrong. All families where each parent takes on work additional to childcare and domestic duties require help with childcare. The scandal of an affluent nation such as the U.S. is that such help is not provided for, and the scandal of American feminism is that for all its efforts in advancing the cause of women, and in spite of the precipitous rise in the number of women in the labor force, it has not fought sufficiently long and hard for this most basic of women's rights.

Had Sesha been the normal toddler, I would have tried to hunt out the few daycare programs that were being established in the 1970s to meet the new demand of women like me who, while not driven by economic necessity, were nonetheless committed to *both* motherhood and some other life's work. But Sesha could not play in the easy way other young children could play. She needed intense stimulation. She mouthed (and continues to mouth) everything. Her attention faded quickly; if left to her own devices, she'd simply stare off in space. Keeping Sesha stimulated was, and remains, hard work.

For a while Sesha was enrolled in one of the pilot projects in early intervention for the developmentally delayed. She made wonderful progress in the first five months of the program. But Sesha's story, unlike so many I have read about[240] was not one of continuing development. After several years in that same program the improvements became more and more minimal. The notion of mainstreaming was taking hold at this time for many disabled children, but it seemed too far from Sesha's condition and Sesha's needs.

While needing childcare was something I shared with other mothers, my daughter's profound disability was the reason I was dependent on house-bound help. Finding good care would be a challenge. Certainly someone could give Sesha perfunctory custodial "care," that is, attend to her bodily needs but without ever seeing the person whose body it is, without tapping into her desires, without engaging her potential, without responding to and returning her affection—her affection which is her most effective means of connecting with others, in the absence of speech and most other capacities required for interpersonal activities.

Some wonderful and some less than wonderful help supplemented our own caring for Sesha. From one young woman, I learned that to enter a child's world, especially one as attenuated as Sesha's, required a talent as precious as an artist's. Childcare work has been viewed as one of the least skillful occupations, second only to janitorial work.[241] To see an exceptional childcare worker engage a child dispels, in an instant, such devaluation of this oldest and most universal of women's work. But to commit to care for Sesha required an ability to give your heart to a child, who, because she would never outgrow the need for your continual care, would not release you from an abiding bond and obligation. While we found a number of talented caregivers, few were willing to yield to the demands of caring for Sesha for an extended time. When done well, caring for Sesha is intensive labor and the relationship enabling such care must also already be intensive.

In the literature on the care of the disabled child, little attention is given to the team of persons doing the hands-on care, those whom I have called "dependency workers," those who attend to the very basic needs of a dependent (needs the dependent is incapable of fulfilling on her own behalf). Perhaps so little is written about dependency workers who are not mothers because, disproportionately, mothers do nearly all the dependency work for their disabled children. Or perhaps writers concerned with the disabled and even with the families of the disabled still are oblivious to the central role of dependency work in the lives of those with disabilities and their families. Even in the saga of disability, the dependency worker remains the invisible stagehand.[242] It is my hope this set of reflections will encourage more discussion about the relation between dependency work and mothering a disabled child; between dependency work and disability; between the dependency worker and the disabled person.

She Came to Stay

As the commitment to egalitarian parenting gave way to professional time demands, my spouse and I moved to a model which, for want of any other adequate term, I'll call "distributed mothering."[243] I am Sesha's one mother. In truth, however, her mothering has been distributed across a number of individuals: her father, various caregivers, and Peggy.

Sesha was four when a woman walked into our lives who came and stayed. How and where we acquired the instincts I don't know, but we knew immediately that Peggy was right. She was scarcely interested in us. Her interview was with Sesha. But she wouldn't take the job. Peggy feared the intensity of the involvement she knew was inevitable. We pleaded and increased the salary. She told me later she would never have taken the job if the agency hadn't urged her to do a trial week. At the end of the week, it was already too late to quit. Sesha had worked her way into Peggy's heart. Twenty-three years later, Peggy told me the following story:

> I had been with Sesha in Central Park and I was working on some walking exercises that the folks at Rusk [Rusk Institute at New York University Medical Center, Sesha's early intervention program] had assigned. I was working terribly hard trying to get Sesha to cooperate and do what I was supposed to get her to do. I sat her down in her stroller and sat down on a park bench. I realized that I was simply exhausted from the effort. I thought, how am I going to do this? How can I possibly do this job, when I looked down at Sesha and saw her little head pushed back against her stroller moving first to one side and then to another. I couldn't figure out what she was doing. Until I traced what her eyes were fixed on. She had spotted a leave falling, and she was following its descent. I said "Thank you for being my teacher, Sesha. I see now. Not my way. Your way. Slowly" After that, I fully gave myself over to Sesha. That forged the bond.

Writing about the relationship between care as labor and care as relationship, Sara Ruddick remarks: "The work [of caring] is constituted in and through the relation of those who give and receive care" (Ruddick forthcoming). Nowhere is this better illustrated than in this story. And nowhere is the notion that the work of mothering and caring requires thought, understanding—again in Ruddick's words, "maternal thinking"—than in this story. Forging the relationship, through this insight into who Sesha is and how she sees the world, made possible the caring labor itself. This caring labor so infused with the relationship, has enhanced the relationship and has made it as solid as the bonds of motherhood.

As I write this essay, a much older Peggy still cares for a much older Sesha in many of the same ways. But as Peggy and Sesha age, we reach the limits of the laboring aspect of caring. The relationship has come to be "in 'excess' of the labor [it] enable[s]" (Ruddick, forthcoming). This is a difficult and troubling state of affairs—for us as parents, for Peggy, and, if Sesha understands it, for her. Sesha's possible future without Peggy troubles me profoundly—not simply because we have come to so rely on her, but because I cannot bear the thought that such a central relationship in Sesha's life could be sundered.

What is this relationship? "A relationship with no name" as my son so aptly said once. Why has no one spoken of such a relationship? Could our family be so privileged as to be unique? Privileged first in having the resources? Privileged above all in having found such a steadfast companion and caregiver for our daughter? What has this daughter and this relationship taught me about mothering? Can anything be generalized and learned from such a perspective of privilege, on the one hand, and anomaly, on the other? For I have come to understand, especially from the exposure to the literature on disability, how extreme my daughter's condition is, how profound is her retardation and her limitations. To us, she is simply Sesha, that unique individual whom we call our daughter.

In time, neither Peggy nor Sesha's father or mother have sufficed for the total care she requires, and we have had to call in others—part-time and mostly weekend help—most of whom have stayed with Sesha for years, until their lives called them to move on. With Sesha it takes more than a village. As Sesha has grown older, we have felt the need for more and more help so that we could pursue our roles as professionals and as parents of our son and as folks entitled to some leisure. We need such gratification and fulfillment not only for their own sake but so that we can love Sesha without resentment that her overwhelming needs rob us of the satisfactions we might otherwise enjoy. "Like other parents in a society" writes Darling (1988, 144),

> parents of children with disabilities hope to maintain a "normal" lifestyle (Birenbaum 1970, 1971). They believe, at least initially, that their children will enjoy the same access to medical care and educational opportunities as children without disabilities. They expect to continue pursuing their careers, participating in recreational and social activities with family and friends, and having as much financial security as others in their social class. When these expectations are not met, parents are likely to feel cheated.

There is something very profound in this expectation because it is part of the expectation of becoming a parent. That expectation does not alter with the birth of a child with disabilities. It is perhaps a fear that this expectation cannot be met when a child is severely disabled that will influence some parents to institutionalize a child and will influence potential parents to choose to receive prenatal testing and abort if the results indicate a significant impairment.

The move to distributed mothering, in the absence of socially provided means of caring for Sesha, has served to inoculate us from the sense of being cheated, and so also has inoculated Sesha against resentment or bitterness that we could not lead lives approximating the lives of those with only "normal" children. Of course, there have been compromises and sacrifices. There are limitations placed on our mobility and the considerable financial cost of Sesha's care. When Sesha is ill (her disabilities make her medically vulnerable) our lives stop. Distributing the mothering no doubt eases the burden. But distributed mothering itself has costs that go far beyond any material ones which I gladly, and with gratitude, pay. To *share* in the intimacy of caring for a profoundly needy child is to engage in an intricate and delicate dance—fraught with stubbed toes and broken hearts, but also yielding its own joys and rewards.

Peggy and I

Peggy and I are like two metals of not very dissimilar composition, each tempered under very different circumstances. Ten years and one month my senior, Peggy was born before the war and lived her youth in wartorn Ireland and Britain. I was born after the war, and grew to maturity in the booming economies of Sweden and the U.S. Both of us are immigrants—she traveled here willingly as a young woman accompanied only by her sister; I came as a reluctant young girl brought by my parents. Peggy was one of thirteen children raised lovingly, but in poverty, in wartime with her father off to battle. I was an only child, the precious projection of hope by two survivors of Hitler's murderous rage against the Jews. She was raised to be fiercely independent; I was overprotected. She was raised to be self-reliant and hardy; I was looked over as a fragile flower. She had to make her own way early, I never *had* to make my own way at all. Peggy and I are not easily compatible. She is always punctual and I am always late. She is a doer while I am a thinker. She insists on routine and I'm incapable of following routine. We come together on politics, on compassion, on a love of books, and most important of all on our passion for Sesha.

Peggy and I respect each other. There may even be love there, but we never speak of it. The worst times are when Sesha gets ill. Sesha's disabilities are multiple, which means her illnesses easily compound. An elevated temperature, a small infection, a bit of nausea will lower her threshold for seizures. When the seizures start up, she becomes sleep deprived and that aggravates her condition. Things can snowball quickly. When Sesha is ill, we don't know what bothers her, what hurts her, what the pain feels like. We are deprived of a vital avenue for diagnosis. This makes her so vulnerable, and makes us crazy. Peggy in her frustration vents her fear and anger on me. I feel guilty: I am not doing enough; why do I not care for her myself? But I also question why I have to cope with Peggy's anger. How long can I continue to live with this tension? This anger? This pain? Can we continue to care for Sesha in our home? What happens when Peggy leaves? Is Sesha's illness life-threatening? What happens when we die?

The threat that Sesha might die, the expectation that we will die— these are always the terminal points for all our questionings concerning Sesha. What is Peggy's terminus? "What happens when I am not here?

Why do I stay? Sesha is not my daughter, I am not her mother. If I don't care for Sesha, will she die?" Peggy has often said to me, "You can get away from concerns about Sesha with your work. But Sesha *is* my work." Peggy can think of leaving. I cannot. But really, can Peggy?

Sometimes I feel that my relationship to Peggy vis-à-vis Sesha is like the patriarchal relation of husband to wife vis-à-vis their children. Peggy accompanies me to doctors' visits with Sesha. Actually it seems more as if it is I who accompany her and Sesha. I deal with the authorities (much as the father does), she undresses Sesha (much as the mother does), although since it is distasteful to me to stand idly by, I "help" (much as an involved father might). I pay the bills, Peggy wheels Sesha out. Some roles we can reverse, others we can't—they are set in the larger practices in which we participate. Each time I see the analogies, it makes my feminist and egalitarian flesh creep. And yet, I can't see my way out of this. I cannot function without this privilege, and yet I despise it. I cannot see how to live my convictions. Of course, even this dilemma is a great luxury. So many other mothers with children like Sesha have to make much more difficult choices.

My choices and my dilemmas are shaped by my personal circumstances and ambitions as they can be realized within the constraints of the social world I inhabit. Distributed mothering as I live it is a privatized model. Many of its discomforts and difficulties are, I believe, attributable to lack of social services, services provided in other nations more attuned to dependency concerns. While the disability community in the U.S. has significantly improved the lives of disabled citizens in the years since Sesha's birth—the same years that have marked the emergence of this movement for the rights of the disabled—the United States remains shamefully behind other, less wealthy industrialized nations in providing a good system of services for the disabled and their families. In a nation with a better social welfare system, would I find myself in this same bind? I believe the answer is no, but I can't honestly say. What I do know is that were services freely and widely available, more mothers would be able to share the dependency responsibilities, not only with a spouse, but with caring others. There would be more places to turn to for help, for relief, and also for sharing the joys of loving a person as special as Sesha.[244]

Alternative Routes—Routes Not Taken

I have been a civil rights activist, an antiwar activist, a feminist activist, and most recently a welfare rights activist. I never joined with other parents of disabled children. Why this abstinence at a time when the disability community was mobilized, when all the rules were changing, when new vistas opened for the disabled? Why did I not see this and the parent's advocacy movement as my movement? I believe that I needed to see Sesha as exceptional, not a member of a stigmatized group. Perhaps it was a form of denial: "Denial is a complex phenomenon that ranges from denying the existence of the handicap altogether to minimizing its severity" (Lipsky 1989, 160). That was part of it, but not all of it.

Due to our material resources and our self-fashioned "coping," combined with my professional ambitions and the degree of Sesha's impairment, the issues other parents were dealing with seemed so different than our own—and it was difficult enough to establish a modus vivendi with our own issues. To some degree we may have been too successful in finding and establishing a good life with our daughter (and in time with her younger brother), to engage in advocacy or activism. Speaking of the turn to activism among parents of disabled children, Darling writes: "When parents continue to encounter needs that cannot be met by existing societal resources, they may embark on a prolonged career of seekership. The goal of seekership is *normalization*, or the establishment of a lifestyle that approximates that of families with only nondisabled children. Seekership results in advocacy and activism when certain situational contingencies or *turning points* occur" (Darling 1988, 150). Such activism, Darling calls entrepreneurship. One has to be socialized into the role of entrepreneur. The entrepreneur works to create the conditions that will answer to their and their children's needs. Darling continues, "For most parents, active entrepreneurship ends after they reach what they consider to be normalization," while for some it continues to "crusadership." These are the parents who continue to work for disabled children and adults even when the needs of their own children are met.[245]

Our journey with Sesha continues. As she reaches her adulthood, a turning point faces us and we may well begin a new seekership, maybe an entrepreneurship to meet new needs, for her and for ourselves. That chapter of our lives together is just commencing. The role of the dependency worker is sometimes to fight for the resources that make dependency work possible—turning the concern for one's own charge to the concern for some other mother's child. And in so doing, creating more equitable conditions in which dependency work is done, by oneself and by others, for one's own charges and for those of others. Facing the less-than-fully-courageous attitudes and the fears that have directed our retreat from advocacy may well alter our path, and thereby shape this next phase of mothering a profoundly disabled child.

7

Maternal Thinking with a Difference

In Chapter Six, I presented a personal narrative focussed on my child and her caregivers. This was the best way I knew to provide my reader with a dimension of living with a person as dependent as my daughter. In this chapter, I wish to expand the vista and think more generally about what it means to mother a severely disabled child, all the while continuing to use my own experiences with my daughter as a source of reflection and as a tether that prevents me from wandering away from the lived reality. What do these experiences of disability and difference tell us about dependency and dependency work? What do they tell us about the particular form of dependency work called mothering? Can looking at the anomalous situation of mothering a severely disabled child help us in reflecting on what is required for a society to be just to all its members and make way for a true equality?

In the literature by and about parents of disabled children, the theme of difference and sameness is persistent. (In this book, *sameness* resonates in the epigraph that introduces the personal narrative of the previous chapter; *difference* occupies the title of that same chapter.) The tension emerges in opposing claims: Parents of disabled children cope as well as parents of normal children; parents of disabled children experience more stress than parents of normal children. There is a sense in which both statements are true. Most mothers and many fathers find the strength to cope with the special burdens of a disabled child—and doubtless more would do so and many would do so better if better resources were available. But read even the cheeriest account, and you will find the enormous cost and pain involved in coming to the point of coping. Nonetheless, every day with even a profoundly disabled child is not a trial, nor does it require virtual sainthood to be a more than adequate parent to such a child.

What I have learned from the experience of mothering Sesha, and what the many accounts of parenting such a child reveal, is that the differences we encounter redefine sameness. Raising a child with a severe disability is not just like parenting a normal child—but more so. It is often very different. Yet in that difference, we come to see features of raising any child that otherwise escape attention or that assume a new valence. One notices aspects of maternal practice that are not highlighted when we begin our theorizing from the perspective of the mother of the normal child.

Considering maternal practice as exercised when children are intact, Ruddick has identified three requirements of maternal work: preserving the life of a child, socializing her for acceptance, and fostering her development. In many important regards these requirements hold for the case of mothering the child with a disability. Nevertheless, the scope and meaning of these practices are altered. In the remainder of this essay, I want to consider how starting reflections about mothering and dependency care with the mothering of a child with severe disabilities reorients our thinking about the meaning of maternal and caring practices in our social life.

Preservative Love

Preservative love seems to be the most fundamental of all maternal requirements. Disability, however, especially if it is severe and manifests itself early, is too often the occasion for *denying* a child preservative love. This is especially so where resources are too meager to keep even a well child functioning.

Nonetheless, where the conditions for maternal care are in place, where the commitment to the child has been made, preservative love comes to occupy an often overridingly central place in one's maternal practice. Whether I am engaged in Sesha's care firsthand or at a distance (when I turn her care over to another), preservative love is foremost. For Sesha, safety and attention to medical needs are the first commandments of her care. Attention to them by her caregivers is paramount. Her fragility elevates this feature of maternal practice and sometimes threatens to overshadow all other aspects of maternal thinking with respect to her. An excerpt from my diary recording my participation in a Hastings Center Project[246] perhaps says it best:

> Reflecting now on one participant's [at the Hastings Center] memory of when her pediatrician told her that he didn't know if her underweight baby would be all right, and her recalling this as the

most terrible moment in her life, I thought what I would answer if someone had asked me if the moment I learned that Sesha was retarded was the most terrible moment in my life. I would have answered, "No." The most terrible moment in my life was when I thought Sesha would die.

The incident I had in mind was one of Sesha's mysterious illnesses. Preservative love propels parent and child into a medicalized world. Corrective procedures for the disability will often involve surgical fixes and even routine illness can go wrong all too easily. Dealings with medical authorities are among the most frequent complaints one hears when listening to mothers of disabled children.[247] One researcher cites a pediatrician saying, "I don't enjoy it. . . . I don't really enjoy a really handicapped child who comes in drooling, can't walk and so forth. . . . Medicine is geared to the perfect human body. Something you can't do anything about challenges the doctor and reminds him of his own inabilities" (Darling 1988, 149; 1979, 152). In the same study, Darling speaks of the mother of a child with cerebral palsy who says, "[Our pediatrician] didn't take my complaints seriously. . . . I feel that Brian's sore throat is just as important as [my normal daughter's] sore throat" (Darling 1988, 149; 1979, 152).[248]

In my own dealings with physicians, it never occurred to me that any physician wouldn't take my daughter's ailments as seriously as those of a normal child. On the contrary, I have always assumed that a disability gives her a priority because of her fragility and vulnerability. Perhaps this assumption has served to shield me from the thought that a physician might value her life and well-being less, although I have had enough negative experiences with the medical profession to alert me otherwise.

The physician who remarked that he didn't "really enjoy a really handicapped child who comes in drooling" still has to understand that regardless of the level of impairment, this child, as every other child, is "some mother's child." It is by virtue of the toil and love of some mothering person(s) that this child stands before him. If the physician or other professional is so limited that he cannot see beyond the disabling trait, might he be open to the child's humanity and need through the loving care lavished on this child?[249]

In the struggle to watch over Sesha, to preserve her, to avoid the catastrophe of her death, it is not just the hard wall of medicine I encounter, but her protracted dependency. Preservative love, when directed at the "normally" functioning child, has its most intense period in the early years of the child's life. The individual with severe disabilities does not outgrow a profound vulnerability, nor can she assume the task of her own self-preservation. The effort of preserving a severely disabled child's life is often accompanied by a *lifelong* commitment to day-to-day *physical* care for the child. For in the case of a severely disabled child, the dependency is protracted over the course of a lifetime, violating what Featherstone characterizes as a "a natural order."

> When parents are young and healthy and energetic, children require vast amounts of exhausting physical care. As both grow older, this demand tapers off, and eventually the children grow independent. . . . A severe disability disrupts this natural order, extending a child's dependence beyond a parent's strength, health, even lifetime (Featherstone 1980, 19).

Sesha's extended dependency has given me a certain vantage point from which to consider how a social organization responds to certain exigencies of human life. Because our own childhood, and even the childhood of our children, is so fleeting—it goes so quickly, even as it is so absorbing at the moment—a sort of amnesia sets in. Consequently, in writing of social organizations, and matters of justice and equality, we too easily think of the child as the future independent being. Because care for Sesha means confronting her irrefutable, inescapable daily and sustained dependency, my own understanding of what social organization and the place of maternal practice in that social organization entails is otherwise oriented. More than any abstract theorizing could, it has made me see that we cannot understand the demands of social organization if we cannot take the fact of dependency as one of the circumstances of justice.

Socialization for Acceptance

Raising children includes more than caring for and protecting them.[250] It means preparing them for a world larger than the family. Mothers who are wary of the social institutions and practices of the society in which they live, and who understand the oppressive nature of these institutions, are reluctant to socialize their children to be acceptable in situations that they themselves view as unacceptable. Yet the most rebellious mother understands that each human is a social being and that some degree of social acceptance is crucial to their own child's well-being.

The task of socializing the child with disabilities also calls upon a notion of "acceptance." But acceptance is now understood against the background of "normalization." Those who are "different" or those who have, to use Featherstone's term, a "difference in the family" very much want acceptance: acceptance of who they are, if they are disabled;

acceptance of the child that they love and the family they have created, if they are parents. *Normalization* is often an avenue to acceptance, but by virtue of the disability, it cannot be the exclusive avenue.

Socializing a disabled child for acceptance may, for instance, encourage a mother to have the child present herself in such a way that the disability is less noticeable—or that the "normal" characteristics of the child are underscored. I often find myself far more concerned with the clothes Sesha wears than I would be with my able child and with making sure her clothes or wheelchair are not in any way soiled, that is, with being certain that Sesha presents a face to the world that is as attractive as possible. This is so that the first response to her is as positive as I can make it.

There is something very sad about this need—but I believe it is a realistic response to the repugnance (as harsh as that word is) of so many people toward disability. The sadness comes from the recognition of that repulsion, the need to do what I can to counteract it, and the knowledge that a pretty dress is such a superficial way to address the fear and ignorance that the response bespeaks. And yet I do it and feel I must do it, for Sesha, for myself, and for our whole family. I do it for Sesha, because I know that she understands when she is approached with a smile, with delight; that she is tickled when people make a fuss over how pretty she looks; that she feels pain at people's indifference to her. I do it for myself, because it is one thing I can do to integrate Sesha into the community of which she is a part, even if her interactions with it are minimal. Finally, I do it for my family because we all feel the pain of the stigma attached to disability. Dressing Sesha nicely, making sure that she goes into the world looking clean and fresh and well-cared for is my way and our family's way of telling the world that this person is loved and cared for, and hoping that the message that she is worth being cared for will be absorbed by others.[251]

That I discuss this feature of Sesha's care under the category of "socializing for acceptance" illustrates a particular feature of what socializing for acceptance means in the case of a child who is disabled. Where we cannot mold the child, we can work to shape attitudes and the environment in which she moves. Socializing for acceptance can mean altering what the child gets socialized into, and what will count as or form the grounds of acceptance.

Maybe there is a fundamental sense in which a mother cannot fully accept the disability of her child, even as she accepts the child. Conflating these two acceptances is all to easy. Adrienne Asch cites one disabled woman:

She [the author's mother] made numerous attempts over the years of my childhood to have me go for physical therapy and to practice walking more "normally" at home. I vehemently refused all her efforts. She could not understand why I would not walk straight. Now, I realize why. My disability, with my different walk and talk and my involuntary movements, have been with me all of my life, was part of me, part of my identity. With these disability features, I felt complete and whole. My mother's attempt to change my walk, strange as it may seem, felt like an assault on myself, an incomplete acceptance of all of me, an attempt to make me over (Rousso 1984, 9; cited in Ferguson and Asch 1989, 117).

Acceptance looms large in the life of each child, but so much more so in the life of the disabled child. In the effort to socialize for acceptance, the messages sent to the disabled child, to oneself, and to siblings[252] are hard to decode. Asch, who is blind, asks, "At what point is it all right, even essential to cease working on eliminating those differences disability can cause in appearance and behavior?" (Ferguson and Asch 1989, 117). She goes on to speak of her own experience:

My parents confronted the same dilemma and responded differently at different times. Repeatedly, but usually with patience and tact, my father pointed out that sitting with my head down and putting my finger in my eyes jarred people and interfered with their getting to know me. Generally he managed to explain without my feeling ashamed or humiliated. As a result, by the age of ten or so, I had learned to sit up straight and now, in fact, must work to slouch in informal gatherings when my friends are disconcerted by my too straight back and shoulders. Eating skills were different. Something about teaching me to use a knife and fork properly and keep my fingers from touching my food frustrated my parents and made them impatient. They gave in, ensuring family peace and my self-consciousness at formal meals to this day. Yet, since they could not be patient they were wise to let it go. I did things differently, yes, but not grossly so, and there was no point in trying to get me to do everything in life as a person with sight would do it (Ferguson and Asch 1989, 117-8).

Contained in what I have said about socialization for acceptance are really two related but distinct notions. There is the "acceptance" which grants the difference, which demands acceptance *of the difference* and *in the face* of the difference. The other is the notion of normalization which, looked at most positively, is the desire to normalize the situation at hand—whatever the situation may be—and, less positively perhaps, the desire for acceptance *despite* the difference. Helen Featherstone cites an instance that brings to the fore the way in which the family normalizes the disabled child, and the outer edge of consciousness that is always alert to the stigma and the non-normality of the situation. She writes of her response to the experience of starting her son Jody, a profoundly retarded boy with cerebral palsy and partial blindness, in a new school:

> On the first day I took him myself, intending to spend the morning. As soon as he was comfortably settled in the classroom, I withdrew to the observation booth. The program pleased me, but after a few moments I realized that I felt depressed . . . [what I saw] evoked a memory. A year earlier I had interviewed a teenage babysitter. Caitlin and I liked him immediately, and his enthusiasm seemed to equal ours—until he met Jody. At that moment his jaw dropped; mumbling something about checking his afternoon schedule, he hastened out the door. Disappointment and chagrin washed over me. I hated to lose this bright, lively babysitter. But even worse, I suddenly found myself looking at Jody through adolescent eyes. I saw not the cheerful, handsome seven-year-old whom I care for every day, but a seriously deviant little boy who drools and makes strange, uninterpretable noises. The forgotten terrors of Jody's babyhood surfaced. I saw my son as I might have seen another seriously handicapped child seven years before. I realized that not everyone has changed as I have, and that not everyone would find our family as attractive as I do. . . .
>
> Sitting in the observation booth at this new school, I felt something similar. This time I looked at my son as a new teacher might. I saw a little boy with severe cerebral palsy and no useful vision. . . .
>
> Familiarity and routine blunt our awareness of disability after a while. Without meaning to, a stranger can upset this internal balance (Featherstone 1980, 41).

I realized as I read that passage that this is why it is so difficult to take Sesha out in public. I don't want to upset that balance. I don't want to see Sesha as others see her. I want them to see her as I see her. The blunting of awareness of disability is part and parcel of a socialization that I, as a mother, have had to undergo—one that is a prerequisite to my socializing my child.

This socialization has two parts. First I refuse to see my child as not "normal"—for what she does is *normal for Sesha.* This is a redefining of normalcy that accepts Sesha in her individuality. Without such acceptance, I would not be able to present to the world a child *I* find acceptable. At the same time, I have to see the child as others see her so that I mediate between her and the others—to negotiate acceptability. The parental task involves then both socializing the child for the acceptance, such as it might be, of the world, and socializing the world, as best you can, so that it can accept your child. Yet a precondition for both requires socializing yourself for the acceptance of the child with her disability, and establishing a sense of normalcy, for yourself and for the face you present to the world.

Fostering Development

> I vividly recall a meeting to discuss my son's annual IEP[253] . . . for the coming school year. [W]e found ten professionals of various species arrayed around the table, each convinced that his or her information was the most essential to Ian's progress and his parent's edification (Ferguson and Asch 1989, 123).

Most "normal" children are remarkably adaptable and their development will take place in many different circumstances. The aim of maternal practice will be to provide, wherever possible, those conditions that are best suited to foster that development. For a child with disabilities, by contrast, development is never a given. It is not only fostering development, but *enabling development* that a mother of a disabled child puts her heart and mind to. Enabling the development of a disabled child involves (as Peggy's story in the previous chapter indicates) attuning oneself to the individual's unique tempo. And it requires parents to navigate complex straits.

First, finding appropriate facilities and teachers is integral to the task. This is at once an individual and a collective effort. If it were not for the activism of other parents, Sesha's schooling would not have been funded. Although Sesha was never a candidate for mainstreaming, the mainstreaming of less involved children means that Sesha receives a better reception in public. As other disabled children and adults move into their communities, they open vistas for all disabled persons, and facilitate enabling development for even the most profoundly impaired individual.

Second, parents of children with disabilities are dependent upon professional help available for their children—help that was hardly imaginable as little as twenty-five years ago. There are, on the one hand, the imposing (often impressive and sometimes worthless)[254] professional knowledges that are being applied to your child. On the other hand, there is one's deep and intimate knowledge of *this* child, a knowledge that is, however, curtailed by one's limitations in training and expertise. Philip Ferguson fantasizes coming to the next school meeting where a team of professionals sits prepared to discuss his severely retarded son's "individualized educational program" (IEP) with the young man in tow, along with his own numerous friends, his son's friends, etc., all armed with prepared statements they then shower on the assembled experts.

The difficulty of negotiating professional and personal knowledges is compounded by the different virtues that guide professional care and maternal care. As Darling remarks, "While professional responses to disabled children are generally characterized by affective neutrality, universalism, and functional specificity, parental responses are affective, particularistic, and functionally diffuse" (Darling 1983, 148).[255] These differences in virtues and perspectives, while marked by a professional or familial relation to the child, are also gendered, reflecting the nature of the often gendered interaction of the parent and professional. The (frequently) male professional, assuming the stance of impartiality and universalism is set against the (generally) female parent, affecting a particularistic concern with the welfare of this child.[256]

No doubt parents generally worry that a professional's "affective neutrality" too often translates as indifference to the particular needs of their particular child. But such "neutrality" can be especially difficult to tolerate when the needs are so urgent and when social stigma continues to attach itself to disability, perhaps most of all to cognitive deficits. Affective involvement may be too much to demand of professionals, and without a doubt, an involvement as intense as that of mothering persons should not be expected. Yet parents and professionals need a mutual respect and partnership in order to enable the disabled child to grow and flourish to whatever extent the physical impairment permits. And there is no question in the minds of the many mothers and fathers of disabled children that professionals of all sorts are inadequately trained in the affective requirements of meeting needs of those who are ill or disabled.

The rift between professionals and mothering persons is further aggravated by that aspect of professionalism that assigns the professional a task that is "functionally specific." This means that the professional "focuses exclusively on a part [of the child], indeed a disabled part" (Darling 1983, 148). To the parent, however, the child's roles as son or daughter, sibling, grandchild, student, playmate, or church member usually supersede his or her disability. This difference is perhaps the source of the greatest dissonance between the mothering person and the professional as they each attempt to ensure a child's thriving.

Professionals also sometimes expect parents to carry out often complex and time-consuming instructions that are unrealistic. Featherstone (1980, 57) quotes a professional who became a parent, "Before I had Peter I gave out programs that would have taken all day. I don't know when I expected mothers to change diapers, sort laundry, or buy groceries" (cited in Darling 1988, 149). Such heedlessness to the enormity of day to day demands inspires in turn parents' resentment toward professionals and guilt vis-à-vis themselves. Such guilt reinforces (especially within mothers) the sense that their role cuts them out for failure.

A failure in preservative love can result in death or injury. A failure in enabling and fostering development is less visible—but its threat is persistent. It is the continual concern: Am I doing the right thing? Am I pushing too hard? Not hard enough? Are there better, more appropriate programs? How do I balance her needs and those of my other child(ren)? How do I balance the demands and all the other aspects of my life, my life with my partner, my obligations to others? Some of these concerns are common to raising any child. But many of these concerns take on special poignancy when the very possibility of your child developing some fundamental skills to stay alive depend on your making the right decisions. The guilt that you may not be doing enough fuels resentment at those who should understand but never seem to understand well enough.

While such self-questioning can evoke a sense of maternal incompetence, the knowledge that you are providing for an especially vulnerable child, that you are providing as best as you can, also becomes a source of pride and accomplishment. But for that pride and sense of accomplishment to be realized, so many conditions need to be fulfilled—you need to know that what you are doing is in fact the best that can be done. This means you need access to knowledge, to financial, medical and educational resources, to making needed physical modifications in the environment, to technology when appropriate, and to financial security.[257] All these are far from realizable under the conditions in which most mothers of disabled children in the United States and in most the world find themselves. But at those moments, when I have been fortunate enough to have the best possible situation, I glean that profound satisfaction. It can vanish in an instance. It can vanish at the next IEP meeting with Sesha's "professional team."

As the disability community is anxious to remind us, handicapping conditions are not simply a product of the impairment itself but also of socially constructed environments and notions of ability. In reflecting on this point, I note an irony: It is a source of great inspiration and insight in the disability community that independent living, as well as inclusion within one's community, should be the goal of education and habilitation of the disabled. But this ideal can also be a source of great disempowerment if applied with too broad a brush. Even as the disability community, including parent advocates, work toward inclusion and the maximum attainable independence, some of their efforts get congealed in concepts and behaviors that have less desirable consequences. Chief among these are the notion that with concentrated parental effort, the child will improve; that providing teams of professionals will "fix" things; that an appreciable degree of independence is the end result of all the appropriate efforts.

Independence, acceptance, and normalcy are generally the goals of parents of disabled children—not very different from the goals of most parents raising most children. But for parents with a severely or profoundly retarded child, development may no longer have as a goal independent living: lifelong dependence may be clearly an inevitability. So it is in Sesha's case. As we try to feed her soul as well as her body, we look for activities that give her joy, activities that tap into her diverse pleasures and that will make her function as well as possible. She loves the water, so we arrange for her to "go swimming." Swimming in Sesha's case means walking in lap lanes—the only time she can walk independently without support, back and forth, providing her pleasure and exercise simultaneously. Music is a perpetual treat, so she has headphones and a walkman that, incidentally, connect her to her teen contemporaries. When we can find the appropriate persons, we supply her with music therapy. We have fought on many occasions for funding for her swim therapy and music therapy. But unlike physical therapy and speech therapy, neither of which are especially applicable to her needs, swim and music therapies are considered luxuries and are not offered to her. They are not seen as necessities, because, in part at least, these do not appear to be geared to "independent living."

What does "development" mean for someone like Sesha? Sesha never focused on images. We slowly interested her in images through her love of music and supplied her with musical videos. She began to get interested in the screen, and now enjoys ballets and movies such as *Mary Poppins*, *The Sound of Music,* and *Beauty and the Beast*, delighting in the children singing and the cartoon characters dancing. For Sesha, learning to fix her gaze on the video screen—something I seriously discouraged in my able child—was development. No, I don't take independent living as Sesha's goal, as much as I admire it as an aim for so many other disabled individuals. Independent living is a subsidiary goal to living as full and rich a life as one's capacities permit.

I believe that a focus on independence, and perhaps even on the goal of inclusion when inclusion is understood as the incorporation of the disabled into the "normal" life of the community, yields too much to a conception of the citizen as "independent and fully functioning." The disability community has achieved enviable recognition of the needs of the disabled by stressing that it is the combination of inherent traits and environmental enablings that result in capabilities, not inherent traits alone. Without sufficient light, the sighted would all be as incapable of seeing as are the blind—and the sighted would be handicapped because those who have lived a life without sight have developed other capacities by which to maneuver around in their environment. The stress on environmental modification to enhance capabilities is crucial in Sesha's life. Without a wheelchair, she would have only a bed from which to view the world. But no modifications of the environment will be sufficient to make Sesha independent.

I fear that the stress on independence reinstates Sesha as less than fully human. With every embrace, I know her humanity. And it has no more to do with independence than it has to do with being able to read Spinoza. So when we think of mothering a disabled child as enabling and fostering development, we must also reconceive development, not only toward independence, but toward whatever capacities are there to be developed. Development for Sesha means the enhancement of her capacities to experience joy.

Care for Disability and Social Justice

Among the sugar cane workers of the shanty town in northeastern Brazil, infants who fail to thrive on the watered-down formula and pabulum mothers feed them are allowed to die, and the mothers bury them without weeping. Nancy Scheper-Hughes (1992) tells us this in her gripping study, *Death Without Weeping*, which takes its name from the tragic phenomena of the dry-eyed burials. Because they lack sterile conditions and have only contaminated water, many young children weaken and become ill. The children most vulnerable are those who perform poorly from birth or shortly thereafter, and are simply allowed to die. The women who mother them do not see themselves as abandoning their babies in a denial of love. To allow the children to die is to allow them "to return to Jesus"—so they believe, or so they rationalize. Their love for these children is not—cannot be—preservative. The situation of abject poverty and harsh physical conditions make a hardiness tested in the first months of life a requirement. The conviction I called the condition for the possibility of mothering (see Chapter Six), which is crystallized in the notion of *preservative* love, is still found perhaps in this limit: a love expressed by allowing the infants "to return to the angels." Maybe it is a requirement of the appalling conditions these mothers and their children endure. Still I cannot easily tolerate such relativity. When mothers must live in the situation Shepherd-Hughes describes, a situation which fosters what to our view looks like maternal neglect, we are witnessing a gross case of injustice. Not perhaps on the part of the mothers, but on the part of the land and sugar cane plantation owners and the corrupt government that permit the conditions of extreme poverty to persist.[258]

Even when material conditions are adequate, the stigma of disability can be sufficient to allow parents of such a child to languish. For instance, a U.S. physician participating in a Hastings Center Project on Prenatal Testing recently reported the case of an infant in his Neonatal Intensive Care Unit with Down's syndrome and an imperforate anus (which necessitated a colostomy that would last a year, if not a lifetime). According to this physician, the social worker relates that the parents no longer visit the child and have placed him for adoption. The social worker also believes that the Down's syndrome and associated medical problems are entirely "unacceptable" for the parents because "of a strong cultural bias." Apparently the parents plan to tell family and friends that the child died. The infant was the child of an immigrant couple, decidedly middle-class and whose financial resources were less at issue than was the social stigma attached to the disability.[259]

Poverty and stigma are twin stakes that pierce the heart of the disabled and their families. They undermine the possibility of love's labor. Beyond the extreme conditions are the denial of services, the insistence that families (often mothers alone) must bear with their child the full brunt of the costs of impairments to which we are each susceptible. All these are part and parcel of a failure to consider the circumstances of dependency as central for an ideal of a well-ordered society. The lack of social supports for the disabled and those who care for dependents constitute a denial of our inherent vulnerability to disability. It is a denial which is at one with the stigma that causes even families who have material resources to abandon their child in a hospital ward.

Disability brings sadness in its wake. There is a loss—of capacities and possibilities. The disaster, however, is not the disability per se, but the callousness and insensitivity, the sheer miserliness of the response to it. Must it be so? Is it inevitable? The sorrow may be, but not the inequality, not the injustice.

Ironically, so much of the injustice masquerades as "fairness," as "impartiality," and as "equality." Darling (1983, 148) identified as a professional virtue "universalism . . . a belief that all cases are to be treated equally," and pointed out that it conflicts with the maternal concern with this particular child. Among the vulnerable, not all cases are equal. Unfortunately, when resources are limited, universality and equality mean only that all are treated *equally poorly*.[260] For parents who must rely on clinics for medical services, the experience of the Massies raising a son with hemophilia is all too familiar:

In the main waiting room, there were long lines of wooden benches. We sat there, as if we were in court, waiting. It was obligatory to be there at 8 A.M. when the clinic opened. No appointments were made. You waited . . .

We all waited there, mothers of every race, tense and worried, with restless, bored children . . .

Mothers were afraid to ask, "When will the doctor see us?" for fear that "Doctor" would get angry.

Whole days slipped away in this manner. But we went on waiting, for there was no other place to go. That was the problem. How well I came to know the sullen anger, the mutinous rage that grows in the helpless. They say nothing. What can they say? But angry thoughts boiled in me (Massie 1975, 75).

Parents served by the private physician are not strangers to the long angry waits. Although the maternal pull will always (and appropriately) be toward the affective and the particularistic, parents could readily accept a rhetoric of universalism and equality, if what was being distributed equally was high quality care and services and if that care and those resources were in fact universally available. Instead, parents are asked to accept injustice and shoddy treatment as "conditions" as inevitable as their children's disability.[261]

The universalism we require is not that all should equally wait for long hours in unstaffed and inadequate clinics, but the sort of universal programs I urged in Chapter Five. We need universal programs serving needs we have when we are disabled, whether we are disabled temporarily when we are ill, or permanently when we suffer from some impairment. As the passage above so well reflects, the needs of the person who is disabled are here (though admittedly not always) at one with those of his caregivers. His ill-treatment is their pain.

The virtue of universality among professionals described by Darling can be exercised only in the perverse form of treating all people equally poorly: where there is no universal health care, where education is funded by property taxes, and where the fates of children and dependents is based on a fundamentally unjust distributive system. The inequalities that affect all children's ability to grow and thrive are mirrored in the treatment of disabled children. While legislation providing for the education of all children with disabilities, and early intervention in the case of disabled infants, may bring the opportunities of some disabled children closer in line with those of non-disabled children, such legislation fails to address the compounding of poverty and racism for poor and non-white children with disabilities. It is hard to do justice to the ways in which racism inflects every aspect of the care of the disabled. Multiplying the anguish of stigma with inequitable allocation of resources based on race makes race a crucial factor in the study of families with disabilities. And yet relatively few studies even include families of diverse racial backgrounds (as is the case of the study I examine below).[262]

As I write this chapter, thousands of children with disabilities face cutbacks in the meager, but essential Supplemental Security Income (SSI) benefits that were swept away with "welfare reform."[263] In addition, many of their mothers or mothering persons (sometimes a grandmother or other familial caregiver) are forced to find employment outside the home in order to continue receiving benefits. Poverty and racism are, furthermore, causally implicated in many cases of disability. Just as the poor are increasingly blamed for their poverty, so the mother of a child with disability is often seen as responsible for that disability. Only a system of benefits for families with disabled children—that are universal rather than means-tested—will *begin* to redress the stigma and hardships that are heaped on the poor and non-white disabled persons and their families. Our own nation, in spite of the wealth that makes such universal services possible, is a long way from enacting the necessary legislation.

Is it utopian to think that a nation could find the political will to provide the services and support required? Waisbren (1980) conducted a study contrasting the social services in Denmark and the United States and the impact of these services on families. Summarizing what was available in the United States for the developmentally disabled child and her family at the time of the study, Waisbren writes:

> [T]he system of services in the U.S. [for the developmentally disabled child and her family] is disjointed and incomplete. Parents must hunt out the programs for their child since central referral agencies are inadequate, slow and overly specialized. Financial support is provided by a variety of agencies that each serve only a specific population; therefore, a definite diagnosis is often required before a family is eligible for assistance. The schools, workshops, and residential institutions for developmentally disabled people in the United States are inferior architecturally, more crowded, and far less community oriented than are those in Denmark. For developmentally disabled adults, halfway houses and training programs for independent living are rare (Waisbren 1980, 346).

Between the time Waisbren wrote and today, many services have improved, and the work of the disability community and the advocacy of parents of the disabled have generated more programs, more community integration, and more flexibility in aid to families. Even the improved services and support garnered by the passage of the ADA (many of which still must be fought for at every point) falls short of what was already available in Denmark in 1980, making the latter seem a utopian dream. The provisions in Denmark include free services and financial support, which are guaranteed for all families with a developmentally disabled child, cash subsidies allowing one parent to remain at home, home counseling, respite care, day facilities, home nursing and parent training. Nor is that all:

> Parents are supported in keeping their developmentally disabled child home until the late teens or young adulthood. At that point, halfway houses or small groups homes as well as supervised apartments are provided. . . . In addition, families are helped to find better homes, with moving costs paid for and rent subsidies granted. Remodeling of the home to adapt it to the handicapped person's needs is also paid for by the government. The government provides special equipment, free diagnostic evaluations and routine checkups, free medical care, early stimulation programs for motor development, and transportation to and from doctors' offices" (Waisbren 1980, 346; cites Bank-Mikkelsen 1969, Sterner 1976).[264]

Such provisions should, it would seem, go a long way in alleviating the tensions, pain, and stigma, parents encounter in mothering the disabled child. Surprisingly, the Waisbren study finds no significant differences in stress levels between the parents of very young developmentally disabled children in Denmark and in the United States when comparing parents of comparable demographic profiles. She remarks, "Evidently, parents in each country tended to accept the developmental services as they existed. *The lack of services was often accepted without question*" (Waisbren 1980, 348, emphasis mine).

It is worth considering the import of this finding. First, the demographic aspects of this study bear scrutiny. The population Waisbren (1980, 346)) examined was white and middle-class families in which both parents were present. Because on the whole, these families were less likely to suffer conditions (poverty, effects of racial discrimination or the responsibilities of single parenting) that aggravate the stress of the disability (and so for whom social supports and financial supports would be especially valuable), the fact of the disability alone could overwhelm all other considerations for the families studied. Doubtless the choice of comparative families in the United States was dictated by the Danish population, largely white and not impoverished (as poverty does not loom as large in Denmark as in the United States). But these methodological concerns may well have skewed the results of the study.

While most of the powerful emotions and needs in the child's infancy center on the pain and sadness of the child's impairment, these recede as a parent accepts the child and her situation.[265] But with this acceptance comes a decreased tolerance for the paucity of services and supports as the child grows older and families must struggle with the demands of caring for the child and assuring her well-being. The concern turns quickly to providing the possibilities for preservative love, for enabling development, and for social acceptance.

Lessons for the Theoretician

The Waisbren study exemplifies the predominant form of social science research in looking at stress levels of families of children with developmental disabilities. There are a variety of competing views supported by different research. The earlier literature was virtually unanimous that these families are marked by pathology; the recent studies are almost as unanimous that these families are coping just fine and that they are not significantly different than families with only "normal" children. The results of the Waisbren study raises the question of how much we should conclude by investigating measurable stress levels. The issue is less how well parents cope and more what it is fair and just to provide to disabled persons and their families. As those who plow the fields of social justice know, an oppression that has lain so heavy on the shoulders of its victims that it has numbed the response to the burden is the most unjust of all. If we believe that social services to support dependency work is required by justice, must we not also and especially think that the vulnerability of the disabled charge requires services and support commensurate with the vulnerability? The principle of *doulia* would mandate that those who serve the child are themselves supported: financially, with additional caregiving help, with counseling, with home improvements and with direct medical, educational and habilitative provisions for the disabled charge.

How do we go about conceiving of equality and justice in the context of disability? The essays in this book have served only as a preparation for what needs to be a systematic theory of equality-in-connection. I want to briefly sketch what such a theory may look like with respect to disabled persons and their caregivers, and propose that Sen's capability model is most useful. That model emphasizes "interpersonal variations in converting incomes (and other external resources) into individual advantage" (Sen 1992, 195). Capability is for Sen "a reflection of the freedom to achieve valuable functionings" (1992, 49). "Functionings" are "constitutive of well-being." Capabilities, he adds, are relevant not only to the *"freedom to achieve well-being"* but also "for the *level of well-being achieved"* (1992, 49). What we seek to equalize then is not a set of goods (not even "primary goods") but the ability to realize those functionings we deem valuable.

Nowhere is the interpersonal variation of which Sen speaks more important than in dealing with disabled persons and those who care for them. Nowhere is what is understood by individual advantage more singular. Even within a single disability, such as cognitive disability, the "space of functionings" (Sen 1992) is so varied that no one set of goals or goods can easily pertain to all affected. Finally, because acceptance of the disability (whether it is our own or that of our child) is so crucial to well-being, and because attempting to achieve acceptance can cut us off from our own expectations of what we ought, in fairness, to have, nowhere is it more important to emphasis the *freedom* in the capability to realize valuable functionings.

So what is to be equalized? Does equality make sense in the context of disability and care of the disabled? What is to be equalized is, on the one hand, the capability space for the individual who is disabled. The disabled person determines alone or along with family and dependency workers the valued functionings as they arise out of his abilities and possibilities. On the other hand, the family and other dependency workers (that is, all who care about and for the disabled person—whether familial or employed) also need to be accorded an equality of capability. They too must be able to determine their valued functionings and have the freedom to realize these functionings. But these functionings, the capability set itself, is not merely a matter of each individual's space of functionings considered apart from the space of functionings defined for others in the relationship. If it were, then this capability equality would be just another form of *individual-based* equality. (See Chapter One, pages 28–29.) If capability equality is to be a *connection-based* equality then there must also be a consideration of how the maintenance of the relationships of dependency can be sustained and how the functioning spaces are to be coordinated. The coordination must be more than merely maximizing the freedom of functioning of each, although that, too, is a desirable outcome. The coordination must provide space for the relationships themselves. The valued functioning of the disabled individual who requires care must be figured in conjunction with valued functionings of those who stand outside of but are needed to support a relationship of dependency. The valued functioning of those who stand outside a relation of dependency must similarly take into account the valued functionings of those within a particular relationship of dependency. Moreover the quality of the relationships themselves is a determinant in considering what is a valued functioning. By viewing our relations to others as nested dependencies and coordinating valued functionings across these nested dependencies, we start to frame equality in terms of our interconnections. A distribution that enables such an equalization in the space of capability and functionings is entirely consistent with the difference and dependence inherent in disability—for the disabled and their caregivers alike. Each gets to be seen as some mother's child.

In writing of social organizations, and matters of justice and equality, we think of the child as the future independent being. We value equal exchanges. Women have been very important in reminding social and political theorists that "independence" is an illusory ideal and have offered up the image of persons as interdependent. But even feminists who have directed us away from the atomistic individualism of much traditional Western philosophy have failed to recognize the full implications of dependency. Lorraine Code, for example, acknowledging that women can achieve satisfactory relationships with both children and men, just as one can with feminist friends and colleagues, insists that equality is a crucial value. "It is a matter of mutuality, where each member of a relationship is prepared to compromise with respect to her or his time, convenience, comfort and success . . . Only for such relationships is it worth relinquishing a measure of autonomy" (Code 1986, 56). This insistence on mutuality, in some usually understood sense of that term, pervades the discussion of most feminists.

But this mutuality is inapplicable when discussing the relation of mothering a child such as Sesha. Clearly Sesha is not "prepared to compromise" in the requisite ways for a mutual equal relationship, yet it does make sense for me to relinquish a portion of my autonomy. And if it is not me, then someone must. Yet this does not mean that I must acquiesce to the "feminine" virtues of self-effacing self-sacrifice. It means that we need a reconfiguration of how reciprocation comes to be possible in the case of dependency work.

While the image of a mutuality and interdependence among persons is an important one, life with Sesha underscores that there are moments when we are not "inter"dependent. We are simply dependent and *cannot* reciprocate. Furthermore, while dependence is often socially constructed—*all* dependence is not. If you have a fever of 105, the dependence you have is not socially constructed. Sesha's dependence is not socially constructed. Neither "labeling" nor environmental impediments create her dependence—although environment modifications are *crucial* for her to have a decent life.

Life with Sesha has also brought to light the ways in which the characterization of citizens in a just society as "free and equal" ignores the maternal requirements that limit one's freedom in the sense that one cannot presume to act always as the self-originator of valid claims, as Rawls would have us think. *This* nonfreedom, while not chosen, may be accepted as a fate to be embraced without injustice when conditions at once permit us to ascertain our valued functionings and provide the capability to realize them. Life with Sesha has then brought to consciousness the way in which the "equal" portion of the formula cannot be met for the mothering person of a truly dependent individual unless the wider society provides resources for caring not only for the dependent, but also for the one who provides the care. This, after all, was the old message in my nursing book. A seriously disabled person may not be as dependent as a nursing infant, but as long as the person sustaining the dependent directs her energies there, she cannot be participating as an "equal" in the economic or social or political order of which she is a part. To have her needs met as she meets the needs of another who is dependent on her becomes the condition of *her* equality—that is, her equal membership in her community. To have one's needs met as one meets the needs of another may not be a feature of the relation between independent persons who have an equal status. Nonetheless it becomes the condition for equality for all those within a relationship of dependency, where someone is significantly and inevitably dependent on another for basic needs.

The young woman who is my daughter will never read a book of philosophy—she will never read—and will never speak English sentences. She will never be independent. The lessons of this book, nonetheless, are the product of her gentle tutoring. The lessons are not over and will continue as long as we have each other. The process of mothering will not end, just as marriages are not supposed to end "till death do us part." Until then, I will continue to learn from my daughter, from those who share her mothering with me, and from the unique and at times also generalizable, aspects of this remarkable relationship with an exquisite person we call Sesha.

Afterword

The acknowledgment of dependency and the quest for equality are the two conceptual poles of this book. The book grapples with the question whether dependency and equality are reconcilable in the lives of women.

If this volume has covered a great deal of ground it is because to speak of human dependency and equality is to embrace a wide sweep of our lives and our hopes. To deal with dependency is to be concerned with our young years, our old age, the times of our own illness and disability, and the times we care for our aging parents, our young children, our ill spouses, friends, and lovers. While dependency is a condition to which men and women are equally vulnerable, the care of dependents occupies mostly women, and for many women, it occupies the better part of their lives.

Equality has served as the basis of the moral, social, and political order for which people have struggled and fought throughout the modern age. But any idea of equality that is located in the autonomous, free, and self-sufficient individual, who joins only with similarly situated others, does not easily recognize the dependency that has so occupied women's lives. By failing to recognize this dependency, such conceptions of equality effectively exclude women.

This book envisions a world where the wider community accepts a social responsibility for the care of dependents and support for their caregivers, and where caring for dependents does not become so costly to dependency workers that they are unable to be equals in a society of equals. In such a world, the requirements for doing dependency work are accepted in turn as requiring reciprocation from the wider community that makes equality possible for all. In this vision, both receiving and giving care are understood to be essential goods, as fundamental and irreducible as political liberty and economic well-being. Only in a world in which dependency work is not determined by gender, race, or class can such a requirement be fulfilled. Only then can this work be compatible with an ideal of full equality of opportunity where positions are open to those with the appropriate skills, interests, and capacities.

This is not the world we currently inhabit. It is not even a world theorized in progressive tracts shaped by a man's vision. The world we know is one fashioned by the dreams of those who, by and large, consider themselves independent. Their self-understanding as independent persons is generally purchased at a price—one set so low and considered so inevitable that few have traditionally considered it pertinent to considerations of social justice. The purchase price of independence is a wife, a mother, a nursemaid, a nanny—a dependency worker. Whether the care of dependents is turned over to a woman with whom one shares an intimate life or to a stranger, unless someone attends to the dependencies that touch our lives, and inevitably touch the lives of all, we cannot act the part of a free and equal subject featured in the conception of society as an association of equals.

Those who do dependency work, be it familial or paid, garner the satisfaction of doing a labor of love. They watch an infant flourish; they comfort a sick person; they return the loving care they received from a person who cared for them. They also become vulnerable to economic deprivation, lack of sleep, disruptions of their own intimate life, loss of leisure and career opportunities, and so on. It is a vulnerability dependency workers incur as they turn their attentions to the needs of one who is entirely vulnerable to their actions, whose comfort, ability to thrive, and even survive—whose most fundamental well-being rests with them. In their labors, dependency workers subject themselves to work conditions which are among the most emotionally and morally demanding. These demands are constitutive of the labor itself.

There are additional hardships not essential to the labor itself: when the efforts of the dependency worker are not reciprocated by others; when they do not receive adequate release time, adequate compensation, emotional support, and when they are not provided the social and technical services a particular form of dependency requires. These are the result of social and political inequities.

The rectification of such injustices is what a public conception of *doulia* demands. A public principle of *doulia* demands a reciprocation that calls upon a social responsibility to the charge and caregiver alike. A commitment to the equality of *all* requires an equality that is connection-based, an equality that acknowledges a common fate and shared humanity which lies as much in our need to care for others and be attended to in caring relationships as in properties we possess as individuals.

If dependency is not a part of one's daily life, it is easy and convenient to ignore it. After all, what does cleaning bedpans or comforting a teary toddler have to do with matters of State, matters of finance, or the world of culture? The answer, of course, is *everything*. Yet our own dependency and the dependency of others has been conveniently kept out-of-sight, tucked away metaphorically and literally, attended to by women who have only aspired to and have not yet achieved full citizenship. As women attempt to gain full citizenship, to become equals in a world created by men, the hidden dependencies become visible. Women cannot leave the home for the marketplace and abandon dependents in the process. Attempting to be in both places at once is either impossible or achieved with strain and struggle—something gets lost, either some of a woman's autonomy and ability to compete as an equal or else the care and well-being of dependents.

We like to think that equality is an inclusive ideal; that its inherent dynamic is to progressively encompass a wider and wider range of individuals. Yet equality always excludes *some* as it includes *others*. When one group defines itself as composed of equals, it so defines itself against those who are not members. Even the most inclusive conception of equality—the equality of all persons—excludes the nonperson. Perhaps we should not be surprised that the very possibility of conceiving of society as an association of equals has been predicated on dependencies which stand outside of the domain of equals. The very young are equals-to-be-once-they-reach-majority—not yet equals. The ill or disabled stand outside the charmed circle of those equally abled. The frail elderly retire and step aside, yielding their place in the company of equals to those who have come of age and are now "independent." In truth, we know that no one is independent. We all are dependent—the fates of each of us hang on those of others. But, at any given historical moment, we know, nonetheless, what relative independence means, what it entitles us to, and what inclusion into the circle of equals signifies.

The right to be thought of as an equal is a right that women today have seized upon with a grip far surer and unyielding than at any other time in history. That is why we can see today that the circle of equals has itself depended on women's care of the inevitable human dependencies—to provide for its new members, to provide succor to those who have had to temporarily step out due to illness or disability, to care for those who retire from the circle. It is women's insistence that they be included that makes visible the need for some persons to care for all those outside it. At the same time, the fact of dependency and women's responsibility for dependency work has been, in large measure, why including women within the political and economic order as equals has been so problematic and slow.

The attainment of equality can be made compatible with the inevitability of dependency. But only under certain conditions: that we develop policies by which those who care for dependents are adequately compensated, supported with services and with the means of participating in the competition for social goods, while and after they care for dependents. Such policies must also assure that dependency work be de-gendered and not racialized, but distributed according to skill and inclination.

The reader may have a reservation here. I may have convinced a skeptical reader that the dependent whose needs are not in the charge of a capable dependency worker is likely to be shortchanged, and that unpaid familial caregivers are handicapped as they enter into competition for the goods of social cooperation under present arrangements. However, it may not yet be clear why the benefits of a social order are not equally available to the dependency worker who avoids an emotional attachment to her charge—who, for example, simply cleans the bedpan, does the laundry and shopping for her elderly charge, collects her pay, and leaves at the end of her shift with no more thought of her charge than the automobile assembly line worker's thought of the car's driver's safety and well-being. Why is *this* dependency worker more vulnerable than a worker on a Ford assembly line?

To answer this question we must first acknowledge that while dependency work may be paid or unpaid, it has traditionally been unpaid labor—and to a large extent continues to be. This fact also means that incorporating dependency work into the accounting of resources and costs is not easily accomplished. For example, as every woman who has had to figure out the costs of childcare knows, childcare is expensive relative to what she brings into the family by her employment outside the home. This means that the compensation for dependency work—as it is now figured—is always on the low end of the wage scale. It will remain so until we put our minds and our political will to figuring out how to adequately compensate this work. Because dependency work is poorly paid it is likely to draw on the most disenfranchised populations—those who are least likely to find better paid employment. At the very least, the paid dependency worker is likely to be vulnerable by virtue of her poverty and her marginal status.

In this respect, however, she is no more vulnerable than the migrant farm worker, for example, or any other poorly paid and disenfranchised worker. But she is at least that vulnerable, and it surely can be argued that these individuals do not currently reap the benefits of participation in what is putatively, if not actually, a free and equal society. Still, a liberal theory, such as that provided by John Rawls, does consider how to build a just society in which the interests of those least well situated economically are considered equally. If this were the full extent of the dependency worker's vulnerability when she is doing her job without the thick involvement that is required to do the job well, then these workers would be excluded from the concerns that I take to be particular to dependency work.

But the dependency worker—even when she refuses an affective engagement with her charge—has a distinctive moral obligation, one that sometimes subjects her to increased legal scrutiny. Contrast her situation to that of an automobile assembly line worker. The latter has a responsibility to do her job properly, which means following the direction of management. There is a hierarchical set of commands that determines the responsibility. If a poorly manufactured automobile endangers its passengers, the assembly line worker who has done her own job properly can rest easily—without moral or legal guilt. But even the assembly line worker who does her work poorly is unlikely to be directly responsible for a defect that can result in injury or loss of life, because it is the worker's manager and ultimately her employer who has the responsibility to oversee the work, to assure that potentially hazardous mistakes are rectified, and to assume accountability. The dependency worker who, by virtue of her detachment and failure of responsiveness to her charge, allows her charge to take a step that should not have been taken, or fails to perceive a precipitous rise in temperature, may in contrast be directly responsible for a dangerous illness or loss of life. In addition to being subject to the moral guilt, she is subject to job loss and even criminal action. This is a vulnerability that is at times heightened by her poverty and her marginal social status.

To become sufficiently responsive, however, is to open oneself to the emotional attachments that characterize dependency work when well done, and such attachments incur still further vulnerability. They make possible the responsiveness characteristic of the "transparent" self (See Chapter Two, pages 51–53) and allow for the willingness to forgo one own's best interest for the sake of another who is entirely vulnerable to one's own actions.[266]

The principle of care—that in order to grow, flourish, and survive or endure illness, disability and frailty, each individual requires a caring relationship with significant others who hold that individual's well-being as a primary responsibility and a primary good—together with the principle of *doulia*—that just as we have required care to survive and thrive, so we need to provide conditions that allow others, including those who do the work of caring, to receive the care they need to survive and thrive—point to an approach that authorizes the use of social resources for the support of relationships of dependency. If equality is to become a reality in the face of dependency and the demands of dependency care, then it must be a *connection-based* equality, an equality that recognizes needs based on our functioning through periods of dependency and caring for dependents. A connection-based equality is one concerned less with resources as such and more with capabilities and functionings. Such a connection-based equality, I have been able only to adumbrate.

Perhaps a full theory of equality adequate to dependency concerns (and sensitive to issues of difference, dominance, and diversity to which other feminist and race theorists have pointed) awaits not only further theoretical developments, but also a change in the practices of organizing dependency work. It may be the case, for example, that we need more experience with ways to incorporate dependency concerns into the public domain, and more public discussion before we can decide how resources can best be allocated to create the conditions for women's equality. For instance, with respect to the dependency of young children we may want to ask if we are better served by supports for those who want to raise their own preschool-aged children at home or by the provision of many more day-care facilities. The conclusions of this book suggest that both efforts are needed, but perhaps a more refined theory, based on more experience in different cultural and economic contexts, can provide a sophisticated and targeted response that better weighs considerations of the diversity of needs, the long-term impact of women's entry into non-gender-stereotyped jobs and the well-being of young children in different circumstances.

The economic dimension of dependency work provides another example of why a theory of equality that embraces dependency awaits both more scholarly work and changes in our practices. Because dependency work has traditionally been unpaid labor, and because so few efficiencies of production are possible in this labor intensive activity, dependency work *always* seems to be considered too expensive. Its costliness is decried whether the payment is made privately in families or publicly through the welfare system. How then, given the special demands of this work, can dependency workers be fairly compensated? How, for example, can some of the proposals of this volume be made economically feasible? Do we need a different system of accounting, just as environmentalists have urged with respect to the costs of environmental protections?

Still another set of questions, which may not be answerable until we set about changing our practices, concerns the extent to which gender identities and stereotypical characteristics attach themselves to this sort of labor. If we begin training for dependency work early—in school perhaps, concentrating on accustoming young boys, as well as young girls, to take on dependency work—will there be new resistances to degendering this labor that we cannot now envision? How are expectations that women will do dependency work integral to our understanding of sexuality, to the shaping of emotional response, and to the creation of personality? While feminists have explored some of these issues, we will not have answers that we can use to build on until we begin altering the social organization of dependency work. Until we begin to see the consequence of some of the changes that are presently occurring and that are possible by insisting on more social responsibility for dependency work, we will not truly understand what genuine equality may look like, or what it is that we demand, when we demand equality that acknowledges dependency.

The call for sexual equality has been with us for a long time. But until relatively recently, the demands of even the most farsighted women have assumed very traditional and gendered arrangements of dependency work. Radical visions in which dependency work is taken out of the family have left many women cold—largely, I suggest, because they have failed to respect the importance of the dependency relationship. A view of society as consisting of nested dependencies, so constituted as to provide all with the means to achieve functioning that respects the freedom and relatedness of all citizens, is a view that can only emerge now, as women taste the fruits of an equality fashioned by men—and find it wanting. This equality has not left room for love's labors and love's laborers. It is time to shape a new vision by creating new theories and by forging the requisite political will. We need to revise our social and political commitment to ourselves as dependents and as dependency workers. Only through these efforts may we come to see what it means for men and women to share the world in equality.

Notes

Preface

1. Mrs. Perry's husband and his brothers paid her $200 a week to care for their mother.
2. The article makes it clear that men, as well as women, engaged in familial dependency work. It speaks about the son of Eldora Mitchell who does the primary dependency work for his mother. Female relatives and friends help with some intimate care for her. However, in the case of Martha Perry, her husband felt that because he could not bathe his mother or do the more intimate care, it was best for his wife to do this work.

Part One

Chapter One

3. Title VII of the Civil Rights Act prohibits discrimination on the basis of sex—even disallowing requirements that adversely impact on women—save in the case where an employer can show compelling reason why gender itself, or a qualification that has an adverse impact on women, is essential for the job. The Pregnancy Amendment to Title VII prohibits employers from dismissing a worker because she is pregnant or from imposing an extended mandatory leave because of pregnancy. According to Title IX, schools must provide equal educational facilities, even in the area of sports. Efforts to attain sexual equality have brought easier access to education—more than 50% of the college population is female—as well as to women's entrance into professions such as law and medicine, and arguably women now experience greater sexual freedom.
4. Between 1940–1994, the percentage of women in the labor force rose from 24% to 46% (Herz 1996, 45, 47).
5. In a comparative study of sexual equality, Pippa Norris writes, "In certain societies such as the United States, one of the most striking phenomena is the marked contrast between the expectations and achievements of the women's movement. . . . The woman's movement has been highly vocal in pressing for equal pay over the last twenty years, but the average pay packet for full-time American women workers compared with that of men is lower than in almost

all European countries. . . . Compared with the European Community, America has one of the highest proportions of women in the labour force, but . . . their average wages are among the lowest" (144). In addition, she comments on the female *nouveau poor* due to high divorce rates, single-parent families, and a less comprehensive and generous welfare system. Norris also remarks on the other objective inequalities American women suffer including the paucity of legislative and other governmental representation.

6. For example, in 1994, 8.5% of all engineers were women (up from 4% in 1981). Women engineers earned 86.5% of men's salaries. Meanwhile 73.8% of teachers, other than college and university level, were women (in 1981 the figure was 70%) earning 87% of men's salaries in the same occupation. Among college and university teachers 36.4% were women, earning 86.6% of men's salaries. While 92.3% of all nurses were women; at the same time, 23.2% of all physicians were women (up from 14% in 1981) earning 76.7% of men's salaries. Among lawyers, 31.0% were women, earning 74.1% of men's salaries, while 98.8% of secretaries were women. (Bureau of Labor Statistics 1994).

7. According to the Department of Justice, for example, "during each year women were the victims of more than 4.5 million violent crimes, including approximately 500,000 rapes or other sexual assaults. In 29% of the violent crimes against women by lone offenders the perpetrators were intimates—husbands, former husbands, boyfriends or former boyfriends" (U.S. Department of Justice 1995).
   See also (Blum, et al, 1993: 49–58) for a staggering array of statistics on rape, violence, sexual harassment and the sex industry.

8. The 1976 Hyde Amendment banned federal funding for abortions, and prohibits Medicaid funding for abortions except in cases of rape or incest (Stone 1996, 178). Furthermore, Title X funding which provided family-planning clinics that many women of color depended on was cut between 1980 and 1990 (*Facts in Brief, Abortion in the United States*, 1991). In addition, 83% of the counties in the U.S. (metropolitan areas among them) are without identifiable abortion facilities (Henshaw 1987, 63). All of these above factors conspire against poor women.

9. Overall women make 76.4 cents for every one of men's dollars. The median weekly salary for women in 1994 was $399 compared to men's $522 (Bureau of Labor Statistics 1994).

10. Although there are women making top salaries in major law firms and corporations, even in 1993, single, female-headed households earned a median yearly salary of $17,413 compared to $26,467 for single, male-headed households. Race exacerbates the difference. The median income for white women who were single parents was $19,962, while the income for black single mothers was $11,905, and income for Hispanic single mothers was $12,047 (Bureau of the Census 1994). Among union workers, white women earned 85.3% of white men's wages; black women earned 86.3% of black men's wages; and Hispanic women earned 79.4% of Hispanic men's wages. Among non-union workers, white women earned 75.2% compared to white men; black women earned 86.3% compared to black men; and Hispanic women earned 91.5% compared to Hispanic men (Bureau of Labor Statistics 1994).

11. Even though women in the United States have had the rights of citizenship since 1920, and participate at all levels of electoral politics, in 1995, only 11% of Congress were women (forty-eight women in the U.S. House of Repre-

sentatives and eight women in the Senate); 26% of statewide elected officials were women; 21% of state legislators were women; and 18% of all mayors were women. The much touted efforts of President Clinton to increase women's visibility in high office only brought that figure to 29%. With the appointment of Ruth Bader Ginzburg to the Supreme Court the number of women on the Supreme Court increased to two (Center for the American Woman and Politics [CAWP] 1995; National Women's Political Caucus [NWPC] 1995).

12. Women working full-time in households shared by adult men do 83% of household chores and childrearing, while women employed full-time outside the home do 70% (Stone 1980, 33).

13. A number of feminist scholars have contributed to my own writings on the relation between equality and dependency. The work of Susan Okin has been immensely valuable in elucidating the role of women's social position in the family as the source of her exclusion from the political domain. Her work, including her discussions of John Rawls, which I both draw upon and take issue with, has been very important in crystallizing my own thinking. Within legal thought Martha Fineman has vigorously pursued what I think of as the dependency critique of equality, especially in the publication of *The Illusion of Equality* but also in the *Neutered Mother*. Much of my earlier thinking had been developed independently of the work of Martha Fineman, and when I found Fineman's work, I found the confluences both illuminating and heartening. My own work draws heavily on the feminist project of a care ethic and the attempt to gain moral, social, and political insight from the caring work of mothering.

14. Martha Fineman's approach is most similar to my own. See note 13.

15. Rawls distinguishes a concept and a conception with respect to justice:

> Thus it seems natural to think of the concept of justice as distinct from the various conceptions of justice and as being specified by the role which these different sets of principles, these different conceptions, have in common. Those who hold different conceptions of justice can, then, still agree that institutions are just when no arbitrary distinctions are made between persons in the assigning of basic rights and duties and when the rules determine a proper balance between competing claims to the advantages of social life (Rawls 1971, 5).

It seems natural to import such a distinction to the discussion of equality.

16. See Rae (1989).

17. See Minow (1991).

18. See Sen (1987).

19. James Bohman points out that a problem with equality is that it is at some times exclusive when it ought to be inclusive, and, at other times, overly inclusive. See Bohman (1996).

20. There have always been feminists who have questioned equality in this form—who have always understood that the meaning of feminism should not be constrained by the measure of man. Even Wollstonecraft who is generally thought to be the "equality feminist" par excellence, was careful to insist that women not merely copy (the myriad follies of) men. Also see note 21.

21. It should be noted that from the eighteenth century onward there have been

two distinct arguments for women's emancipation. One insisted on the egalitarian argument: Men and women share essentially the same the same human character and that denial of these commonalties has kept women out of positions of privilege and away from resources. The other has insisted on the value of women's difference, arguing for women's suffrage because were women to be introduced into the political and social arena, they would inject new characteristics into these areas; that women's difference from man would benefit all humanity.

22. Christine Littleton, a difference feminist, has remarked that the problem with the model of androgyny is that women's values tend to be too little valued to get fair representation, and citing Carrie Menkel-Meadow, she remarks, "The trouble with marble cake is that it never has enough chocolate" (Littleton 1987a, 224). Also see Littleton (1987b).

23. The issue emerges most clearly as it pertains to pregnancy. The equality strategy is to analogize or assimilate pregnancy leaves to disability leaves. See Williams (1985). Williams argues for an understanding of pregnancy as disability, not because pregnancy is inherently a disability, but because in the context of the workplace pregnancy can be disabling to a person *as a worker*. Responding to arguments that the equality position simply integrates women into a male world, Williams, a feminist, writes: "The goal of the feminist legal movement . . . is not and never was the integration of women into a male world any more than it has been to build a separate but better place for women. Rather, the goal has been to break down the legal barriers that restricted each sex to it's predefined role and created a hierarchy based on gender."

24. MacKinnon puts it this way: "On the first day that matters dominance was achieved, probably by force. By the second day, division along the same lines had to be relatively firmly in place. On the third day, if not sooner, differences were demarcated . . . " (1987, 40).

25. MacKinnon puts it this way: "You can be the same as men, and then you will be equal." or "You can be different from men, and then you will be *women*." (DuBois, et al. 1985, 21).

26. MacKinnon, characteristically puts it more tendentiously. Speaking of comparable worth, she asks how you compare when there are no men around to make the needed comparison—men have found better things to do.

27. See Adams (1980, 2, 3, 6, 7, 26).

28. For example, Catharine MacKinnon has urged such policies with respect to sexual harassment and together with Andrea Dworkin has drafted an antipornography ordinance that explicitly signals pornography as a harm directed at women and against which women ought to have special recourse. For a statement of what I call the dominance critique, see especially MacKinnon (1987).

29. See Drucilla Cornell's critique of MacKinnon (1991, 119–164).

30. "Intersectionality" is the term employed by Kimberly Crenshaw (1991) to denote the ways in which women's multiple identities create problems which are not addressed when women of color are seen on the one hand as "women," on the other hand as "persons of color," but never as "women of color."

31. See especially Fishkin (1983), who examines the issue in considerable detail.

32. Perhaps then it is simply time to rid ourselves of the vestiges of the head of household equality and hold fast to the individual-based equality. The problem here, as I will argue in more detail later (Chapter Three), is that there remain important reasons why the one responsible to a dependent needs to have a

certain jurisdiction, and so treating a dependent as a fully independent citizen is not without difficulties.

33. I would include here the very act of bearing children, as in the practice of "surrogate" mothering, which is often undertaken by poorer women on behalf of middle-class women. For an interesting discussion of the moral ramifications of this, see the discussion stimulated by Keane (1981) in Singer (1985, 105–6).

34. For instance, Virgina Held points out—citing a U.S. Department of Labor publication—that on a scale from 887 (the lowest skill level) to 1 (the highest skill level) "the skill thought to be needed by a homemaker, childcare attendant, or nursery school teacher was rated . . . 878" (Held 1983, 9). See also Young (1983) and Bart (1983).

35. One can say that the relational move is an analogical one. In a case such as *Hernandez v. New York* discussed above, it requires that we locate those variables in the juridical peerage that translate across the linguistic difference between Anglos and Latinos.

36. Carol Gilligan (1982), Sara Ruddick (1989), Nel Noddings (1984), Annette Baier (1994), and Virginia Held (1993). For an attempt to formulate a politics based on principles of care see Tronto (1993).

37. That is to say, the greater inter-gender equality may contribute to a greater intra-gender inequality among women, not only because the ceiling is raised for some women, but because the floor is lowered for others. See Sen (1993). As distasteful a prospect as this presents, the question cannot be evaded when the rise of some women into fields and high income-earning professions previously closed to them is temporally, at least, coincident with the impoverishment of many other women. These concerns echo MacKinnon's claim that gender-neutral policies only benefit those women who, in their situation, are already most like men. However when the comparison among women is made with respect to dependency work, it is as often women as men who exert the power over the worse situated women.

38. See Held (1995), Clement (1996), and Bubeck (1995).

39. The cite continues "come to full maturity, without all kind of engagement to each other" (Hobbes 1966, 109).

40. Another interesting competitor is equal opportunity for welfare, see Arneson (1989) and Cohen (1993). Equal opportunity for welfare is an interesting alternative to both resource and the welfare equality, however, the criticisms that pertain to each from the perspective I'm developing, pertains as well to equal opportunity for welfare. The equality of capability is a view that I believe is most consistent with my aims here, but this view also begins with the individual. Also see Sen (1987), Nussbaum (1988a), Dworkin (1981), and Williams (1973a).

41. Chodorow (1978) offers a convincing argument that this is key to different responses to parenting by men and women. For some contrary views see essays in Trebilcot (1987).

42. Although it takes place at a time which was perhaps especially oppressive for women, Kate Chopin's *The Awakening* attests to the difficulty of even conceptualizing what a mother does, when she leaves her child for reasons that men so often do, as anything but pathological.

43. See Stack (1974, 63–89) for a discussion of "child-keeping." Within the community Stack studied, a trusted member of the primary parent's domestic kinship or domestic network would be asked to "keep" a child for a short or

an extended period in case the primary parent, usually the mother, became unable to care for the child because of illness or other stress, work opportunities elsewhere, new sexual or domestic arrangements, and so forth.

44. Under very harsh conditions, climatic, economic, etc., strong commitments to care for the frail elderly or severely ill may be too demanding and too costly to the welfare of the community to become a social expectation. Just as conditions of extreme scarcity impact on the very norms of a just distribution of goods, so, too, harsh survival conditions may alter the very norms of decency which demand the care of dependents. This is one way to understand the vaunted Eskimo custom to abandon the frail elderly. But it can hardly serve to justify the callous neglect of the elderly within societies where such conditions do not apply.

45. Recently, Bubeck (1995) has developed an argument of care work on the model of the Marxist understanding of exploitation.

46. See Fineman (1995, 161–64).

47. With the rise of the disability movement in the U.S. for example, the inevitable relation between disability and dependency has been importantly contested. In appropriate environments, a physical impairment or incapacity need not be a handicap. A person who is physically dependent on a wheelchair for mobility may be capable of living a fully independent life, or at least a life no less dependent on others than one not requiring a wheelchair—especially when the person's environment is accommodating to wheelchairs. Without a wheelchair, the individual would be dependent in the sense relevant to this book. However, the dependency would be the consequence not of biology only, but of biology as it is lived in a particular (social and technological) circumstance (Silvers and Wasserman 1998 [forthcoming]). Nevertheless, there are some forms of disability in which the biological basis of dependency cannot be overcome by social (or technological) circumstance. See Chapter Seven.

48. Furthermore, not all caring involves the actual labor in dependency work. (Tronto 1993).

49. This may be a more controversial point than it appears at first. In part, much hangs on how narrowly we construe sexuality. I argue (Kittay 1990) that sexuality tends to be thought of largely without reference to specifically female aspects of sexuality, such as childbirth and nursing. Nursing, clearly dependency work in my sense, does, I believe, have a sexual component which is not inappropriate.

50. Bubeck (1995) includes a wonderful thought experiment illustrating how the labor saving robots we envision to do housework are horrific when imagined as substitutes for the caring labor I identify as dependency work.

51. See Ann Ferguson (1989), especially Chapter Four for a discussion of a related notion *sex/affective production*. It would be worthwhile, on another occasion, to describe how differing organizations of dependency work figure in differently organized sex/affective production systems. But also see the discussion of dependency work in the extended sense on page 37ff. above.

52. Noddings (1984, 30–58) calls the dependency worker the "one-caring." She is speaking of a wider range of activities than those underscored here. I prefer dependency worker even in those cases where the extension of our terms overlap, however. First, because as I said above, I am interested in underlining the idea of labor involved in such caring. Second, because one can do dependency work poorly, and so not be caring. This would leave us with the notion of "one-caring," who may *not* be caring.

53. Noddings (1984, 59–78) calls the benefactor of care the "cared-for." See note 55.
54. Jane Martin (1989) argues that the three Cs need to be taught in schools along with the three Rs. The three Cs are the orientations and skills required to prepare individuals to take responsibility for the moral domain.
55. Especially where the cared-for is incapable (in the sense I specified above) of meeting essential needs alone.
56. I owe the first two of these observations to Diana Meyers and the third to Anthony Weston—all in personal correspondence.
57. This is a point that Bubeck (1995) also argues with great force.
58. "Practices," says Ruddick, building on the work of Winch (1972), "are collective human activities distinguished by aims that identify them and by the consequent demands made on practitioners committed to those aims. The aims or goals that define a practice are so central or "constitutive" that in the absence of the goal you would not have that practice" (Ruddick 1989, 13–14).
59. McDonnell, speaking of her experience with her son who is autistic writes about Ruddick's *Maternal Thinking*, reminding the reader that not all children are "intact," that is to say, "not handicapped in some way, not blind, deaf, autistic, retarded, paraplegic, dyslexic, etc." (McDonnell 1991).
60. See Conover (1997) for an example of such vulnerability in the case of the frail elderly.
61. Whether the relationship is just may also be a feature of whether its demands result in obligations for persons within it that render them incapable of responding to the more urgent moral demands outside the relationship. (Scheffler 1997). In addition, the moral nature of the relationship is a function of the moral nature of the practice in which it is situated.
62. Some writers, Noddings (1984) and Tronto (1993) for example, speak of the obligations of the one cared for to "complete" the care by their appropriate reception of the caring. I am most interested in the relation between dependency work and the ways the dependency worker becomes vulnerable. The inappropriate reception of care is one of several harms to which the dependency worker becomes vulnerable.
63. For example, the caregivers of an elderly woman report her uncontrollable piercing and abusive screams throughout the night, screams she cannot even recall during the day. The woman's demonic behavior is a sore trial to the caretakers, but they cannot vent their anger or frustration at her abuse of them during these periods (Conover 1997) for her behavior is itself a part of her affliction. This restraint on the part of the dependency worker is one of the most demanding of the requirements of the work.
64. Also see Bartky (1990).
65. While he is still a minor that social inequality plays a lesser role than when the son reaches adulthood. But there are subtle manifestations of the social disparity throughout – often played out with good humored references to "the little man of the house." And yet, the extent to which sons feel entitled to "graft the substance" of their mother to their own and the extent to which women accede to these deeply harbored expectations should not be underestimated. It requires a great deal of vigilance for the feminist mother to resist these socially shaped impulses. They are often harder to detect and so harder to resist than expectations made by other men.
66. See Audre Lorde's essay entitled "Man Child: A Black Lesbian Feminist's Response" (1984). See also the discussion of Gloria Naylor's work on page 36.

67. Robert Goodin (1985) develops the position that a moral commitment ensues when one individual is vulnerable to the action of another. I discuss this position in Chapter Two.

68. Of course, everyone who is employed is subject to being exploited by the need that makes them seek employment. That is not specific to the dependency worker, although paid dependency work is often done by those who are poorly positioned to seek more lucrative opportunities.

69. For a particularly sensitive account of the self-deception those who are caretakers often engage in, see Bartky (1990), especially Chapter Seven.

70. For an important discussion of trust and its relation to women's lives, see Baier (1986).

71. Those creatures to which we have given much care, or from which we have received care are ones to which we tend to bond. Such bonding can perhaps be extended to nonsentient beings in a unidirectional fashion, such as ties we feel toward physical landscapes which have comforted or nurtured us and in which we have invested care.

72. Although Naylor describes the relation between a mother and her grown son, which is not my paradigm of a dependency relationship, this line shows how difficult it is to draw the temporal boundary of the dependency relationship between mother and child.

73. So, too, is the "dial-a-mom" or "dial-a-wife" described by Margaret Talbot in a recent article (Talbot 1997).

74. As always, these things are not clear-cut. An elderly person, or one severely physically disabled, but who is in full command of his or her intellectual powers, may require extensive assistance by what I would call a dependency worker in the primary sense. Insofar as they are in the care of the dependency worker, they are charges of their caretaker. Yet, the disabled or elderly individual will have the capacity to hire and fire her aide much as a secretary is hired or fired by her boss. What distinguishes the cases is that the frail older or disabled persons are in need of life-sustaining help. On the other hand, we can imagine a very pampered individual who has grown so dependent on a servant for very basic needs that the individual is virtually incapacitated if he must fend for himself—and may fare very badly if he must take care of his own needs. And yet it seems counterintuitive to say that this individual is "the charge" of his servant. The fact that the incapacity is not grounded in an impairment that makes him both practically and in principle unable to perform these functions for himself appears to work against the idea that he is dependent in this primary sense.

75. See Darling (1983) who uses this distinction with respect to the care of a disabled child. See also the discussion in Chapter Seven below.

76. See Ruddick (1989) for a discussion of the intellectual skills required for maternal work. Important attacks on the concept that mothering skills and capacities are merely "natural" have been available in the feminist literature for quite a while. See the work of Held (1993).

77. See Susan Reverby (1987) for an interesting account of the troubled shift in nursing from work that is in the spirit of dependency work to its professionalization.

78. I suspect that in localities where the interventionist character of the work is stressed over its sustaining nature, that is, where the work is not conceived as similar to dependency work, one will tend to find more practitioners who are male.

79. I do not address women's special vulnerability to sexual abuse and exploitation in circumstances where she is not performing dependency work. Either an additional argument is required to relate sexual abuse to dependency work as performed under present conditions, or the distinctly sexual nature of much of woman's oppression must be located elsewhere. There may well be a link between sexual exploitation (and abuse of women more generally) and our traditional role as dependency workers. This may be related to the ambivalence of the male child to the principal dependency worker in his early life, his mother. The work of Nancy Chodorow (1978) and Dorothy Dinnerstein (1977) is surely suggestive in this respect. But I also urge a non-reductive account of women's subordination. See Kittay (1984). We should not insist that all the forms of sexist oppression must be rooted in any single phenomenon.

80. The term "patriarchal marriage" is adopted from Okin (1989b). See also her discussion of this point with the accompanying documentation.

81. See Pateman (1989). I describe what is thought of as the "non-pathological" case, understanding all the while that this fiction is *serviceable* only for those who do not suffer the unhappy fate of the reality of domestic abuse, a predictable accompaniment of the sexual contract. (See the discussion of "cooperative conflicts" p. 42ff.)

82. Contemporary feminists have, of course, challenged the concept that women must take on dependency work—or that this work is primarily the responsibility of women. But there has been little organized effort, especially among equality-minded U.S. feminists, to alter the distribution of dependency work along non-gendered and classless lines. For a discussion concerning the problems in putting childcare on the national agenda in the United States. See Sonya Michel (forthcoming).

83. This will be more extensively argued in the following chapter.

84. The locus classicus is Stack (1974) for African-American communities. See Scheper-Hughes (1992).

85. See, for example, the essays in Sassoon (1987). These essays pertain to legislation prior to the demise of Aid to Families with Dependent Children. The new welfare "reform" has opened the door to controlling women through new programs such as "workfare," "learnfare," "the family cap," and so forth. Workfare demands employment at substandard wages for a mandated number of hours; learnfare cuts back benefits to families when children skip school; the family cap restricts benefits for any children born to a woman while she receives public assistance.

86. Fineman (1995) speaks of the "derived dependency" of caretakers. Since Fineman and I developed these ideas independently, it is interesting to see how naturally a similar structure to the argument unfolds.

87. Some family structure has, in most cultures globally and historically, has been the favored "social technology" for meeting the needs of dependents.

88. Its favored status persists despite the statistical reality of its demise. Today less than 12.9% of all American households fit the traditional model in which the primary responsibility of the husband (where there is one) is that of the provider while the wife has the primary responsibility for dependency work (U.S. Bureau of the Census 1988). Despite its anachronistic nature, the workplace remains tailored to the traditional model.

89. Sen is primarily speaking of familial arrangements in developing nations. However, the structure of conflicting needs and cooperative aims is entirely translatable to families in industrial nations.

90. The pattern described here is replicated in other caring domains, for example, nursing, where nurses are "ordered to care" but are given little or no control over the resources they need to do the caring work. See Reverby (1987).

91. The precise economic arrangements vary with different historical periods, cultures, and classes. Where married women cannot control or own property, men are always the providers—regardless of where the resources originate. The subjective understanding of who contributes resources to the relationship comes to be identified with who controls the resources. Exit options for a woman whose husband has full control of her resources are as poor as those of a woman who enters a relationship without wealth. If she leaves the relation, she is generally obliged to leave her wealth and often her child. Dostoyevsky gives a poignant description, in *The Brother's Karamazov*, of the fate of Karamazov's first wife who contributed substantially to Karamazov's income through her dowry, but still suffered cruelly from the tyranny of her husband. That Karamazov received his wealth from his marriage to her did little to offer her protection from his abuse and did nothing to contribute to her exit options.

92. Rawls speaks of the participants in the Original Position (Rawls 1971, 1992) as being equally situated and being equally empowered. I argue, in Part Three, that we can understand the relation of dependency worker to provider and to other citizens who do not carry the responsibilities of dependency care, as a relation of inequality *in situation*; while the inequality of the dependent (vis-à-vis the dependency worker, but also vis-à-vis the "independent" citizen) is an *inequality of power* or, more specifically, of capacity.

93. Please note the distinction between an *extended* sense of dependency, that is a situation in which the needs of the one catered to are not those of a charge, and a *secondary* dependence, that is a situation in which the dependency worker is herself dependent on a provider.

94. It is the custom within families in Japan for the husband to hand over the entire pay check to the wife. She has total financial control of the resources the husband brings into the household. The social pressure for women not to enter the workplace, however, is strong. This is not the sort of autonomy most Western feminists envision.

95. Legally, it is an achievement for women to have gained the right to keep her children upon the dissolution of a marriage. Having this right has expanded marital exit options for women. But while women now can expect to continue to care for her children, she often lacks access to the same material means she had within her marriage and so caring for her children is financially more burdensome for her.

Chapter Two

96. This point is discussed in the Introduction.

97. Reference to the term "moral parity" is found in Elfie Raymond (1995). Elizabeth Wolgast uses the term "moral peer" (1980).

98. Chodorow (1978), Keller (1986), Gilligan (1982), Belenky, et al. (1986), Kittay and Meyers (1987), Irigaray (1985), Manning (1992), Hekman (1995) are among the many writers who speak of the relational self in some variety.

99. Catherine Keller (1986).

100. Robin West (1987).

101. See Friedman (1997) for a review and discussion of feminist critiques of the idea of autonomy and of attempts to develop relationally conceived ideas of

autonomy. Such efforts treat "social relations and human community as central to the realization of autonomy" (1997, 40).

102. I use the term in the extended sense that Ruddick (1989), gives to it. For Ruddick, the term "mother" includes any individual, regardless of gender, who does the primary caretaking. Virginia Held also speaks of a "mothering person" (1993, 197–8). Nonetheless, I adopt a convention of using the feminine pronoun for the dependency worker, reflecting at once the predominance of women who do this work *and* the possibility of generalizing the feminine as well as the masculine pronoun to speak of someone whose gender is not specified.

103. In Chapters Six and Seven the reader can, for example, see how this pertains in the case of the care of a severely disabled person.

104. See Benhabib (1987).

105. Similar points have received a great deal of philosophical attention, especially since Bernard Williams made his now famous remark with respect to the utilitarian calculator who considers if he should save his drowning wife before he saves others, that he asks one question too many. See Williams (1973b) and Friedman (1987).

106. This is a point I argue below and in Part Two. It is also a point nicely argued in Ruddick (1995).

107. One writer who has attended to this is Nel Noddings. She speaks of responses of care coming out of memories of our best caring (Noddings 1984, 80). I believe that this identification is (and is meant as) a psychological and not a normative source—that is, not a source of the obligation, but of the desire to care for another. Accordingly, she identifies the distinctly moral character of caring actions as those responses that are generated not simply by that desire but by our sense that we have the obligation to care. My approach is somewhat different: I want to identify the source in a normative sense, but say that a response motivated by another need is already a moral response.

108. We ought to note that the parties in the relationships discussed are individuals. However, there is no reason not to talk about the parties as groups—social groups or ethnic groups or groups formed on a given occasion, bystanders at an accident, let us say. Goodin discusses the responsibilities codified in professional codes, group responsibilities more generally, and the responsibility of an individual as a member of a group. To think in terms of group responsibility may be a useful way in considering how different systems of oppression interact, given that there are important dependency relations achieved among distinct social groups. Furthermore, when we understand what it is for an individual to be especially well-situated to meet the needs of another, it may be a situatedness that is mediated by her membership in a particular social group. Thus, for example, when the earthquake in Armenia occurred, Armenia-Americans were the ones who were most vigorous in their response. By virtue of their membership in that ethnic group, they saw it as their special responsibility to meet that need. Stereotyping, unfortunately, will create expectations that members of a particular group will assume certain responsibilities. Women sometimes find themselves with responsibilities foisted upon them that are the result of other's expectations of them as women. Once these expectations are in place, a person can find herself so situated that another is now vulnerable to her actions merely in virtue of stereotyped expectations of the group to which she belongs.

109. The move to a relational construal of notions previously considered on an individualistic model is found in several authors. Earlier we cited relational accounts of autonomy. Martha Minow (1990) attempts a reconstruction of rights along a relational model. A right, she emphasizes, is not something we possess regardless of the actions of another. Rights are what we hold against the actions of another. While compatible with my own position, Minow still supposes a ethical model in which the obligations and responsibilities incurred are *reciprocal* in a standard sense. In focusing on dependency relations, I am considering moral relations that often *cannot* be reciprocal.

110. See Scheffler (1997) for a defense of a non-reductive account of obligations in special relations.

111. Goodin's own Principle of Group Responsibility (see Goodin 1985, 136), does acknowledge if not cultural practices as such, group-based obligations. I think we require something stronger, namely, an answer to the question "who in a group is vulnerable to whom as a matter of (cultural) practice?" However, it may be possible to refine the principle in ways that satisfy the stronger requirements to which I point.

112. In a very tender scene in the movie *Fried Green Tomatoes*, the responsiveness of the heroine is portrayed in her willingness to treat the town alcoholic to a shot of whiskey. Her action is depicted as an act of kindness that transcends moralizing when, during dinner, the poor fellow excuses himself from the table to avoid the humiliation and miserable exposure of the shakes. In the absence of other available means of response, giving an alcoholic a drink may be the most compassionate action. For the alcoholic struggling with the pain of abstinence, but determined to stay dry, giving her a drink is a very poor response to an apparent need.

113. I speak primarily of coercion here, but I use the term to cover all sorts of unjust circumstances that might result in our being in, and staying in, positions where we are the one upon whom seemingly vulnerable-responsive obligations fall.

114. See Sommers (1987) and Daniels (1988), for examples.

115. See Gilbert (1996) for an interesting discussion of the formation of obligation as a consequence of relations. Gilbert, however, is not confining her discussion to moral obligation.

116. In *Subjection and Subjectivity*, Diana Meyers suggests that in such cases we question the "kind of person" we would be if we failed to respond appropriately (1994). The question gets framed precisely this way in Doctorow's novel (most recently made into a musical play) *Ragtime*. The female protagonist, wife of a successful fireworks manufacturer and adventurer, residing in an all-white suburban town, finds a newly buried yet still alive black infant as she digs in her garden. She tries to understand what she ought to do. As a dutiful wife, she knows that her husband—away on an adventure to the North Pole—would want her to give the child away immediately to a charity that would handle such a case. As a caring woman, who knows all too well the indifferent treatment such a throwaway child would receive, she cannot determine to do her wifely duty to obey what she knows would be her husband's wishes. In the musical, she sings in one chorus, "What kind of wife would I be?" if she kept the child, and responds in the next with: "What kind of woman would I be?" if she gave up the child. She resolves to keep the child and raise it in her own home. She responds to the pressing need of one who, by mere happenstance, is

totally vulnerable to her actions rather than to an unquestioned duty to obey her husband.

117. While intuitions may be less uniform with respect to the fetus, I take it to be a desideratum of a model of moral obligation that an argument defending a woman's right to an abortion can be made plausibly. My quarrel with Thomson is not with her conclusion, but with the argument. The situation of pregnancy is not, I believe, adequately analogized to other situations that lend themselves to voluntaristic models. Historically, pregnancy has not been a consciously-consented-to-action that is characteristic of voluntarism. More often, a woman just finds herself pregnant and must respond to the situation in some way. But an adequate defense of abortion is not within the scope of the present project. Nonetheless it is an interesting challenge to the vulnerability model to attempt to mount a defense of abortion that respects the largely involuntary nature of the relation between pregnant woman and fetus.

118. See Part Two for a defense of this claim with respect to the liberal tradition of contract theory as revived by John Rawls. For a feminist critique of obligations based on the social contract, see Hirshman and DiStefano (1996).

119. In Chapter Three, I make the case for the limitations of this conception in the face of dependency.

120. See Chapter Five, p. 133ff., for a discussion of the Family and Medical Leave Act of 1993.

121. It is interesting to hear the vulnerability model echoed in this response. The assumption of obligation is neither freely chosen nor coerced. It is, however, expected. The expectation arises out of the fact that the speaker's mother cared for her own mother. The speaker's mother is vulnerable to the speaker's actions first because of the expectation, and second because there is no one else who can help. The demand is morally warranted moreover because of an expectation backed by a similar response on the part of the one who now needs care—the care was justly deserved and justly demanded of the speaker. Also see note below.

122. At the same time the response is situated in a context where dependency work is gendered by social convention. What is the moral justification for the gendered assignment of care? Does the speaker have any male siblings who could share her obligations? That the mother has a justifiable claim to care from her children seems plausible enough, but the further question can be asked, why is there no one else who can do the care?

123. See Ruddick (1989).

124. This method is not discussed in ethical reasoning frequently enough, but it is doubtless of great importance for ethical judgments. It is a separate project to work out the precise nature of such analogical moral thinking.

125. Virginia Held suggests that the maternal relation be substituted for the contractual relation as the fundamental model of moral relations. My suggestion follows upon that of Held except that I generalize these to dependency relations and do not confine them to maternal relations. See Held (1987b and 1987c).

126. On the other hand, *in spite* of the condition of slavery, a certain fellow feeling may have developed between his master and him. This fellow feeling may become a more legitimate basis for an obligation arising out of his master's vulnerability to his actions. Such fellow feeling could only come about if the master had similarly provided evidence of fellow feeling toward the slave. A

truly brutal master could not even warrant such a basis for response. Relationships of dependency often invoke some affective bonds which make clear-cut moral injunctions difficult—especially since (I want to insist) these affective bonds (of which fellow feeling is perhaps the mildest and most general) are themselves the ground of moral obligation.

Part Two

127. A number of feminist theorists have regarded the work of Rawls and other liberal philosophers with an eye toward issues of dependency without articulating the dependency critique. Although feminist criticism of liberal political philosophy has now become too extensive to list in a work such as this one, some have been more closely tied to dependency. Those writers have spoken of "the need for more than justice," as Annette Baier entitles one work expounding this theme. Baier expands on this theme in a number of other works. See Baier (1985, 1986, 1987, 1994). Others, e.g., Minow (1990), Pateman (1989) and Held (1978, 1987a, 1987b) have shed light on the unacknowledged gender considerations that undergird legal theory and a social contract engaged in by men. Also see essays in Phillips (1987). Fineman (1991, 1995) comes very close to articulating the dependency critique as I conceive it. Susan Okin brings both the historical and the contemporary neglect of women's involvement in dependency to the forefront of her political considerations (Okin 1979, 1989a, 1989b). I owe much to her systematic analysis and feminist, but sympathetic, critique of Rawls. My examination of Rawls is deeply indebted to these and others too numerous to mention, and intends to carry these discussions further.

128. See, for example, Rawls (1992, xxviii–ix) for the characterization of his project. Rawls acknowledges that a conception of justice "so arrived at may prove defective" (1992, xxix). My claim is that it is defective because it is so arrived at.

129. I am not assuming that any features of human life are untouched by social factors, nor that these social factors can be neatly bracketed. Nonetheless, development, decline and disease are inescapable conditions for natural beings, and these set the parameters for the dependency that is equally inescapable. See discussion of these issues in Chapter One, especially pp. 29–30 above.

130. In one sense, the inability to reciprocate is a function of dependency only in the context of certain socially based distribution policies. Socially based distribution policies also make those who are or become dependent especially vulnerable to impoverishment, and so unable to reciprocate benefits they have received. In an other sense, however, while we are very ill or very young, we are at the mercy of others to dispense whatever resources we have. In *this* sense, the infant heir and the beggar's child both require a third party intervention to repay their caretaker. I focus on the second sense because the book looks at dependency through dual lenses, that of the dependent and that of the dependency worker. It may be helpful to see the difficulties here raised by dependency in terms of capability, rather than resources. See Sen (1992). Thus, although the children of the poor and of the wealthy have differing resources, by virtue of their dependency their inability to convert those resources into functionings and capabilities is more similar than their resources are different.

131. The person who intervenes may or may not be the same person who provides hands-on care. But the person who provides hands-on care is virtually always

in a position in which she has to interpret the needs and desires of their charge. She is not always, however, the person empowered to translate those needs into socially understood interests. See Chapter One, especially pp. 33–37 above.

132. See Kittay (1994) for a bibliography of Rawls's feminist critics and a discussion of his response to these criticisms.

133. Rawls says that equality operates on three levels: 1) the administrative and procedural, i.e., the impartial and consistent application of rules, constituted by the precept to treat likes alike; 2) "the substantive structure of institutions" (Rawls 1971, 505) requiring that all persons be assigned equal basic rights; and 3) the situation of the original position addressing the basis of equality, those "features of human beings in virtue of which they are to be treated in accordance with the principles of justice" (Rawls 1971, 504).

There are inequalities for dependency workers and dependents at the first level which could be defended. One can argue, for example, that persons unable to fill a job because of a disability, or because they have dependency responsibilities, cannot be eligible for equal opportunity considerations. At the second level, we can justify some inequalities as well. Minors do not have the right to vote. Severely retarded individuals cannot be assigned rights and freedoms requiring higher mental abilities. Rights, after all, can be granted only to those capable of understanding and acting on them. Responsibilities of dependency work, in contrast, should not affect the equal assignment of basic rights.

Note that formerly, women's responsibilities as dependency workers have been deemed sufficient to exclude them from many economic and political rights. If we count pregnancy as "dependency work"—insofar as it is the care and nurture of a completely dependent being—then, as the abortion debate (along with controversies concerning surrogate mothering, suitable work environments of pregnant women, and the prosecution of pregnant women abusing drugs) show, the assignment of equal basic rights to these dependency workers is still not a resolved issue.

The burden of this book is to show that even while we can grant that some inequalities are justified, there is a more elemental problem for the achievement of full moral equality at the third, and most fundamental, level.

134. The method is characterized by Rawls, first as a procedural interpretation of Kantian moral conceptions (particularly those principles regulative of the kingdom of ends [1971, 256]), then as *Kantian Constructivism* (1980), and later as *political constructivism* (1992). The alterations do not affect the argument presented here. The method is supposed to be constructivist in that "it does not accept any intuitions as indubitable and does not begin with the assumption that there are first principles in moral theory" (Baynes 1992, 55).

135. Rawls's later writings are intended to answer criticisms that the conception of the person is a metaphysical one specific to certain liberal theories and that the principles of justice chosen are not as purely constructivist as Rawls's claims. See especially Nagel (1973), Hart (1975), and Sandel (1982). Rawls's response is to distinguish "political liberalism" from liberalism as a "comprehensive moral doctrine" (1992; also 1985). He also clarifies the basis on which parties in the OP adopt the basic liberties and their priority, avoiding both metaphysical conceptions of the person and particular psychological propensities (1982; 1992). The argument in this paper is, nonetheless, that the individualism at the core of the theory—which Nagel (1973, 228) notes is augmented by the

motivational assumption of mutual disinterestedness—does predispose the parties in the OP to ignore the concerns of both dependents and dependency workers.

136. Also see Rawls (1975b, 542f).

137. In *Political Liberalism*, Rawls writes, "To model this equality in the OP we say that the parties, as representatives of those who meet the condition, are symmetrically situated. This requirement is fair because in establishing fair terms of social cooperation (in the case of the basic structure) the only relevant feature of persons is their possessing the moral powers . . . and their having the normal capacities to be a cooperating member of society over the course of a lifetime" (1992, 79). The OP is regarded as fair because it presumably models this equality. He also writes, "citizens are equal in virtue of possessing, to the requisite minimum degree, the two moral powers and other capacities that enable us to be normal and fully cooperating members of society. All those who meet this condition have the same basic rights, liberties and opportunities and the same protections of the principles of justice" (1992, 79). He then continues, "To model this equality in the OP we say that the parties, as representatives of those who meet this condition, are symmetrically situated" (1992, 79).

138. Rawls (1980) writes simply: "[T]he idealization means that everyone has sufficient intellectual powers to play a *normal* part in society, and no one suffers from *unusual* needs that are *especially difficult* to fulfill, for example *unusual and costly medical requirements*" (emphasis mine, 546]). The idealization requires the condition of adulthood as well as health. Since both children and the temporarily disabled merely temporarily and contingently fail to meet the requirements for equal moral worth, they are included in the category of equal citizen. See Rawls (1971, 509). The appropriate treatment of those who are permanently disabled seems to be another matter.

139. In *Political Liberalism* Rawls drops the term "self-originating source of claims" (1980, 544) and substitutes the term "self-authenticating source of valid claims" (1992, 32). See pp. 96–99 for a discussion of this difference.

140. Rawls acknowledges that some will have a more developed sense of justice than others. Equality with respect to a sense of justice demands only that persons have a sense of justice "equally sufficient relative to what is asked of them" (1980, 546) insofar as they are "fully cooperating members of society over a complete life" (1980, 546).

141. See note 140. Rawls also writes of "the equally sufficient capacity (which I assume to be realized) to understand and to act from *the public conception of social cooperation*" (emphasis is mine, 1980, 546).

Chapter Three

142. According to the *New York Times* (14 Nov. 1989, A1, B12) a 1985 survey found that "about one in five employees over the age of 30 was providing some care to an elderly parent." The same article reports that almost one third of part-time workers spent more than twenty hours a week helping older relatives and, of those not employed who had had jobs, twenty-seven percent had taken early retirement or resigned to meet their responsibilities.

143. Rawls is not concerned here with the dependencies with which we are concerned, at least not insofar as these are the ones to which *women* usually attend. This is evident in his language: "Nevertheless, since it is assumed that a

generation cares for its immediate descendants, as *fathers say care for their sons*, a just savings principle ... would be acknowledged" (emphasis is mine, 1971, 288). And on the following page he writes, "Thus imagining themselves to be *fathers*, say, they are to ascertain how much they should set aside for their *sons* by noting what they would believe *themselves* entitled to claim of their *fathers*" (emphasis is mine, Rawls 1971, 289). No mothers or daughters appear on these pages. In a discussion with Professor Rawls (April 1993), he indicated to me that he meant to include both parents—the mother as well as the father— in the representative head of household. How different would the theory look if fathers *and mothers* had been included among the parties in the OP? That would depend, I think, on whether the dependency concerns for which mothers are traditionally responsible are included as well.

144. So she admonished her husband. Still, the representation granted the paterfamilias is different than the one necessitated by dependency work, when the head of household represents those who are capable of speaking for themselves. The dependency worker must represent needs of those too young, frail, weak or ill to come to a public forum and speak for themselves.

145. Okin (1989b) makes the additional point that the phrase "head of household" is gendered masculine, for a "female head of household" invariably denotes a household in which there is no healthy adult male.

146. This stands in contrast to what Rawls calls the "relevant positions" of "equal citizenship and that defined by his place in the distribution of income and wealth" (Rawls 1971, 96.)

147. The representatives in the OP are envisioned by Rawls to all be of the same generation. One who adopts the point of view of the OP assumes a "present time of entry" into the OP and assumes that they can communicate with other parties in the OP. See Rawls (1971, 136–142) If parties represent generational lines, there is little point in asking what temporal position they occupy relative to one another with respect to the issue of mutual disinterestedness. But if the representatives represent individuals, the question is pertinent. Now, however, the requirement of mutual disinterestedness is questionable. We could have one representative representing an individual living today and another representing the other's ancestor, and then it is not clear if we can say that the parties are mutually disinterested.

148. It may seem possible to construe an ambiguity in Rawls's notion that each individual in a future generation should have someone who cares about them: an ambiguity between each assuming a special responsibility for someone in the next generation, as in the case of a parent to a child, or each acting responsibly to the next generation. But Rawls himself seems to see not an ambiguity but a relation between these seeming alternatives. He writes: "Those in the OP know, then, that they are contemporaries, so unless they care for at least their immediate successors, there is no reason for them to agree to undertake any savings whatever" (Rawls 1971, 292.)

149. Rawls distinguishes between the rational and the reasonable. Persons are *rational* in that they satisfy each person's view of their rational advantage. They are *reasonable* (in that they recognize and accept that not all have the same ends in engaging in social interaction.

150. This, however, is culturally relative and such a decision is generally more socially acceptable for men than for women, even within liberal societies where no moral stigma attaches to such a decision. See Meyers (1993). For a

different cultural view represented, see the powerful drama of Federico Garcia Lorca, *Yerma*.

151. Sen argues that because people have very different needs, an index of primary goods is not a sufficiently sensitive measure of interpersonal comparison of well-being. Primary goods are the "embodiment of advantage," while advantage ought to be understood as "a *relationship between persons and goods*" (Sen 1987, 158; author's emphasis). Rawls replies that he assumes citizens do have "at least to the essential minimum degree, the moral, intellectual, and physical capacities that enable them to be fully cooperating members of society over a complete life" (Rawls, 1992, 183). "The aim is to restore people by health care so that once again they are fully cooperating members of society" (Rawls 1992, 184). Variations in physical capacities due to disability or disease can, claims Rawls, be dealt with at the legislative stage.

152. I thank Annette Baier for calling this alternative interpretation to my attention. The reading consistent with the weaker claim gains support first in Rawls (1971, Part Three, especially 77), where he is careful to insist that the mere potentiality to have the features of a moral person is sufficient to bring into play the claims of justice. This reading gains further support in Rawls (1982, 15), and again in Rawls (1992, 301), where he identifies the point of entry and exit into the society as birth and death.

153. See for example, the moral psychology Rawls outlines (1992, especially 86). If these included dependency concerns and relational capacities, then perhaps there would be motivation sufficient for all parties to consider that they may be taking on responsibilities for dependents.

154. See Schwarzenbach (1986) on the notion that parents are "stewards" to their children.

155. I use the term in a manner similar to Sen (1992), Nussbaum 1988a; 1988b).

156. In the *Dewey Lectures,* Rawls writes, "slaves are human beings who are not counted as self-originating sources of claims at all; any such claims originate with their owners or in the rights of a certain class in society" (Rawls 1980, 544). In analogous passage in *Political Liberalism*, he writes: "[S]laves are human beings who are not counted as sources of claims, not even claims based on social duties or obligations. . . . Laws that prohibit the maltreatment of slaves are not based on claims made by slaves, but on claims originating from slaveholders, or from the general interests of society (which do not include the interests of slaves). Slaves are, so to speak, socially dead: they are not recognized as persons at all" (Rawls 1992, 33).

157. One might reply, as did one reviewer, that the valid claim is the *child's*. The mother may have a valid claim to her own education, but the claim to her child's education should not be expressed as *her* claim. To this I say that the child's is *one* relevant valid claim, and usually, at least when the child is very young, not a self-originating one. The claim originates with an adult responsible for the child's well-being. In fact, the child's claim lacks efficacy as long as her status as a minor excludes her from political participation. The claim not only originates with, but must also be pressed by, an adult whose voice can be heard in the relevant arena.

158. The communitarian critique expounded by Sandel (1982) raises some similar points about a self-definition that includes centrally the well-being of others. Sandel's account locates the difficulty in Rawls's prioritization of the self over its ends (1982, 19). I locate it in a conception of self so individuated that

dependency concerns are not normally comprehended as intrinsic to it and the consequences for one's understanding of oneself as free.

159. Rousseau's writings not only embodied this image, linking it to an enlightenment ideal of freedom for male citizens, but also exerted much influence in women's actual behavior. See Rousseau (1762, 1979), Wollstonecraft (1792, 1988), and Badinter (1980). Also see Held (1993), especially Chapter Six.

160. Although even in the *Dewey Lectures*, he writes, "These remarks . . . [are] to indicate the conception of the person connected with . . . the principles of justice that apply to its basic institutions. By contrast, citizens in their personal affairs or within the internal life of associations, may . . . have attachments and loves that they believe they would not, or could not, stand apart from . . ." (Rawls 1980, 545)

161. This way of putting the criticism is taken nearly *verbatim* from some very interesting and useful comments provided by John Baker.

162. Consider the horror that yielded the *New York Times* story about the physically and mentally handicapped children who were abandoned in a besieged Bosnian hospital. The reporter writes about Edin, one of the children who died, "Unlike 200,000 others whom the Bosnian Government estimates to have died in the war, Edin was not blown apart by heavy artillery, cut down by snipers, tortured or burned alive. He was simply left to fend for himself, an infant in a cot who was so severely handicapped that he had spent most of his life at the hospital." (Burns, John, *New York Times*, 20 July 1993, 1.) The sentiment expresses the moral horror of abandoning such helpless individuals: "It's monstrous," said Brig. Gen. Vere Hayes, Chief of Staff for the United Nations protection force in Bosnia. "There is, at least prima facie, a special obligation not to abandon such helpless persons—regardless of the cost to the staff."

163. See, for example, Beauvoir (1952), Chodorow (1978), Dinnerstein (1977), Gilligan (1982), and Bartky (1990), etc.

164. See the essays in Trebilcot (1987).

Chapter Four

165. Rawls later (Rawls 1992, 308–9) gives essentially the same list but accompanies it with an explanation of why each is included. Conspicuously absent from the considerations adduced in the explanations are the elements of "nurture," "interdependence," and "phases of life," all of which are mentioned as general facts about human life on the preceding page. Effectively, these elements are still omitted in the hard-core center of the theory.

166. See Nagel (1973), for the criticism that ignorance concerning one's own conception of the good does not necessarily result in an index of primary goods that is equally fair to all parties, "because the primary goods are not equally valuable in pursuit of all conceptions of the good" (1973, 228). One may try to assimilate my argument to Nagel's by assuming that dependency concerns are important to some conceptions of the good, more important perhaps than many of the other goods currently in Rawls's index. But the criticism that I put forward differs from Nagel's. I am arguing that, regardless of one's conception of one's own good, dependency concerns would belong on a list of primary goods. For a good discussion of the controversy surrounding the claims that such an index is the best way to make interpersonal comparative assessments of well-being, see Daniels (1990). See Rawls (1992, 1982) for his answer to this objection.

167. See Arrow (1973) and especially Sen (1987, 1992) for arguments that the variations in capabilities between persons may be so significant that one index cannot be adequate to meet the needs of all citizens. And see Rawls (1992, 182 ff.) for his answer to this objection.
168. See Meyers (1993, 1994) who speaks of the necessity of empathetic thought as a feature of a moral person. What I am considering is such a moral capacity.
169. This argument is made on pages 85ff. of the previous chapter.
170. As I remarked above, a number of writers have urged the need for "more than justice." See especially Baier (1987), Held (1993), Tronto (1993), and Ruddick (1995).
171. Health care is an obvious candidate for inclusion in a list of primary goods. Norman Daniels (1990) argues that the Rawlsian primary good of opportunity can be extended to cover health-care needs of persons. Health needs of the "normally active and fully functioning" are first calculated at the legislative stage, and then "special needs" can be considered. Health care demands "those things we need in order to maintain, restore, or provide functional equivalents (where possible) to normal species function" (1990, 280). Daniels emphasizes the relevance of normal functioning to equality of opportunity, and proposes the concept of "normal opportunity range." Appropriate health care, as determined partially by culture and partially by individual talents and skills, can allow a person to "enjoy that portion of the range to which his full array of talents and skills would give him access, assuming that these too are not impaired by special social disadvantages (e.g., racism and sexism)" (1990, 281). The handicap with respect to normal functioning refers to one of Rawls's two moral powers, the power to form and revise our own vision of the good. Rawls takes up this suggestion: "The aim is to restore people by health care so that once again they are fully cooperating members of society" (Rawls 1992, 184ff). While health care is an integral part of dependency care, Daniels's solution will not be adequate for three reasons. First, "normal opportunity range" is ill-defined for many sorts of disabilities and illnesses, for example, Down's Syndrome and especially severe mental retardation. Second, providing the "functional equivalents" to "normal species functioning," even when that is far short of a complete restoration, can require resources extensive enough that an explicit commitment in the founding principles themselves may itself be needed for its realization. And third, we need to consider whether a social commitment to restore, when possible, the dependent to full functioning will also compensate dependency workers without exploiting them. This final point is not Daniels's concern, but it is integral to any adequate reckoning of justice that includes dependency. Since few dependents can be restored to any degree of functioning without a significant infusion of caring labor, we have to ask about the cost to the dependency worker and the level of compensation.
172. See also Schwarzenbach (1990). I emphasize that (3) calls for the *capacity*, not for the response itself. We must understand such a capacity (along with a sense of fairness) as fundamental to moral persons, if we want basic institutions to incorporate principles ensuring support for relations in which dependents are cared for without sacrificing the interests of caretakers.
173. This view, espoused by many when the ethic of care was first expounded, has been revisited by a number of feminists. See, for example, Bubeck (1995), Bowden (1997), Tronto (1993, 1997, 1995), Held (1995) and Ruddick (1995).
174. See Rawls (1982), where Rawls stresses that we assess needs in many different

contexts and for many different reasons, adding that the index of primary goods includes only those needs relevant to justice.

175. Sen (1990) has criticized Rawls's use of primary goods. Sen argues that guarantees of primary goods do not serve justice for those so handicapped that they cannot make use of the goods. Sen's important argument is orthogonal to my own. The demands of care are primary goods that reflect a relation between persons and the resources for their well-being. See also note 151 above.

176. In *Political Liberalism* Rawls (1992) characterizes social cooperation as more than just efficiently organized social activity. It involves the "fair terms of cooperation" which in turn articulate "an idea of reciprocity and mutuality": All who cooperate must benefit, or share in common burdens, in some appropriate fashion judged by a suitable benchmark of comparison (1991, 300).

177. See note 171 for a discussion of Norman Daniel's efforts to include considerations of the just distribution of health care.

178. Rawls writes, "We take the two moral powers as the necessary and sufficient condition for being counted a full and equal member of society in questions of political justice. Those who can take part in social cooperation over a complete life, and who are willing to honor the appropriate fair terms of agreement are regarded as equal citizens" Rawls (1992, 302). This is a very strong claim and a puzzling one. For why should the contingent fact that some people are born, let us say, sufficiently mentally disabled, necessitate their exclusion from citizenship? There are some political activities they may not be able to engage in—for example, they may be incapable of enough political understanding to vote—but surely they need to receive the protections of political justice all the same. (I thank Susan Okin for discussions on this point.) The only rationale that is consistent with the theory is that although their condition is no less due to contingent factors, they will never be able to participate in the social cooperative situation as understood by Rawls.

179. This point is also discussed in Chapter Two above under the consideration of "exchange reciprocity."

180. See Aronow (1993). One of the *doulas* "recalls arriving at homes late morning to find mothers who haven't eaten or dressed. They are so concerned that the baby is O.K., they forget to take care of themselves" (1993, 8).

181. I wish to thank Elfie Raymond for helping me search for a term with the resonance necessary to capture the concept articulated here.

182. See the discussion in Chapter Two, pages 67–69. The importance of this ethic within the African-American community was documented by Stack (1974).

183. It may be unclear whether either Rawls's new principle of intergenerational justice or my principle of *doulia* are truly instances of reciprocity, not only because we are enjoined to give back to a party other than the one from whom we have received, but also because both principles enjoin us to give what we would have *wanted* to receive, not necessarily what we have *in fact* received. Nonetheless, the survival of a generation depends on having received a world not entirely depleted of resources, and the survival of an individual depends on care sufficient to bring us to adulthood, so there is a minimal sense in which both are principles of reciprocity, for we are not only enjoined to give, but enjoined to give *back*. That is, we would not be in a position to consider what we would want others to provide us, if we were not already recipients, even to a minimal degree, of those goods. But neither Rawls's principle of intergenerational justice nor my principle of doulia are notions of reciprocity

in the sense of returning either *to the same party* or *in the same measure* that which we have received.

184. I do not mean to suggest that we have a duty to *have* children because we have been cared for, but I do suggest that we owe to any children we do have the care we would have wanted to receive (and, at the very least, the care that was necessary to allow us to survive and thrive). And moreover, that the care bestowed on us—and some care must have been bestowed on us if we survived—is, in fact, *reciprocated* through care to the next generation.

185. Even a Hobbesian state of nature is barely conceivable without some principle of care (however attenuated). *Contra* Hobbes, we mischaracterize social organizations if we conceive of men springing from the earth "like mushrooms," already fully grown. See Hobbes (1966, 109).

186. For a just society to incorporate the concerns of dependency must mean it not only promotes the well-being of the dependency worker and the dependent, but also ensures the integrity of the relation between them. This integrity was very much threatened by the 104th U.S. Congress, which seriously entertained orphanages as suitable placement for children whose parents could not provide for them without government assistance.

187. The difference principle is the distributive principle applicable to certain goods on the list of primary goods (especially income and wealth) and not others (e.g., the basic liberties). To determine if it would be applicable to the added primary good(s) concerning care, it would be necessary to consider whether and how the Rawlsian project could coherently be reworked to include dependency concerns. This is too large a project for the current study whose aim is a critique and not a reconstruction. But I do not mean to suggest that a difference principle that applies to distributive problems concerning dependency care and dependency work is, in theory, not possible.

188. For some of the most recent work on the effects of this "restructuring," see Mushaben (1997), and Clayton and Pontusson (1997).

Part Three

Chapter Five

189. This is the Social Security Act of 1935, which was created during Roosevelt's presidency. See Davis (1993, 7–8).

190. However, it is important to note that, contrary to popular misconceptions, whites represent the largest racial group utilizing welfare. In 1993, of the 14 million recipients of Aid to Families with Dependent Children, 39% were white, 37% were black and 18% were Latino (Albelda, Folbre and the Center for Popular Economics 1996, 107).

191. The title of this section is borrowed from Tillmon (1976).

192. Many of these feminist writers see welfare in terms of both gender and race. For some examples of these analyses see Abramovitz (1996), Sassoon (1987), Skocpol (1992), Gordon (1990, 1994), Mink (1995).

193. Delivered at the Teach-In on Welfare at SUNY Stony Brook, Stony Brook, N.Y. March 1997.

194. Tillmon was a welfare mother and National Welfare Rights Organization leader. She spoke of welfare as "a supersexist marriage" in which we trade in "a" man for "the" man (1976, 356).

195. It is important to point out that the empirical facts do not support claims that welfare payments to impoverished women with children influenced the inci-

dence of single-parent households, never-wed mothers, mothers having additional children while on welfare, or teenage pregnancy. See Center on Hunger, Poverty and Nutrition Policy (1995).

196. That power is sometimes retained even where men cannot find work by doling out benefits to unemployed men for the support of their families. The money goes to the unemployed "breadwinner." A powerfully ironic description is to be found in Frank McCord's memoir of life in Cork County, Ireland, before the outbreak of World War II, *Angela's Ashes*. Relief money was obtained by McCord's father through the unemployment bureau. This dole money, while meager, was substantial in comparison to the charity meted out by the church to his mother. The mere presence of a man was adequate to put food on the table, because only "breadwinners" were eligible for the more "respectable" relief.

197. Few notions are as sexist and unjust: A child is made to suffer for the actions of its parents, and the stigma attaches itself to the woman and the children she has borne outside of marriage, but not to the man who sired these children.

198. The figure is 50 million dollars a year beginning in fiscal year 1998 through 2002.

199. States must apply for the funds and must conduct programs that conform to the Act's definition of abstinence education (PL104–193, sec. 912). In addition to promulgating the views already mentioned, a program must also:

   1) have as its exclusive purpose education about the psychological and health gains of abstaining from sexual activity
   2) teach that monogamy is the expected standard
   3) teach that sex outside marriage is likely to have harmful psychological and physical effects
   4) teach young people how to reject sexual advances and how alcohol/drug use increases vulnerability to sexual advances
   5) teach the importance of attaining self-sufficiency before having sex

200. According to the NOW Legal Defense and Educational Fund, at present the welfare plans of twenty-one states in the U.S. include a "family cap" provision. See note 209 for further explanation of "family cap" provisions.

201. A recent study released by the McCormack Institute and the Center for Survey Research, both at the University of Massachusetts, Boston, found that among a representative sample of the Massachusetts Transitional Aid to Families with Dependent Children (T.A.F.D.C.) caseload, 65% would be considered victims of domestic violence by a current or former boyfriend or husband using the Massachusetts state law's definition of abuse.

202. Some have argued that consumption is as central as production in the assumption of citizen rights. For this view worked out with respect to the Welfare Rights Movement, see Kornbluh (1998) who discusses the demand for consumer rights of credit by the women of the National Welfare Rights Organization (NWRO) and the action against Sears department stores initiated by the NWRO.

203. For an excellent discussion of how the term "independent" came to be associated with wage labor and "dependent" became attached to those who were excluded from wage labor, see Fraser and Gordon (1994). They point to three groups who epitomized a dependent status: paupers, slaves, and women. In the semantics of dependency, children, the disabled, and the frail elderly do not figure in the primary use of the term.

204. Even as the Left tries to protect residualist programs from being eviscerated,

the target of the Right is broader. Many programs such as social security, progressive taxation, and even public education are targets. I want to argue that by restricting a defense of welfare to residualism, especially with respect to welfare's impact on women, supporters of the welfare state may lose the opportunity to respond adequately to both the narrow and the broad attack.

205. Sometimes these conditions are taken as inevitable barriers to employment when they are not. The fruitful work of the disability community has demonstrated the extent to which "disabling conditions" are as much a consequence of the social environment which does not provide adequate access as are the impairments themselves. Also, persons without adequate education or training are generally incapacitated in ways that bespeak injustice, not an inherent incapacity. In all these cases the just solution to a person's inability to participate in paid employment is to provide the enabling conditions. But even when we recognize all the ways in which social efforts to enable persons to participate fall short, there remain conditions that severely limit persons' ability to engage in paid employment.

206. Ironically, Adam Smith himself saw one of the benefits of capitalism and the division of labor to be the production of sufficient wealth to be able to support a very substantial population of persons who did not labor. He took this to be an advance over other means of production. See Smith (1921, 2–3).

207. In fact, the victims of social circumstances not infrequently blame themselves especially harshly in an environment of equal opportunity rhetoric. See Bartky (1990).

208. Diana Pearce put the point this way at a panel on women and welfare at Yale University, May 1995. I borrow my formulation from her.

209. This is a remark I have heard time and again from women who considered themselves "liberal" and "feminists." One officer of NOW Legal Defense and Educational Fund remarked that she had rarely seen so much negative mail and threats to withdraw support as when the organization took up the fight against the "family cap" provision of state welfare plans. The family cap provision prohibits the use of public assistance for any child born while the mother was receiving welfare. The very availability and legality of contraception and abortion, victories of feminism, make the situation of those women who do not or cannot avail themselves of these reproductive means, more precarious still. They now are blamed for their condition not only by conservatives, but by many liberals as well.

210. They were also responsible for protective labor legislation, which protected women from some of the abuses of employers, but also reduced the earning capabilities of low income women—the income of the very mothers they were concerned to help. Because the benefits provided by Mother's Pensions were kept very low, it was difficult for the families to survive without women's (and children's) supplemental wage labor, labor made less accessible to them by the protective labor laws.

211. It also resonates with efforts to question the fixity of the public-private divide. Both facets emerge in the suggestive use of Daniel Bell's term "the public household" (Bell 1976) by feminist theorist Michele Moody-Adams (1997). She points to social policy "that seeks to use public power and the vast resources of the public household to legislate against certain behavior rather than to provide positive social support that might help prevent the behavior in the first place" (1997, 12). Although she argues that such "reactive" policies are inimi-

cal to the viability of truly liberal democratic institutions, I have argued in Chapters Three and Four that the principles of liberalism, as articulated by John Rawls, are not adequate grounds for what both Moody-Adams and I agree are the more positive policies implied by the notion of the public household. Developing a basis for arguing for positive policies such as socially responsible family policy is the purpose of what follows.

212. For the notion of social citizenship with respect to women see, for example, Pateman (1989), Piven (1985), Siim (1988), Gordon (1990), Orloff (1993), and Skocpol (1992).

213. Orloff (1993), offering a gendering of the "power resources" school of analysis, argues that social citizenship for women is not centrally about the decommodification of labor, as it is for men within a market economy. Instead, she argues, social citizenship for women involves both women's ability to be economically independent of men and their capacity to form and sustain autonomous families. As economic independence is understood as a good for *all* citizens, women's right to such a good cannot be questioned. That women should have a right to form and sustain autonomous families does not immediately follow from the sorts of rights usually presumed for citizens of a liberal democracy or even a social democracy. While such a right seems to me to be exactly what is necessary, the question is whether it can be justified on grounds acceptable to those who also accept the premises of a liberal/social democracy and whether it can serve as a justification for welfare. This argument is not made in the excellent article under discussion. Instead, the argument Orloff makes is that as social citizenship is understood as desirable, and since decommodification is a condition of social citizenship, but is gendered and more appropriate to men then women, we need to find a condition that corresponds to the lives lead mostly by women. This is an argument that can motivate feminists, but one still needs to show that the corresponding condition disadvantages women unfairly—that is, that it amounts to an inequitable distribution of the benefits and burdens of social cooperation between men and women; that this condition benefits the larger social group and simultaneously disadvantages women. That is the point of the argument in this section of the book.

214. In Schmidtz and Goodin (1997), a later work, Goodin takes these matters into account. His is a superb defense of the notion of collective responsibility against those who maintain the primacy of "personal responsibility."

215. The question can be raised, "What happens when the government is the provider?" But where the provider is not privatized and individualized as it is in families, the dependency worker has an option that is available to other workers—and that is to organize. This doesn't mean that the dependency worker take the option of strikes—walking out on dependents. But they have available mobilization strategies used by other politically organized groups. The model of the National Welfare Rights Organization is perhaps useful here.

216. The importance of the affective component of care is found in recent studies indicating that "After birth ... in humans, the inflowing stream of sights, sounds, smells, touches—and most importantly, language and eye contact—literally makes the brain take shape." In other words, not only do infants require feeding and clothing, they require high quality interaction with their caretaker to develop well cognitively. Such interactions are most likely to be found in on-going relationships with caretakers (Blakeslee 1997).

217. These points are discussed in greater detail in Chapter Two above.
218. See Handler (1987) for an extended discussion of these models with respect to medical care, special education for the mentally retarded and care for the elderly. Handler takes a communitarian approach to meeting needs of dependents.
219. See Adams and Winston (1980, 88–99) for a comparative study of welfare and family assistance in the different economic systems of the U.S., Sweden, and China.
220. See Sen (1987).
221. I thank Joan Tronto for calling my attention to what might appear as an undue bias for a goods-based assessment of equality. At the conclusion of Chapter Seven, I briefly discuss the benefit of a capability approach in dealing with distributional issues surrounding disability.
222. Public Law 103–3, 5 February 1993, 107 Stat., 6–29.
223. For a study evaluating who uses the FMLA and for what purposes see Gerstel (1998).
224. On the morning of the day I was to read this portion of this chapter at the Feminist Theory and Social Policy Conference held at the University of Pittsburgh in October 1993, the public radio station announced on its news program that in Pittsburgh the figure was one-third of all households.
225. Only forty-four percent of women workers and fifty-two percent of men workers are covered by the current act which exempts employers with fewer than fifty employees. See Spalter-Roth and Hartmann (1990, 44).
226. This idea can be found in Kaplan (1993).
227. Fraser (1997) has listed a number of criteria by which to evaluate proposals for the welfare state. The criteria are guided by an ideal of gender parity. I invite the reader to consider the proposals put forward here in terms of those criteria.
228. This is a close to the vision articulated by the 1996 vice-presidential candidate Jack Kemp in one of the vice-presidential debates. He envisioned an economy that could support a family with one breadwinner and one stay-at-home parent, although he was quick to add that the stay-at-home parent would not have to be the woman! It is interesting to have the ideal of the "family wage," a concept fought for by the Left in this country, reemerge as a proposition by the Right, at the same time when the Right is legislating the entrance of welfare recipients (women usually without male support) into the labor force at minimum wage salaries, even those raising children as young as two years of age.
229. Orloff (1993) points out that one way of characterizing the difference between welfare programs geared to men and those targeted at women is that the former are meant to shield the citizen against the worst effects of market failures, while the latter are meant to shield against familial failures. In this respect it is important to see that when the benefits are intended to deal with familial failures, it is the fate of the children rather than the adult women which is most likely to have public sympathy. Women again come to be seen as conduits rather than as persons and citizens in their own right.
230. According to the *Current Population Survey* of March 1994, 9% of married couples were poor, and single mothers comprised 46% of the poor; of all poor families 12% had at least one year-round, full-time worker and 32% had at least 1 member who worked at least thirty weeks during the year. These figures are based on a rate of poverty that all experts agree is set too low.

231. Center on Hunger, Poverty & Nutrition Policy, citing the Bureau of Labor Statistics, U.S. Department of Labor.

232. Why this is so is an interesting sociological question. It is also interesting to contemplate the possibilities for gender equity within the family if such an arrangement within the home is coupled with genuine gender equity in the public domain of paid employment and political and social power. But in spite of all of women's advances, this remains a utopian vision.

233. Strictly speaking, universality is too strong a claim, for there are occupational exclusions and eligibility rules that restrict who can receive these benefits. Nonetheless, all workers within those limits are eligible—their eligibility is not income dependent. When writers on welfare and the welfare state speak of "universal" programs they mean either that all citizens receive the benefit or that all within a certain category do. The contrast is generally with programs in which benefits depend on income or occupation. For example, neither AFDC nor farm subsidies are universal benefits.

234. See Sen (1992, 39–42).

235. But it also recognizes that all these specificities are called into play when the need is defined. How it is to be satisfied is something that must be negotiated by those in the dependency relation. See Fraser (1987).

Chapter Six

236. This notion, readers will recognize, presaged the concept of *doulia* I have been elaborating in this work.

237. Some readers will note that I am using the categories of Sara Ruddick's (1989) *Maternal Thinking*. In the following chapter, I will be working with these categories more fully. There I will both use and challenge them since, as Jane McDonald (1991) has noted, in formulating these categories, Ruddick seemed to assume that all children are "intact."

238. Another important question is whether this commitment is marked by birth or adoption, or marked by an awareness of a conception, especially one that is planned and desired. How one answers this question bears on the moral desirability or opprobrium of genetic testing and selective abortion for disability. See Kittay and Kittay (forthcoming).

239. I have in mind Rawls's use of Hume. See Chapter Three above.

240. See, for example, Jablow (1982), and Bérubé (1996).

241. See note 34 in the Introduction.

242. I borrow once again (see Chapter One) Marilyn Frye's metaphor for the role of women on the stage of world history and culture (Frye 1983). One writer who does discuss this relationship is Barbara Hillyer (1993).

243. As in cognitive science, where models of processing are being developed in which a given task is not only broken into serially performed operations, but into a set of parallel operations distributed over several processors, so the mothering that Sesha has had over these many years has been one in which tasks have been assigned across a set of mothering persons.

244. In Chapter Seven, I will discuss questions of resources that ought to be devoted to disabled persons and their families. For now I merely raise the issue.

245. A sadder group are those who assume a *retreat* adaptation. These are parents who "abandon the entrepreneurial role even though they have not achieved normalization . . . . Doubly isolated, they lack access both to opportunities for normalization and to involvement in advocacy groups" (Darling 1988, 156).

Chapter Seven

246. The project concerned prenatal testing and selective abortion based on disability.

247. Ferguson and Asch remark: "If there is any one dominant rhythm to most parents' narratives, it must be the constant drumbeat of dissatisfaction with the medical profession's handling of, or approaches to families with disabled children" (1989, 122).

248. Parents of the disabled have decried the excessive medicalization of disability and the pathologizing of parental responses. See for example, Ferguson and Asch (1989) and Lipsky (1985). Yet parents are also grateful for medical procedures that are now available. For an eloquent statement of the improvements in medical care and habilitation for Down's Syndrome children, see Bérubé (1996, especially Chapter Two).

249. And should it? These questions need to be pursued within the same professional ethics that presents problems of triage, the morality of physician-assisted suicide, and cost-benefit analyses.

250. See Ruddick (1998) for a discussion of this distinction.

251. To be sure, dressing her nicely and keeping her in unsoiled clothes is not *the same as* loving and caring for her—but it is sending a message loudly and clearly.

252. In a conversation with my son concerning prenatal testing for genetic disability, my son speaks of the "message" that he thinks a sibling would receive if a parent aborted because of an impairment in the fetus. He writes:

> If a child believes his membership in the family is contingent on not being retarded or otherwise disabled, he might at first value his place in it more highly because it was *earned*. . . . But the positive feeling that love has been earned can subside, and the child might instead feel a constant pressure to prove himself to be worthy of his place in the family. He will not view his family's love for him as unconditional love. (Kittay and Kittay, 1998)

253. "IEP" refers to the "Individualized Educational Program." Every program for developmentally disabled children is required to come up with an individualized set of goals and tasks for each student. In the U.S., the legislation which brought about the IEP was PL 94–142, The Education for All Handicapped Children Act of 1975. Gartner, Lipsky, and Turnbull explain that "With the 1986 Education of the Handicapped Act Amendments (PL 99–457), which extended earlier legislation, children with disabilities are provided for from birth . . . " (Gartner, Lipsky and Turnbull 1991, 134).

254. On the excessive medicalization of disability and the pathologizing of parental responses, see for example, Ferguson and Asch (1989) and Lipsky (1985).

255. Although both professionals and parents are engaged in caring work, the virtues that are characteristic of the professional participate more markedly in virtues that are often thought to characterize a "justice orientation," while partiality, affect, and particularity are valued within the "care orientation" (Gilligan 1987; Kittay and Meyers 1987). The gendered flavor of these moral orientations has stimulated much discussion in feminist scholarship and is not surprising in this context. As we have remarked throughout this book, feminists today are more likely to see the distinction as problematic, or at least as

more complicated than a simple dichotomy. In fact, in the context of disability the oppositions arise within a *practice* of care. Furthermore, the task of this book has been to insist that care must be brought into the domain of justice, and that justice can be realized only when those who do the work of caring are treated with justice. Nonetheless, Darling's analysis directs us to how different virtues, each of which is associated with these moral orientations, can clash.

256. The female professional also assumes the virtues (and some of the status) of the male, while the parental male figure gets feminized, both in the virtues he assumes and his status relative to professionals. (Sesha's father has sensed this with respect to himself in the company of medical professionals.) I believe that the feminization of which I speak is behind the following odd study. Cummings (1976) found that "Compared to the healthy control group, fathers of the mentally retarded group were rated higher on the Order and lower on the Dominance and Heterosexuality variables.... [which suggests] a constricted male accentuating his compulsive tendencies in order to suppressive his aggressive and sexual drives" (Cummings 1976, 251). In other words, Cumming's study claims to have shown that, at least with respect to certain parameters (the ratio of Order and Dominance and Heterosexuality variables), fathers of mentally retarded children were more likely to repress their sexual and aggressive drives than fathers of healthy children. The assumptions behind such a finding are in serious need of deconstruction. Not only is the study heterosexist, but it also pathologizes what may be perfectly appropriate responses. These fathers may be perfectly sexual when not focusing on (as they must be when they are filling out these questionnaires) the serious disability of their child who must face a hostile world. Order is invaluable when you are dealing with a difficult situation of any sort, so the finding that fathers have a strong need for order should not be so surprising. The question that should be asked is not how having a disabled child "distorts" one's personality, but whether the personality traits that are found are helpful or destructive in dealing with the situation at hand. Mostly, it appears odd that the question of the "masculinity" of the father of a developmentally delayed or otherwise disabled child should even be raised.

257. A continual sense that one's own efforts in mothering are inadequate may begin to gnaw at one's self-esteem. Nonetheless, it appears that activism and the reduction of stigma of the disability are operative in reducing the lowering of a parent's self-esteem. See Cummings, Bayley and Rie (1966). While mothers of retarded children experienced more dysphoria than mothers caring for autistic and chronically ill children (this was found to be replicated with fathers in a later study in Cummings [1976]), they also did not experience themselves as having any less self-esteem. These mothers were apparently largely recruited from "militantly active associations for retarded children where considerably higher morale appears to obtain than when parents have no such affiliation" and were enlisted at a time when the stigma of retardation was diminishing in response to the Kennedy family's activism in this area and "the recent activation of government service programs for the retarded" (Cummings, Bayley and Rie 1966, 606). This raises the question of how stress and unhappiness in the mothering of a child with disabilities arises from the stigma of disability and how the provision of social services can itself serve to decrease stigma.

258. Scheper-Hughes traces the causes of this misery to the chain of responsible parties. As she does, we find that the blame extends to the U.S. and to

multinational corporations who profit from this misery. The extent of the misery is commensurate with the amount of blame there is to go around.

259. Personal Communication by Jeffrey Botkin, M.D., M.D.H. (Salt Lake City, Utah). For sake of confidentiality I cannot reveal much more about the case. Suffice it to say that the couple was Muslim and although a Moslem cleric was called in and informed the parents that the Muslim faith regards such children as a gift from God, the parents refused to accept the child. Another researcher of the Hastings Project, a genetic counselor (Diana Punales Morejon), tells of a Hasidic couple who sent their Down's infant to Israel to be cared for by relatives so that the presence of this child would not endanger the marital prospects for their other children. The stories can be multiplied and the cultural sources will vary. But the stigma remains widespread and is often interwoven with other social concerns.

260. I am reminded of one of the many wise and humorous stories about philosopher Sidney Morgenbesser. He tells of being one of the few faculty among the students who were beaten and arrested during the anti-Vietnam War sit-ins at Columbia in the 1960s. When he was brought before the judge, the judge asked the young professor: "So, you think you were treated unfairly by the police?" Morgenbesser replied: "Oh no, Judge, I was treated very fairly. The police were being equally vicious to everyone." A mother's sense of fairness, especially when her children's well-being is involved, is not so ready to accommodate to this sort of equality.

261. The point is best expressed in this passage by Josh Greenfield, writing about his experiences with his son, Noah:

> Noah's school called: the school would be closed, the roof is leaking. I called the local school board: Could they furnish facilities, if we furnish the teachers? They told me it was out of their hands legally and not a good idea educationally. They would offer no substitute site during the period in which we lacked a school structure.
> I don't mind accepting the conditions of life. It's just that I resent like hell the disadvantages that are heaped upon the already disadvantaged and then described as "conditions" (Greenfield 1978, 93).

262. As race is often combined with ethnic and cultural differences, professionals are often not well equipped to understand how multicultural differences aggravate the difficulties of not being a white parent of a disabled child. See Groce and Zola (1993).

263. Eunice Kennedy Shriver (1997), explains that "Despite the fact that in 1994 the Social Security Administration had markedly tightened the criteria for SSI eligibility so that only thirty percent of child applicants qualified (fewer than among adult claimants), Social Security is now interpreting the new legislation in the most stringent way. About 135,000 needy, disabled children will be disqualified, and many more in the future will not be eligible." Also see Giordano (1996), Pear (1996), Stewart (1996), and Lelyveld (1996). For general information on the Supplemental Security Income (SSI) and Social Security Insurance for Adult Disabled Children (SSDI), see Gartner, Lipsky and Turnbull 1991, (120–121).

264. Denmark is not alone in offering substantial support to families of disabled

children. For a comparative overview of different services offered to families with a child with a disability see Gartner, Lipsky and Turnbull (1991).

265. Although some biographical accounts, for example Jablow (1982) and Bérubé, (1996) indicate the difference such early services make for both parents and children.

Afterword

266. In the United States this has been in place since the Civil War. (For a discussion and a development of the relation and analogy between the establishment of mother's pension and aid to veteran's see Skocpol 1992). Other occupations also have some degree of "selflessness" incorporated in the job requirements. Monks and nuns are poorly compensated and are expected to give over their lives to the service of God or God's work with the poor and needy. They, too, are expected to renounce the interests of self—at least a worldly one. This service has institutional recognition and support, however, through the church. Soldiers, too, are expected to give of themselves *selflessly* in the service of their country. Yet, it is on the basis of the vulnerability soldiers thereby incur that a series of institutional supports have been put into place.

While these supports are not always as good as they ought to be, the fact of institutional supports alone is a recognition of particular vulnerability of services that are also understood to be crucial to the society they serve. While the traditional family, with its requirement that the husband provide for his wife and children, has been one institution that recognizes the vulnerability incurred through dependency work, it can itself be the source of additional vulnerabilities for unpaid dependency work, and it is not responsive to the condition of paid dependency workers.

References

Abramovitz, M. *Regulating the Lives of Women.* South End Press, 1996.

Adams, C. T., and K. T. Winston. *Mothers at Work: Public Policies in the United States, Sweden, and China.* New York: Longman Inc., 1980.

Alan Guttmacher Institute. *Facts in Brief, Abortion in the United States.* New York: The Alan Guttmach Institute, 1977.

Albelda, R., N. Folbre, and the Center for Popular Economics, *The War on the Poor: A Defense Manual.* New York: The New Press, 1996.

Arneson, R. J. "Equality and Equal Opportunity for Welfare." *Philosophical Studies* 56 (1989):77–93.

Aronow, I. "Doulas Step In When Mothers Need a Hand." *New York Times,* Sunday, 1 August 1993, p. 1, Westchester Section.

Arrow, K. J. "Some Ordinalist Utilitarian Notes on Rawls's *Theory of Justice.*" *Journal of Philosophy,* 70 (1973):245–63.

Badinter, E. *Mother Love: Myth and Reality.* New York: MacMillan, 1980.

Baier, A. C. "Caring about Caring." In *Postures of the Mind: Essays on Mind and Morals,* 93–104. Minneapolis: University of Minnesota Press, 1985.

———. "Trust and Antitrust." *Ethics* 96 (1986):231–60.

———. "The Need for More Than Justice." In *Science, Morality & Feminist Theory,* ed. M. Hanen and K. Nielsen, 41–56. Calgary, Canada: University of Calgary Press, 1987.

———. *Moral Prejudices: Essays on Ethics.* Cambridge, MA: Harvard University Press, 1994.

Bank-Mikkelsen, N. E. *Changing Patterns in Residential Services for the Mentally Retarded,* ed. R. B. Kugel and W. Wolfensberger. Washington, D.C.: U.S. President's Committee on Mental Retardation, 1969.

Barber, B. "Professions and Emerging Professions." In *Ethical Issues in Professional Life,* ed. J. Callahan, 35–39. New York: Oxford University Press, 1988.

Bart, P. "Review of Chodorow's *The Reproduction of Mothering.*" In *Mothering Essays in Feminist Theory,* ed. J. Trebilcot, 147–52. Totowa, NJ: Rowman and Allanheld, 1983.

Bartky, S. *Femininity and Oppression.* New York: Routledge, 1990.

Bayles, M. "The Professions." In Callahan, *Ethical Issues in Professional Life*, 27–31.

Baynes, K. *The Normative Grounds of Social Criticism: Kant, Rawls, and Habermas.* Albany, New York: State University of New York Press, 1992.

Beauvoir, S. de. *The Second Sex.* trans. H. M. Parsley. New York: Alfred Knopf, 1952.

Belenky, M. F., B. M. Clinchy, N. R. G. Goldberger, and J. M. Tarule. *Women's Ways of Knowing: The Development of Self, Voice, and Mind.* New York: Basic Books, 1986.

Bell, D. *The Cultural Contradictions of Capitalism.* New York: Basic Books, 1976.

Benhabib, S. "The Generalized and the Concrete Other." In *Women and Moral Theory*, ed. E. F. Kittay and D. T. Meyers, 154–77. Totowa, NJ: Rowman and Littlefield, 1987.

———. *Situating the Self: Gender, Community and Postmodernism in Contemporary Ethics.* New York: Routledge, 1992.

Bérubé, M. *Life as We Know It: A Father, a Family, and an Exceptional Child.* New York: Random House, 1996.

Birenbaum, A. "On Managing a Courtesy Stigma." *Journal of Health and Social Behavior* 11 (1970): 196–206.

———. "The Mentally Retarded Child in the Home and in the Family Cycle." *Journal of Health and Social Behavior* 11 (1971): 196–206.

Blakeslee, S. "Studies Show Talking with Infants Shapes Basis of Ability to Think." *The New York Times*, 17 April 1997, p. D21.

Blum, A., J. Harrison, B. Ess, and G. Vachon, eds., *Womens' Action Coalition Stats: The Facts About Women.* New York: The New Press, 1973.

Bohman, J. "Capabilities, Resources and Opportunities." Delivered at the American Philosophical Association Eastern Division, December 30, 1996.

Bowden, P. *Caring: Gender Sensitive Ethics.* New York: Routledge, 1995.

Bubeck, D. *Care, Gender, and Justice.* Oxford: Claredon Press, 1995.

Bureau of Labor Statistics. *Current Population Survey 1948–1994 Annual Averages.* Washington D.C.: Bureau of the Census, 1994.

Bureau of the Census. Current Population Survey, March 1994. Unpublished data. Washington D.C., 1994.

Center for the American Woman and Politics (CAWP). 1995. *Statewide Elective Executive Women 1995 Fact Sheet; Women in State Legislatures 1995 Fact Sheet; Women in the U.S. Senate, 1922–1995 Fact Sheet; Women in the U.S. House of Representatives 1995 Fact Sheet.* Rutgers, NJ: CAWP, 1995.

Chodorow, N. *The Reproduction of Mothering: Psychoanalysis and the Sociology of Gender.* Berkeley, CA: University of California, 1978.

Clayton, R., and J. Pontusson. "Welfare State Retrenchment and Public Sector Restructuring in Advanced Capitalist Societies." Paper presented. Revisioning the Welfare State. Cornell, 3–4 Oct., 1997.

Clement, G. *Care, Autonomy and Justice: Feminism and the Ethic of Care.* Boulder, CO: Westview Press, 1996.

Code, L. "Simple Equality Is Not Enough." *Australasian Journal of Philosophy*, 64 supplement (June, 1986):48–64.

Cohen, G. A. "Equality of What? On Welfare, Goods, and Capabilities." In *The Quality of Life*, ed. M. C. Nussbaum and A. Sen, 9–29. New York: Oxford University Press, 1993.

Conover, T. "The Last Best Friends Money Can Buy." *The New York Times Magazine*, (1997):124–32. November 30.

Cornell, D. *Beyond Accommodation: Ethical Feminism, Deconstruction, and the Law*. New York: Routledge, 1991.

Crenshaw, K. "Demarginalizing the Intersection of Race and Sex: A Black Feminist Critique of Antidiscrimination Doctrine, Feminist Theory, and Antiracist Politics." In *Feminist Legal Theory: Readings in Law and Gender*, ed. K. T. Bartlett and R. Kennedy, 57–80. San Francisco: Westview Press, 1991.

Cummings, S. "The Impact of the Child's Deficiency on the Father: A Study of Fathers of Mentally Retarded and Chronically Ill Children." *American Journal of Orthopsychiatry*, 46 (1976): 246–255.

Cummings, T. S., H. C. Bayley, and H. E. Rie. "Effects of the Child's Defiency on the Mother: A Study of Mothers of Mentally Retarded, Chronically Ill and Neurotic Children." *American Journal of Orthopsychiatry*, 36 (1966):595–608.

Daniels, N. *Am I My Parents' Keeper?: An Essay on Justice Between the Younger and the Older*. New York: Oxford University Press, 1988.

———. "Equality of What: Welfare, Resources, or Capabilities?" *Philosophy and Phenomenological Research*, supplement, 50:273–96.

Darling, R. B. *Families Against Society: A Study of Reactions to Children with Birth Defects*. Beverly Hills, CA: Sage, 1979.

———. "Parent-Professional Interaction: The Roots of Misunderstanding." In *The Family with a Handicapped Child: Understanding and Treatment*, ed. M. Seligman, 95–121. New York: Grune and Stratton, 1983.

———. "Parental Entrepreneurship: A Consumerist Response to Professional Dominance." *Journal of Social Issues*, 44 (no.1) (1988):141–58.

Davis, M. F. *Brutal Need: Lawyers and Welfare Rights Movement, 1960–1973*. New Haven, CT: Yale University Press, 1993.

Dinnerstein, D. *The Mermaid and the Minotaur: Sexual Arrangements and Human Malaise*. New York: Harper and Row, 1977.

DuBois, E. C., M. C. Dunlap, C. J. Gilligan, C. A. MacKinnon, and C. J. Menkel-Meadow. "Feminist Discourse, Moral Values, and the Law—A Conversation." *Buffalo Law Review*, 34 (1985).

Duras, M. *The Lover*. New York: Pantheon Books, 1985.

Dworkin, R. "What is Equality? Part 2: Equality of Resources." *Philosophy & Public Affairs* (1981) 10:283–345.

English, J. "Justice Between Generations." *Philosophical Studies*, 31 (1977):91–104.

Featherstone, H. *A Difference in the Family*. New York: Basic Books, 1980.

Ferguson, A. *Blood at the Root: Motherhood, Sexuality and Male Domination*. London: Unwin Hyman: Pandora Press, 1989.

Ferguson, P. M., and A. Asch. "Lessons from Life: Personal and Parental Perspectives on School, Childhood, and Disability." In *Schooling and Disability— Eighty-Eighth Yearbook of the National Society for the Study of Education, Part II*, ed. K. J. Behage, 108–40. Chicago: The University of Chicago Press, 1989.

Fineman, M. A. *The Illusion of Equality*. Chicago: University of Chicago, 1991.

———. *The Neutered Mother, the Sexual Family and Other Twentieth Century Tragedies*. New York: Routledge, 1995.

Fishkin, J. S. *Justice, Equal Opportunity, and the Family*. New Haven, CT: Yale University Press, 1983.

Fraser, N. "Women, Welfare and the Politics of Need Interpretation." *Hypatia* 2, no. 1 (Winter 1987):103–21.

———. "Struggle Over Needs: Outline of a Socialist-Feminist Critical Theory of Late-Capitalist Political Culture." In *Women, the State, and Welfare*, ed. L. Gordon, 199–229. Madison, WI: University of Wisconsin, 1990.

———. "After the Family Wage: A Postindustrial Thought Experiment." In *Justice Interruptus: Critical Reflections on the "Postsocialist" Condition*, ed. N. Fraser, 41–68. New York: Routledge, 1997.

Fraser, N., and L. Gordon. "A Genealogy of Dependency: Tracing a Keyword of the U.S. Welfare State." *Signs* 19, no. 2 (Winter 1994):309–36.

Friedman, M. "Beyond Caring: The De-Moralization of Gender." In *Science, Morality and Feminist Theory*, ed. M. Hanen and K. Nielsen. Calgary: University of Calgery Press, 1987.

———. "Welfare Cuts and the Ascendance of Market Patriarchy." *Hypatia: A Journal of Feminist Philosophy*, 3, no. 2 (1998):145–49.

———. "Autonomy and Social Relationship: Rethinking the Feminist Critique." In *Feminists Rethink the Self*, ed. D. T. Meyers, 40–61. Boulder, CO: Westview Press, 1997.

Frye, M. *The Politics of Reality*. Trumansburg, NY: The Crossing Press, 1983.

Gartner, A., D. K. Lipsky, and A. P. Turnbull. *Supporting Families with a Child with a Disability: An International Outlook*. Baltimore: Paul H. Brookes Publishing Co., 1991.

Gerstel, N. "The Third Shift: Gender, Difference and Women's Caregiving." Lecture delivered to Women's Studies Colloquium, State University of New York at Stony Brook, New York. December, 1991.

——— and K. McGonayle. "Taking Time Off for Family: Job Leaves, the Family and Medical Leave Act and Gender." Lecture presented at Fifth Women's Policy Research Conference. *Women's Progress: Perspectives on the Past, Blueprint for the Future*. Washington, DC, June 12–13, 1998.

Gilbert, M. *Living Together: Rationality, Sociality, and Obligation*. Lanham: Rowman & Littlefield Publishers, 1996.

Gilligan, C. *In a Different Voice*. Cambridge, MA: Harvard University Press, 1987.

———. "Moral Orientation and Moral Development." In *Women and Moral Theory*, ed. E. F. Kittay and D. T. Meyers, 19–33. Totowa, NJ: Rowman and Littlefield, 1982.

Giordano, R. "Crisis Looms for Disabled Kids." *The Philadelphia Inquirer*, 21 November 1996.

Glenn, E. N. "From Servitude to Service Work: Historical Continuities in the Racial Division of Paid Reproductive Labor." *Signs: Journal of Women in Culture and Society*, 18, no. 1 (Autumn 1992):1–43.

Goodin, R. *Protecting the Vulnerable*. Chicago: Chicago University Press, 1985.

———. *Reasons for Welfare*. Princeton, NJ: Princeton University Press, 1988.

Gordon, L., ed. *Women, the State and Welfare*. Madison, WI: University of Wisconsin, 1990.

———. *Pitied but Not Entitled: Single Mothers and the History of Welfare*. New York: The Free Press, 1994.

———. "Thoughts on the Help for Working Parents Plan." *Feminist Economics* 1, no. 2 (1995):91–94.

Greenfield, J. *A Place for Noah*. New York: Holt, Rinehart and Winston, 1978.

Groce, N. E., and I. K. Zola. "Multiculturalism, Chronic Illness, and Disability." *Pediatrics*, 91(5 May 1993):1048–55.

Handler, J. *Dependent People, the State, and the Modern/Postmodern Search for the Dialogic Community*. Special Publications. The Institute for Legal Studies, University of Wisconsin, Madison, Special Publications, 176. Madison, WI: University of Wisconsin, Madison, Law School, 1987.

Hanisberg, J. and S. Ruddick, eds. *On Behalf of Mothers: Legal Theorists, Philosophers, and Theologians Reflect on Dilemmas of Parenting.* New York: Beacon Press, 1999.

Hart, H. "Rawls on Liberty and its Priority." In *Reading Rawls: Critical Studies of Theory of Justice*, ed. N. Daniels, 230–52. New York: Basic Books, 1975.

Hartmann, H. I., and D. M. Pearce. *High Skill and Low Pay: The Economics of Child Care Work.* Prepared for Child Care Action Campaign. 1400 20th Street, NW Suite 104, Washington, D.C. 20036: Institute for Women's Policy Research. 1–47.

Hekman, S. J. *Moral Voices Moral Selves Carol Gilligan and Feminist Moral Theory.* University Park, PA: The Pennsylvania State University Press, 1995.

Held, V. "Men, Women, and Equal Liberty." In *Equality and Social Policy*, ed. Walter Feinberg, 66–81. Urbana, IL: University of Illinois Press, 1978.

———. "The Obligations of Mothers and Fathers." In *Mothering: Essays in Feminist Theory*, ed. Joyce Trebilcot, 7–20. Totowa, NJ: Rowman & Allanheld, 1983.

———. "Feminism and Moral Theory." In *Women and Moral Theory*, ed. E. F. Kittay and D. T. Meyers, 111–28. Totowa, NJ: Rowman and Littlefield, 1987.

———. "Non-Contractual Society: A Feminist View." *Canadian Journal of Philosophy*, 13 (198b):111–37.

———. "Non-Contractual Society: A Feminist View." *Canadian Journal of Philosophy*, supplementary vol. 13 (1987):111–35.

———. *Feminist Morality: Transforming Culture, Society, and Politics.* Chicago: The University of Chicago Press, 1993.

———. "The Meshing of Care and Justice." *Hypatia* 10, no. 2 (Spring):128–32.

Henshaw, S. and J. V. Vort. "Abortion Services in the U.S." *Family Planning Perspective*, 19:63 (1987).

Herz, D. E. and B. H. Wootten. "Women in the Workforce." In *The American Woman 1996–1997: Where We Stand: Women and Work*, ed. Cynthia Costello and Barbara Kivimae Krimgold, 44–78. New York: W.W. Norton & Co., 1996.

Hillyer, B. *Feminism and Disability.* Norman, Oklahoma: University of Oklahoma Press, 1993.

Hirschmann, N. J., and C. Di Stefano. *Revisioning the Political.* Colorado: Westview Press, 1996.

Hobbes, T. "Philosophical Rudiments Concerning Government and Society." In *The English Works of Thomas Hobbes*, ed. S. W. Molesworth, 1966.

hooks, b. "Feminism: A Movement to End Sexist Oppression." In *Equality and Feminism*, ed. Anne Phillips, 62–76. New York: New York University Press, 1987.

Hughes, E. C. *Ethical Issues in Professional Life.* ed. J. Callahan, 31–35. New York: Oxford University Press, 1988.

Irigaray, L. *This Sex Which Is Not One.* trans. Catherine Porter. Ithaca, NY: Cornell University Press, 1985.

Jablow, M. M. *Cara Growing with a Mentally Retarded Child.* Philadelphia: Temple University Press, 1982.

Kaplan, M. "Intimacy and Equality: The Question of Lesbian and Gay Marriage." Stony Brook Philosophy Colloquium Series. State University of New York at Stony Brook (4 March 1993).

Kaplan, T. "Female Consciousness and Collective Action." *Signs* 7 (1982), no. 3:545–566.

Keane, N. and D. Breo. *The Surrogate Mother.* New York: Everest House, 1981.

Keller, C. *From a Broken Web*. Boston: Beacon Press, 1986.

Kittay, E. F. and L. Kittay. "On the Ethics and Expressivity of Selective Abortion," 1998. "Conversations with My Son: On the Expressivity and Ethics of Selective Abortion for Disability." In *Norms and Values: Essays in Honor of Virginia Held*, ed. J. G. Haber, M. S. Halfon. Totowa, NJ: Rowman and Littlefield.

Kittay, E. F., and D. T. Meyers, eds. *Women and Moral Theory*. Totowa, NJ: Rowman and Littlefield, 1987.

Kittay, E. F. "Pornography and the Erotics of Domination." In *Beyond Domination*, ed. C. C. Gould, 145–74. Totowa, NJ: Rowman and Littlefield, 1984.

———. Rereading Freud on "Femininity." In *Hypatia Reborn*, ed. A. Al-Hibri and M. Simon, 192–203. Bloomington, IN: Indiana University Press, 1990.

———. "Human Dependency and Rawlsian Equality." In *Feminists Rethink the Self*, ed. D. T. Meyers. Boulder, CO: Westview Press, 1996.

Kornbluh, F. "The Goals of the National Welfare Rights Movement: Why We Need Them Thirty Years Later." *Feminist Studies* 24 no. 1 (Spring 1998) 65–78.

Lelyveld, J. "The President's Next Welfare Text" (editorial). *The New York Times*, 11 November 1996.

Lipsky, D. K. "A Parental Perspective on Stress and Coping." *American Journal of Orthopsychiatry* 55 (4 October 1985):614–17.

Littleton, C. A. "Reconstructing Sexual Equality." *California Law Review* 75, no. 4 (1987a):201–59.

———. "Equality Across Difference: A Place for Rights Discourse?" *Wisconsin Women's Law Journal* 3, no. 189 (1987):189–212.

Lorde, A. *Sister Outsider*. Freedom, CA: Crossing Press 1984.

Lugones, M. C. "On the Logic of Pluralist Feminism." In *Feminist Ethics*, ed. C. Card, 35–44. Lawrence, KS: University Press of Kansas, 1991.

Lugones, M., and E. Spelman. "Competition, Compassion, and Community." In *Competition: A Feminist Taboo?* ed. V. Miner and H. Longino. New York: The Feminist Press, 1987.

MacKinnon, C. A. *Feminism Unmodified: Discourses on Life and Law*. Cambridge, MA: Harvard University Press, 1987.

Manning, R. C. *Speaking From the Heart: A Feminist Perspective on Ethics*. Lanham, MD: Rowman & Littlefield, 1992.

Marmor, T. R., J. L. Mashaw, and P. L. Harvey. *America's Misunderstood Welfare State: Persistent Myths, Enduring Realities*. New York: Basic Books, 1990.

Martin, J. "Transforming Moral Education." In *Who Cares? Theory, Research, and Educational Implications of the Ethic of Care*, ed. M. M. Brabeck, 183–96. New York: Praeger, 1989.

Mason, M. A. *The Equality Trap*. New York: Simon & Schuster, 1988.

Massie, R. and S. Wassie. "Journey." *Journey*. New York: Alfred A. Knopf, 1975.

McDonnell, J. T. "Mothering an Autistic Child: Reclaiming the Voice of the Mother." In *Narrating Mothers: Theorizing Maternal Subjectivities*, ed. B. O. Daly and M. T. Reddy. Knoxville, TN: University of Tennessee, 1991.

Meyers, D. T. "Moral Reflection: Beyond Impartial Reason." *Hypatia* 8 (1993): 21–47.

———. *Subjection and Subjectivity*. New York: Routledge, 1994.

Michel, S. *Children's Interests/Mothers' Rights: The Shaping of America's Child Care Policy*. New Haven, CT: Yale University Press, forthcoming.

Mill, J. S. *The Subjection of Women*. Buffalo, NY: Prometheus, 1986.

Mink, G. *Wages of Motherhood*. Ithaca, NY: Cornell University Press, 1995.

Minow, M. 1990. *Making All the Difference*. Cambridge, MA: Harvard University Press, 1990.

———. "Equalities." *The Journal of Philosophy* LXXXVIII (11 November):633–44.

Moody-Adams, M. "The Social Construction and Reconstruction of Care." In *Sex, Preference, and Family: Essays on Law and Nature*, ed. D. Estlund and M. Nussbaum, 3–17. New York: Oxford University Press, 1997.

Moon, D. J. "The Moral Basis of the Democratic Welfare State." In *Democracy and the Welfare State*, ed. A. Gutman, 27–53. Princeton, NJ: Princeton University Press, 1988.

Mushaben, J. M. "The Gender Politics of Social Welfare Reforms: Germany and the U.S.," 1997. Lecture delivered at "Revisioning the Welfare State: Feminist Perspectives on the U.S. and Europe." Cornell University, Ithaca, New York. October 1997.

Nagel, T. *The Possibility of Altruism*. Oxford: Claredon Press, 1970.

———. "Rawls on Justice." *Philosophical Review* 82 (April 1973):220–34.

National Women's Political Caucus (NWPC). *Fact Sheet on Women's Political Progress; Fact Sheet on Executive Appointments of Women*. Washington, D.C.: NWPC, 1995.

Naylor, G. *The Women of Brewster Place*. New York: Penguin Books, 1983.

Nelson, B. J. "The Origins of the Two-Channel Welfare State: Workmen's Compensation and Mothers' Aid." In *Women, the State, and Welfare*, ed. L. Gordon, 123–52. Madison, WI: University of Wisconsin, 1990.

Noddings, N. *Caring: a Feminine Approach to Ethics*. Berkeley: CA: University of California, 1984.

Norris, P. *Politics and Sexual Equality: The Comparative Position of Women in Western Democracies*. Colorado: Rienner, 1987.

Nussbaum, M. "Nature, Function, Capability: Aristotle on Political Distribution." *Oxford Studies in Ancient Philosophy*, supplemental vol. 1 (1988):145–84.

———. "Non-relative virtues: An Aristotelian Approach." In *Midwest Studies in Philosophy, 13*, 1988b.

Okin, S. *Women in Western Political Philosophy*. Princeton, NJ: Princeton University Press, 1979.

———. "Humanist Liberalism." In *Liberalism and the Moral Life*, ed. Nancy Rosenbaum. Cambridge, MA: Harvard University Press, 1989a.

———. *Justice, Gender and the Family*. New York: Basic Books, 1989b.

Olson, E. "U.N. Survey: Paid Leave for Mothers." *The New York Times*, 16 February, 1998, A5.

Orloff, A. S. "Gender and the Social Rights of Citizenship." *American Sociological Review* 58 (June 1993):303–28.

Pateman, C. *The Sexual Contract*. Stanford, CA: Stanford University Press, 1989.

Pear, R. "U.S. to Review Disability Aid for Children." *The New York Times*, 28 November, 1996, A1, B21.

Phillips, A., ed. *Feminism and Equality: Readings in Social and Political Theory*. New York: New York University Press, 1987.

Piven, F. F. "Women and the Welfare State." In *Gender and the Life Course*, ed. A. Rossi, 265–87. New York: Aldine, 1985.

Rae, D. *Equalities*. Cambridge, MA: Harvard University Press, 1989.

Rawls, J. *A Theory of Justice*. Cambridge, MA: Harvard University Press, 1971.

———. "A Kantian Concept of Equality." *Cambridge Review*, February 1975a.

———. "Fairness to Goodness." *Philosophical Review* 84, 1975b.

―――. "Kantian Constructivism in Moral Theory: The Dewey Lectures 1980." *The Journal of Philosophy*, LXXVII (9 September 1980):515–72.

―――. "Social Unity and Primary Goods." In *Utilitarianism and Beyond*, ed. Amartya Sen and Bernard Williams, 159–85. Cambridge, U.K: Cambridge University Press, 1982.

―――. "Justice as Fairness." *Philosophy and Public Affairs* 14 (1985):227–51.

―――. *Political Liberalism*. New York: Columbia University Press, 1992.

Raymond, E. "On the Authority of Conscience." *Contemporary Philosophy*, XVII (3 May 1995):15–19.

Reverby, S. M. *Ordered to Care*. Cambridge, U.K.: Cambridge University Press, 1987.

Rhodes, D. L. *Justice and Gender: Sex Discrimination and the Law*. Cambridge MA: Harvard University Press, 1989.

Rich, A. *On Lies, Secrets, and Silence*. New York: W. W. Norton & Company, 1979.

―――. "Compulsory Heterosexuality and Lesbian Existence." *Signs* 5, no. 4 (1978):632–60.

Rimer, S. "Blacks Carry Load of Care for Their Elderly." *The New York Times*, 15 March 1998, 5, 1.

Rousseau, J. J. *Emile or On Education*. trans. A. Bloom. New York: Basic Books, 1762, 1979.

Rousso, H. "Fostering Healthy Self-Esteem." *Exceptional Parent*, 14 (December 1984):9–14.

Ruddick, S. *Maternal Thinking*. New York: Beacon Press, 1989.

―――. "Injustice in Families: Assault and Domination." In *Justice and Care: Essential Readings in Feminist Ethics*, ed. V. Held, 203–23. Boulder, CO: Westview Press, 1995.

―――. Forthcoming. "'Care' as Labor and Relationship." In *Norms and Values: Essays in Honor of Virginia Held*, ed. J. Haber and M. Halfon. Totowa, NJ: Rowman and Littlefield.

Ruddick, W. "Parenthood: Three Concepts and a Principle." In *Family Values: Issues in Ethics, Society and the Family*, ed. L. D. Houlgate. Belmont, CA: Wadsworth, 1998.

Sandel, M. J. *Liberalism and the Limits of Justice*. Cambridge, U.K.: Cambridge University Press, 1982.

Sapiro, V. "The Gender Basis of American Social Policy." In *Women, the State, and Welfare*, ed. L. Gordon, 36–55. Madison, WI: University of Wisconsin, 1990.

Sassoon, A. S., ed. *Women and the State*. London: Hutchinson, 1987.

Scheffler, S. "Relationships and Responsibilities." *Philosophy & Public Affairs*, 26 (3 Summer 1997):189–209.

Scheman, N. "Individualism and Psychology." In *Discovering Reality: Feminist Perspectives on Epistemology, Metaphysics, Methodology, and Philosophy of Science*, ed. S. Harding and M. Hintikka. Dordrecht, Holland: Reidel Publishing Co., 1983.

Scheper-Hughes, N. *Death Without Weeping: The Violence of Everyday Life in Brazil*. Berkeley, CA: University of California Press, 1992.

Schmidtz, D., and R. E. Goodin. *Social Welfare as an Individual Responsibility: For and Against*. New York: Cambridge University Press, 1997.

Schwarzenbach, S. "The Concept of a Person in Hegel: Is There a Third Moral Power?" American Philosophical Association, Pacific Division. Los Angeles, Spring 1990.

————. "Rawls and Ownership: The Forgotten Category of Reproductive Labor. In *Science, Morality and Feminist Theory*, ed. M. Hanen and K. Nielsen. Minneapolis, MN: University of Minnesota, 1986.

Sen, A. "Equality of What? The Tanner Lecture on Human Values" (delivered 1979). In *Liberty, Equality and Law: Selected Tanner Lectures*, ed. S. M. McMurrin, 137–62. Cambridge, England: Cambridge University Press, 1989.

————. "Gender and Cooperative Conflict." In *Persistent Inequalities*, ed. Irene Trinker, 123–49. New York: Oxford University Press, 1989.

————. "Justice: Means v. Freedom." *Philosophy and Public Affairs* 19(2) 1990, 111–121.

————. *Inequality Reexamined.* Cambridge, MA: Harvard University Press, 1992.

————. "Positional Objectivity." *Philosophy and Public Affairs* 22, no. 2 (Spring 1993):126–45.

Sevenhuijsen, S. "Feminist Ethics and Public Health Care Policies." In *Feminist Ethics and Social Policy*, ed. P. DiQuinzio and I. M. Young. Bloomington, IN: Indiana University Press, 1996.

Shriver, E. K. "Targeting the Most Vulnerable." *The Washington Post*, 10 April 1997.

Siim, B. "Toward a Feminist Rethinking of the Welfare State." In *The Political Interests of Gender*, ed. K. Jones and A. Jonasdottir, 160–86. Newbury Park, CA: Sage, 1988.

Silvers, A., and D. Wasserman. *Disability, Difference, Discrimination.* Lanham, MD: Rowman and Littlefield, 1998.

Singer, P. and D. Wells. *Making Babies.* New York: Charles Scribner's Sons, 1998.

Skocpol, T. *Protecting Soldiers and Mothers: The Political Origins of Social Policy in the United States.* Cambridge, MA: Harvard University Press, 1992.

Smith, A. *Wealth of Nations.* New York: MacMillan, 1921.

Sommers, C. H. "Filial Morality." In *Women and Moral Theory*, ed. E. F. Kittay and D. T. Meyers. Totowa, NJ: Rowman & Littlefield Publishers, 1987.

Spalter-Roth, R. M., and H. I. Hartmann. *Unnecessary Losses: Cost to Americans of the Lack of a Family and Medical Leave.* Washington, D.C.: Institute for Women's Policy Research, 1990.

Stack, C. B. *All Our Kin: Strategies for Survival in a Black Community.* New York: Harper and Row, 1974.

Sterner, R. *Social and Economic Conditions of the Mentally Retarded in Selected Countries.* Brussels, Belgium: The International League of Societies for the Mentally Handicapped, 1976.

Stewart, J. Y. "For Thousands of Children, Aid Rides on a Definition." *Los Angeles Times* (Washington Edition), 17 October 1996.

Stone, A. J. "In Review: January 1, 1988–July 3, 1989." In *The American Woman 1990–91: A Status Report*, ed. S. E. Rix, 33–68. New York: W. W. Norton & Company, 1990.

————. 1996. "In Review." In *The American Woman 1996–97: Where We Stand: Women and Work*, ed. C. Costello and B. K. Krimgold, 177–245. New York: W. W. Norton & Co., 1996.

Talbot, M. The "Next Domestic Solution: Dial-A-Wife." *The New Yorker*, 20, 27 October 1997, 196–208.

Taub, N. "From Parental Leaves to Nuturing Leaves. *Review of Law and Social Change*, 13 (1984–1985).

Taylor-Gooby, P. "Welfare State Regimes and Welfare Citizenship. *Journal of European Social Policy*, 1 (1991):93–105.

Thomson, J. J. "A Defense of Abortion." *Philosophy and Public Affairs*, 1, (no. 1 Fall):47–66.

Tillmon, J. "Welfare is a Woman's Issue." In *America's Working Women: A Documentary History—1600 to the present*, ed. R. Baxandall, L. Gordon and S. Reverby, 356. New York: Vintage Books, 1976.

Trebilcot, J., ed. *Mothering: New Essays in Feminist Theory*. Totowa, NJ: Rowman and Littlefield, 1987.

Tronto, J. C. *Moral Boundaries: A Political Argument for an Ethic of Care*. New York: Routledge, 1993.

———. "Women and Caring: What Can Feminists Learn About Morality from Caring?" In *Justice and Care Essential Readings in Feminist Ethics*, ed. V. Held, 101–15. Boulder, CO: Westview Press, 1995.

———. "Can the Welfare State Really Care for People?" Lecture delivered at the *Revisioning the Social Welfare State: Feminist Perspectives on the U.S. and Europe Conference*. Cornell University, Ithaca, N.Y., 3–5 Oct. 1997.

U.S. Bureau of the Census. *Current Population Reports*. P-20. Washington D.C.: U.S. Government Printing Office, 1988.

U.S. Department Of Justice, http://www.famvi.com/deptjust.htm. 1995. "Women Usually Victimized By Offenders They Know," August 16th.

Waerness, K. "On the Rationality of Caring." In *Women and the State*, ed. A. S. Sassoon, 207–34. London: Hutchinson, 1987.

Waisbren, S. E. "Parents' Reaction after the Birth of a Developmentally Disabled Child." *American Journal of Mental Deficiency*, 84, no. 4 (1980):345–51.

Walker, M. *Jubilee*. New York: Bantham Books, 1967.

Walzer, M. *Spheres of Justice*. New York: Basic Books, 1983.

West, R. L. "The Difference in Women's Hedonic Lives: A Phenomenological Critique of Feminist Legal Theory." *Wisconsin Women's Law Journal*, 3 (1987):81–145.

Wikler, L. "Family Stess Theory and Research on Families of Children with Mental Retardation." In *Families of Handicapped Persons: Research, Programs, and Policy Issues*, 167–97. Baltimore: Brookes, 1986.

Williams, B. "The Idea of Equality." In *Problems of the Self*. Cambridge, U.K.: Cambridge University Press, 1973a.

———. *Utilitarianism, For and Against*. ed. J. Smart and B. Williams. Cambridge, U.K.: Cambridge University Press, 1973b.

Williams, P. "On Being the Object of Property." In *At the Boundaries of the Law*, ed. M. A. Fineman and N. Thomadson, 22–30. New York: Routledge, 1991.

———. "Scarlet, The Sequel." In *The Rooster's Egg*, ed. Patricia Williams, 1–14. Cambridge, MA: Harvard University Press, 1995.

Williams, W. W. "Equality's Riddle: Pregnancy and the Equal Treatment/Special Treatment Debate." *New York University Review of Law and Social Change*, XIII (1985): 325–79.

Winch, P. "Understanding a Primitive Society." In *Ethics and Action*. London: Routledge and Kegan Paul, 1972.

Wolgast, E. H. *Equality and the Rights of Women*. Ithaca and London: Cornell University Press, 1980.

Wollstonecraft, M. *A Vindication of the Rights of Woman.* 2d ed. trans. C. Poston, ed. New York: W. W. Norton and Company, 1792, 1988.

Young, I. M. "Is Male Gender Identity the Cause of Male Domination." In *Mothering: Essays in Feminist Theory*, ed. Joyce Trebilcot, 129–46. Totowa, NJ: Rowman & Allanheld, 1983.

Young, I. "Mothers, Citizenship, and Independence." *Ethics* 105 (3 April 1995): 535–57.

Zack, N. "Mixed Black and White Race and Public Policy." *Hypatia* 10, no. 1 (Winter 1995):120–32.

Index